Bundok

ADRIAN DE LEON

Bundok

A Hinterland History of Filipino America

The University of North Carolina Press *Chapel Hill*

This book was published with the assistance of the Authors Fund of the University of North Carolina Press.

© 2023 Adrian De Leon
All rights reserved
Set in Arno Pro by Westchester Publishing Services
Manufactured in the United States of America

Library of Congress Cataloging-in-Publication Data
Names: De Leon, Adrian, author.
Title: Bundok : a hinterland history of Filipino America / Adrian De Leon.
Other titles: Hinterland history of Filipino America
Description: Chapel Hill : The University of North Carolina Press, [2023] |
    Includes bibliographical references and index.
Identifiers: LCCN 2023040813 | ISBN 9781469676470 (cloth ; alk. paper) |
    ISBN 9781469676487 (pbk ; alk. paper) | ISBN 9781469676494 (ebook)
Subjects: LCSH: Filipinos—Race identity—Philippines—Luzon. | Indigenous
    peoples—Philippines—Luzon—History. | Peasants—Philippines—Luzon—
    History. | Filipino diaspora—Archives. | Philippines—Colonization—Social aspects. |
    Luzon (Philippines)—Race relations—Historiography. | Luzon (Philippines)—
    Race relations—Archives. | Luzon (Philippines)—Race relations—Economic
    aspects. | United States—Territories and possessions—Race relations. | BISAC:
    SOCIAL SCIENCE / Ethnic Studies / American / General | POLITICAL SCIENCE /
    Labor & Industrial Relations
Classification: LCC DS668 .D37 2023 | DDC 305.8009599/1—dc23/eng/20230906
LC record available at https://lccn.loc.gov/2023040813

Cover illustration: Naujan Lake in Philippines by Replicant.Army/stock.adobe.com.

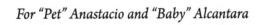

For "Pet" Anastacio and "Baby" Alcantara

Contents

Illustrations

Acknowledgments

At the end of this journey, which began when I was as an undergraduate student at the University of Toronto Scarborough, I have countless people to thank, and this work is all the better for the generosity of these mountains of support.

With its unique commitment to politically driven historical work (not to mention as the publisher of many of my favorite historians), the University of North Carolina Press is a dream home for my book. Thank you to the team, especially to my editor Mark Simpson-Vos, for pushing ahead through a global pandemic to find reviewers, round up contracts and permissions, and put my work between covers. I am thankful that you understood the potential of a sutured history from the get-go. My gratitude as well to María García, Dominique Moore (in 2020), and Brandon Proia (for the assurances and encouragement early in the process). And to my anonymous reviewers, thank you profusely for taking the time to engage with me so generously when a devastating public health crisis might dictate otherwise.

My boundless gratitude to Dorothy Cordova and the Filipino American National Historical Society community for welcoming me into your community archives in Seattle. My gratitude also goes to the staffs at these various institutions: the National Archives in Manila; the Rizal Library at the Ateneo de Manila University, especially Von Totanes; the Hawaiian Collection at the University of Hawaiʻi at Mānoa; the Hawaiʻi State Archives; the Hawaiian Mission Houses Historic Site and Archives; the Special Collections at the University of Washington; the Bancroft Library at the University of California, Berkeley; the Newberry Library; the Bentley Library and Graduate Library at the University of Michigan; the National Archives and Records Administration in Washington, D.C.; the Schomburg Center in New York; the Canadian National Exhibition Archives in Toronto; and the National Archive of the Indies in Seville.

With various sources of financial support, which were privileges during an otherwise precarious graduate school experience, I was able to take the time to travel broadly, write deeply, and produce something that people might hopefully find meaningful. These sources include the School of Graduate Studies at the University of Toronto, Massey College, the University of

Michigan, the Social Sciences and Humanities Research Council, the Fulbright Scholarship, and the Dornsife College of Letters, Arts, and Sciences at the University of Southern California.

Thanks to the many audiences with whom I could brainstorm and clarify these analyses, including the Department of Indo-Pacific Languages and Literatures at the University of Hawai'i; the Wing Luke Museum; the Newberry Library; the Global Philippine Studies Forum at New York University; the Huntington Library; Concordia University; Simon Fraser University, the University of British Columbia; the Asian and Asian American Studies Program at the University of Nevada, Las Vegas; the History Department and the Southeast Asian Studies Initiative at Brown University; and various academic conferences. Special thanks go to the Association for Asian American Studies and the Native American and Indigenous Studies Association conferences for being particularly engaging interlocutors.

As an undergraduate at the University of Toronto, I was blessed with wonderful mentors who, even though I did not end up becoming a literary scholar, laid the foundations for the cultural analysis that I took up. I thank especially Neal Dolan, Maria Assif, Claudia Hoffmann, Jay Rajiva, and Sonja Nikkila. Special thanks to Marjorie Rubright (now at the University of Massachusetts Amherst), for being my first research mentor, and to my dear friend Daniel Scott Tysdal, for the invigorating time together in the classroom and the creative writing career that we shaped together.

As a doctoral student, I found two wonderful communities at the University of Toronto with whom I could share intellectual space but, most importantly, whom I can now call friends. At Massey College, to name a few, are Dina Fergani, Delila Bikić, Claire Jensen, Ariana Ellis, Anthony Quincy Briggs, Andrew Kaufman, Amela Marin, Lily Cho, Gia Ting, and Oris Chekeche. Special thanks to Julian Posada and Michael O'Shea for being the warmest of friends. Around our little corner of East Asian studies are Brenton Buchanan, Melanie Ng, Michael Roellinghoff, and Asako Masubuchi. My special gratitude to Chris Chung for our late nights in Chinatown and more.

Despite the difficulties of working in such a space as the University of Toronto (and there were many), I am thankful for the wonderful mentors who helped me along the way. My teachers Brian Gettler and Russell Kazal, of Indigenous economies and US history, respectively, shaped my reading lists for years to come. The inimitable Lisa Yoneyama taught me what a decolonial transpacific critique could do, and I can only hope to follow in her footsteps. I also thank the creative Kevin Coleman, for visual culture and imperial history, not to mention a sterling example of good allyship, and my adviser,

Takashi Fujitani, for modeling the radical transpacific history I wish to follow and the endless solidarity and support I hope to pay forward.

A certain scholar said that after the toil of a University of Toronto graduate education, I landed on my feet. I have to slightly disagree: I found myself soaring in Los Angeles, one of the great scholarly cities. This is an unironic statement; in this city, I have had the pleasure of meeting and thinking with some of the most brilliant people I have ever met. In the Department of American Studies and Ethnicity, I thank superstar colleagues for chatting with me and showing me the ropes, especially Evelyn Alsultany, Juan de Lara, Chris Finley, Sarah Gualtieri, Edwin Hill, Dorinne Kondo, Oneka LaBennett, Shawn McDaniel, Natalia Molina, Viet Thanh Nguyen, John Carlos Rowe, Nayan Shah, Karen Tongson, and Francille Wilson. Across departments, I also thank Brian Bernards, Brandon Bourgeois, Reighan Gillam, Sarah Kessler, Lon Kurashige, Paul Lerner, Rhacel Salazar Parreñas, Grace Ryu, Marlon Twyman, Cristina Visperas, and madison moore. In addition, my gratitude goes to colleagues who have become dear friends (as well as perfect interlocutors): Fiori Berhane, Joan Flores-Villalobos, Jonathan Leal, Alaina Morgan, AE Stevenson, and Jackie Wang.

As someone from a city and a country without ethnic studies, I am privileged to teach it now as a profession and to be inspired by students who push the envelope further than what I could ever imagine. I especially found it fulfilling and urgent to be part of your academic journey during a global pandemic. At the undergraduate level, I thank Dylan Locke, Kiana Taylor, Tiffany Wong, Jordan Trinh, Bo Kim, Bao Nguyen, Megan Chao, and Jennifer Dam. At the graduate level, I thank Angela Kim, Layla Zbinden, Deena Naime, Ana Briz, Cathy Calderon, Adrienne Adams, Ann Tran, Jason Vu, Karlynne Ejercito, Carlo Tuason, Jiakai Jeremy Chua, Melissa Chadburn, Rojeen Harsini, and Megan Awwad.

Outside the University of Southern California, thank you to other colleagues and mentors who have shaped my work in so many ways. In Southern California, JoAnna Poblete, Oona Paredes, J. A. Ruanto-Ramirez, Simeon Man, Katsuya Hirano, Joy Sales, Evyn Lê Espiritu Gandhi, Elizabeth Bennett, Jenny Ferguson, Judy Wu, Jane Hong, Preston McBride, and Young Oh Jung. Elsewhere, Thy Phu, Ashanti Shih, Tessa Winkelmann, Javon Johnson, Mark Padoongpatt, Constancio Arnaldo, Coll Thrush, Vicente Rafael, Moon-Ho Jung, Julian Lim, Madison Heslop, Roneva Keel, Anna Nguyen, Jorge Bayona, Vernadette Vicuña Gonzalez, Candace Fujikane, Dean Itsuji Saranillio, Chloé Brault-McKinnon, Christopher Capozzola, Kristin Oberiano, Alex Orquiza, Kristie Flannery, Minyong Lee, Theresa Ventura, John Paul Catungal,

Robert Diaz, Jonathan and Soksamphoas Valdez, Neferti Tadiar, Emilie Tumale, Ethan Caldwell, Paul Michael Atienza, Martin F. Malanansan IV, Robyn Magalit Rodriguez, Nozomi Nagakaneku Saito, and Maya Singhal. Special gratitude goes to the Filipinx group chat: Alden Sajor Marte-Wood, Paul Nadal, Genevieve Clutario, Josen Masangkay Diaz, Allan Lumba, Karlynne Ejercito, Sony Coráñez Bolton, and others. And many thanks to my Canadian crew: Christine Noelle Peralta, Wesley Attewell, and Gym Pangalinan.

Like many scholars, I adore working in bars and coffee shops. But I have the fortune of calling so many service industry workers my dear friends. In Toronto, Voodoo Child, especially, Mel, Jason, Kat, Alex, Steve, and the "other Adrian." In Los Angeles, Jay's Bar (Constantine and Maya), Tribal Café, the Bourgeois Pig (which I miss dearly, especially Nadia and Andrew), Doubting Thomas, Coffee Commissary in Burbank, and Bé Ù Vietnamese Kitchen. Special thanks to Ali Mama in Silver Lake, and to Amin and Lilliana, who always keep a warm station and some hot coals set up for me into the late hours of the night.

Thank you to my friends in Los Angeles outside of the academy for helping me maintain a full life: Dolly Li and Austin Williams, Alex and Christian Eloriaga, Kierra Lewis, Sulafa and Nina Zidani, Abed Hathot, and Royce Files. Special thanks to Dolly Li for being my go-to collaborator and coconspirator. From television shows to taco runs, I love creating with you.

Out at the end of Toronto's eastbound train, past the recycling plant and into the blistering cold or the sweltering heat, is my chosen family of Scarborough and adjacents: Yusef Dualeh, Diriye Hassan, Hassan Mohamud, Natasha Ramoutar, Téa Mutonji, Daniela Spagnuolo, and Patrick Simeon. A special thanks to Jason Edward Pagaduan for your friendship. You taught me love and care, mutual conspiring and creating, and with an amazing soundtrack at that.

My love to Ying Li and Phil Omorogbe for a transnational friendship and support across industries.

Boundless gratitude to my therapist.

Thanks to my family, immediate and extended, in Scarborough, New York, Chicago, Los Angeles, Dubai, and the Philippines. My grandmother and my mother are the driving force of my work. My father is the embodiment of Philippine migrant life. My brother is creativity and stubborn joy.

شكراً يا حبيبتي سلافة زيداني.

Notes on Terminology and Use

Terminologies of race and nation will be in flux, and this study will attempt to work through the deployment of labels (e.g., "Philippine" or "American") while recognizing their occasional usefulness. The text deploys "Ilocos" and the "Cordilleras" as the place-names in Northern Luzon and addresses specific provinces in Central Luzon accordingly. Occasionally, "Amianan" (Ilocano for "northern region") will be used in place of "Northern Luzon." "Ilokano" (with a *k*, instead of "Ilocano") designates both the language and the ethnic group. "Igorot" (rather than the Spanish-era "Ygolote" or American "Igorotte") is the preferred spelling for the collective name of Cordilleran groups, especially in colonial and non-Cordilleran contexts. Recognizing its violent uses in colonial anthropology, the term will be substituted appropriately with specific peoples such as the Ifugaos and the Bontocs when it can be specified. However, I maintain its usage in accordance with contemporary activists from the Cordilleras and its diaspora, such as BIBAK International, who have imbued Igorot with a Pan-Cordilleran political fervor.

Furthermore, the term *manongs* will occasionally designate the Filipino prewar diasporas in the American West, while the term *sakadas* will occasionally denote the labor diaspora in Hawai'i until 1946. The transhistorical Filipino migrant or migrant worker differs from my later discussions on the overseas Filipino worker, which is a late twentieth-century formal category for overseas workers who pay remittances to the nation-state and their families. In the Philippines, I denote some Spanish colonial formations of race and mixed-race status. They are *criollo* (so-called full-blooded Spaniards who were born in the Philippines), *mestizo* (mixed Spaniard and native Filipino), and *mestizo de sangley* (or simply *sangley*, who are mixed Chinese and native Filipino). Lastly, the *Visayas* designates the archipelago in the Central Philippines, while *Bisaya* is the term for people in and from that region.

Bundok

Prologue

Dos Hermanos de los Selváticos

Perhaps folklore will provide the fount for a Philippine poetry, a poetry
inspired by Philippine subjects, and born in the minds of Philippine prophets. . . .
These traditions and superstitious practices which you are making known could
one day inspire great poets, and enthusiastic lovers of the strange beauties of this
rich garden.

—Isabelo de los Reyes, *El Folk-lore Filipino* (1887), 15

[I learned to make *doayen*] from the Igorots in the mountains of Baguio. . . .
I lived with them when the revolution was broken in southern Luzon. I fought
with them, and we were called guerrillas. Someday you will understand, and
maybe when you grow up you will see my Igorot friends.

—Carlos Bulosan, *America Is in the Heart* (1946), 26

In Vigan, the colonial trading post at the northwestern shores of the island of
Luzon, Isabelo de los Reyes had just published his landmark study of Philippine customs, through which he hoped to respond to the dominance of
científicos peninsulares (European-trained scientists) in anthropology. Don
Belong, as he was endearingly known, came from a family of writers and intellectuals who called Ilocos their home. Like his mother—Leona Florentino,
a pioneer of Philippine written poetry—before him, Don Belong imagined
the ways in which the "tools of the master," such as written text, the Spanish
language, and new social sciences of folklore and anthropology, might be
used for the purposes of interethnic solidarity and rural justice. In *El Folk-lore
Filipino* (1887), his study of Philippine peoples and their customs, he declared himself "hermano de los selváticos" (a brother to the people of the
forest). For a well-traveled intellectual of the Philippines, de los Reyes's declaration would have been an unusual, even distasteful, claim: the *ilustrados* of
Manila, such as Dr. José Rizal, condemned the representation of Luzon's
highland tribes as a shameful stain on the dignity of an emerging Philippine
nationalism. Whereas Rizal and other Tagalog ilustrados conceived of a bourgeois cacique nationalism, de los Reyes instead fertilized his politics by living
among the landless peasants, the emergent working class, and the uncolonized
highland peoples.

For his revolutionary activities against the Spanish Empire, Don Belong was exiled to Europe, where he studied socialist thought and developed his labor politics. Upon his return to the Philippines in 1901, to the ire of other political leaders and the new American government, Don Belong established the first national labor union and advocated against American capitalism. Not fitting the mold of official nationalist politics, he was made out to be a political maverick and was denied recognition from the mainstream Philippine political culture. Indeed, as the Philippine nationalist canon was consolidated around the ilustrados and their ideas, Don Belong remained marginalized. Isabelo de los Reyes, a Marxist and the cofounder of the revolutionary Philippine Independent Church whose *Weltanschauung* was forged out of a Northern Luzon geopolitics, was dis-membered from the nation he helped imagine from its margins.[1]

Fifty-nine years later, another notable writer-activist recalled this fraternity between the people of Northern Luzon. Writing from the American West, the Ilokano author Carlos Bulosan honed his craft between stints as a migrant worker, from Alaskan canneries to southern California produce farms. In his 1946 novel *America Is in the Heart*, he paid homage to the historical ties between Ilokanos and Igorots in the north, even though he had only known a family life displaced south to the plantations of Central Luzon. In the novel, the protagonist's father teaches his son how to cook with bamboo, which he himself had learned from the Igorots, with whom he lived and fought as a guerrilla.[2] Today, Bulosan's writing is recognized as foundational to Filipino American literature and culture. However, unlike his contemporaries, Bulosan was not a high-profile recruit of the Rockefeller and Fulbright Scholar programs. He did not attend prestigious universities, nor did he frequent the New York literary circles of the Beat Generation. While his writing was, at least at first, not armed with the financial and cultural capital to make an immediate splash among Anglophone literature, he emerged as a potent Filipino writer through his fiction, poetry, and polemics.

Unlike the *pensionados* of the Philippine elite, Bulosan did not emerge from the Tagalog intellectuals and ilustrados in Manila. Instead, his personal journey might be understood best through his migrant worker contemporaries, many of whom hail from Ilocos. Bulosan's politics, grounded in the slopes between Ilocos and the Cordilleras, the plantations of Luzon, and the transnational mobilization of agricultural labor, hearkens back to the work of Isabelo de los Reyes as well. As Ilokano intellectuals, Don Belong and Bulosan were marginalized from the mainstream of the Philippine national canon. However, like their homeland of Northern Luzon, they were central not only to the rise of the modern nation but also to its labor diasporas and their transnational cultures. Through Northern Luzon, both the native history and the workers' history of the Philippines—and, this project suggests, Filipino America—pulls into focus with sharpness and clarity.[3]

In the period between Don Belong and Bulosan, Northern Luzon became swept up in the tumult of Philippine geopolitics between three empires (Spain, the United States, and Japan), churning to the south in Manila. The Philippines changed hands between two colonial masters before being granted formal independence but not without the bloody mess of political controversy and military turmoil. *El fraternidad entre los Ilocanos y los igorrotes*,[4] though remembered by Isabelo de los Reyes and Carlos Bulosan, diverged under US imperial occupation. Interethnic politics between Ilokanos and Igorots were never completely friendly during Spanish occupation, but a long-established political economy of commerce and knowledge exchange flourished in the mountain slopes of the Cordilleras. Some had indeed fought together during the 1898 Philippine Revolution, and still others worked together in Spanish and American colonial industries, such as gold mining and roadbuilding. However, the imperial knowledge production of American imperialism in the archipelago sought to sunder these long-forged kinships. Through ethnological surveys and the first census under the Philippine Commission, communities in the Philippines became known as separate races or tribes. In order to justify colonial rule, the Philippine Commission declared that there are no Filipino people—only a conglomerate of "Christian" and "non-Christian" tribes along a sliding scale of civilization, devoid of collective consciousness and incapable of self-government.[5]

To its Ilokano-speaking native peoples, this colonial heartland at the edges of the US Pacific empire was the Amianan, or the North: a place of colonial struggle and tenacious Indigenous economies at the marginal purview of the metropole. But to Tagalogs down south around Manila Bay, Northern Luzon was merely a mountainous rural hinterland, or a *bundok*. Tagalog *mestizo* intellectuals such as Rizal, de los Reyes's contemporary, regarded people from the hinterlands (*taga-bundok*) as unruly and less civilized than their southern native counterparts. During the genocidal campaigns of the Philippine-American War, US soldiers adopted this word into their slang to describe their sense of bewilderment as they engaged in guerrilla warfare across rural Luzon. For this reason, the English language now refers to a remote nonurban area and its unsophisticated populations as the boondocks.[6]

From the crucible of the colonial boondocks, a sort of Filipino ethno-national consciousness did emerge. As scholars in the past two decades have explored, the Philippines transformed from a multicultural mosaic of tribes into a governable nation composed of an entangled process of race making across an American empire whose power reached beyond its shores. The majority of those ensnared within these transnational racial formations—those who became Filipino America—were made Filipino through their migrant work. Indeed, the social and cultural activity of Filipinos in the US empire is well documented. The *sakadas* of Hawaiian plantations and the *manongs* of the food industries in the American West (Carlos Bulosan among them) were some of the most politically active workers in the Asian American community whose organizing efforts found resonance with other migrant workers such as Chicanos and Native Americans in California. But the cultural view of the Philippines that proliferated most readily in the American imagination was propagated through the photographs, films, and World's Fair midway performances of "savages." To the dismay of Filipino nationalists, dog eating, exotic dances, and head hunting constituted the most popular visions of the Philippines in the early twentieth century United States.[7]

Furthermore, white supremacy in America was built in part through colonialism in the Philippines. Politicians such as Theodore Roosevelt and Henry Cabot Lodge, designers such as Daniel Burnham, and writers such as Dean Conant Worcester and Rudyard Kipling sharpened their racial awareness through the public cultures around the genocides in the Philippines. Through the yellow press, World's Fair midways, and visual memorabilia, the later phases of American imperialism in the Philippines forged a racial consciousness among the American middle class. Finally, for the white working class, the wages of whiteness proved to be a potent weapon in the legal fight for stricter immigration exclusion against Filipinos on the West Coast, especially after World War I and through the Great Depression years.[8]

Scholars of US-Philippine relations have potently shown the exercise of power and the formation of culture on both sides of the Pacific. However, a sharper focus on the source materials as well as the geographical specificities of these relations draws attention to the limits of nation-bound history. The "Philippines" and the "United States" as well as "Filipinos" and "Americans" together emerged into their modern forms at the turn of the twentieth century, taking shape through the global conditions of capitalist production and the material conditions of imperial practice. Furthermore, the 7,000 islands and waterways that comprise the "Philippines" under American power were not subject to colonial rule in uniform ways.

Tugging at the threads of white supremacy, Philippine ethno-nationalism, Igorot savage representations, and agricultural migrant labor, we might find them tangled in a Gordian knot, irreducibly looping and tightening in one particular place: Northern Luzon. The hallmark of American-built environments in the Philippines was not Manila, as left by the Spanish, but rather Baguio: the colonial hill station in the Cordilleras whose temperate microclimate was believed to be favorable for white soldiers' bodies. Most of the early migrant men and their families, whose labor is inextricable from America's commodity empire, hail from the Ilokano-speaking regions of Luzon. The savage iconography of the World's Fairs, with which Filipino America and its historical scholarship still struggle, can be traced to the ethnological projects in Benguet. Finally, the early novels and polemics of the working-class community, most especially by Carlos Bulosan, cannot be appreciated fully without an eye toward the politics of land and labor of Luzon's plantations. Therefore, the history of Filipino America regarding both race relations in the United States and migrant workers across the Pacific must ground itself not in the Philippine nation-state but instead in the material environment of Northern Luzon.[9]

But following those threads away from that knot, we find that the stories of lowland and highland native peoples split into separate paths: Christianized migrant peasants across the Pacific, on one hand, and non-Christian "savages" at the spectacles of empire, on the other. Recognizing their common lands and mountain slopes reveals that the two histories were coconstituted through the economic conquest of a frontier hinterland. The resulting trajectories exist in tension with each other precisely because lowland and highland lives have long been intertwined. And just as de los Reyes and Bulosan saw the suturing of these native kinships as part of their futures, so too in this late capitalist present does this book attempt to reweave the fabric of a globalized Northern Luzon.

Introduction

Histories from the Hinterlands

Bundok is a retelling of the history of "Filipino America" from the *bundok*—the hinterlands—of Northern Luzon. Outside dominant historiographies of Philippine and American histories, which are written primarily from the perspectives of metropolitan people, the formations of the "Filipino" across the US empire appear out of differentiated practices of knowledge production that sought to document and control native people in an encroaching plantation economy. Industrial and corporate imperialists, in addition to the communities built along the infrastructures of their wealth extraction, produced and circulated archives in their efforts to taxonomize an industrial labor force in Luzon and beyond. In response, those subject to practices of data collection and human resource management responded in earnest through the archival media used to racialize them and through producing materials and knowledge systems of their own. As racialized images, Philippine indigeneity and Filipino migrant labor emerge from these conflicts between the massive multimedia colonial archive, natives' elusive resistances to knowledge production, and the alternative practices of archiving enacted by native and diasporic peoples themselves.

In particular, this study follows the transnational coconstitution of the "savage" and the "peasant" from the nation-state known as the "Philippines" through the archival economies of global imperialism. However, rather than trace a particular feature of identity across the Pacific, I take disparate aspects of ethnic culture and roots their production to the historical archives of environmental change, Indigenous politics, and colonial industry. I examine cultural histories of dog-eating shows and ethnological photographs, male-dominated agricultural migration, racial subservience and vagrancy, and anthropological films and workers' novels and trace the predominance of Northern Luzon in their production. Likewise, by following these histories, I demonstrate the ongoing presence of Northern Luzon's native people—highlands and lowlands—even in the diasporic decontextualization of their lifeways as "Filipino" cultural productions. In doing so, I chart the history of a racial dialectic—the savage and the peasant, the Indigenous and the native—grounded in geographies and lives beyond articulations of the Philippine and US nation-states.

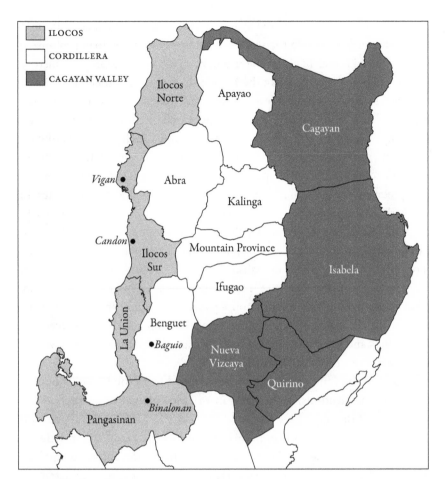

MAP I.1 Northern Luzon.

Bundok builds upon three fundamental premises in the myriad fields known problematically as Philippine studies, Filipino studies, Filipino American studies, and the history of US-Philippine relations. First, this study recognizes that the racial construction of the "Filipino" preceded—and proceeded independently of—the making of the "Philippines" as a modern nation-state. Second, the "Filipino" could have existed independent of American imperialism, albeit perhaps only in the minds of Tagalog nationalist elites in the late nineteenth century.[1] Third, the myriad native peoples of the archipelago that has come to be known as the Philippines did not all converge upon (if ever) a homogeneous idea of nationhood, racial identity, and communal belonging.[2]

These premises all point to the persistent problem of the nation-state in the articulation of native, diasporic, and working-class subjects.[3] The stories of migrant workers to the United States do not begin upon their arrival within its formal borders, nor do the stories of native peoples eventually colonized by the United States begin at the moment of US occupation. The history of US-Philippine relations, like the broader history of US imperialism itself, was necessarily a project that was international (that is, "between" the United States and a "foreign" place). This dialectic is well established in the scholarship on US empire and US-Philippine relations, including in landmark works such as Paul Kramer's *The Blood of Government*, though these at times continue to reify a US-centric perspective that privileges the experiences and interpretations of US colonial administrators, soldiers, and political elites. In his work, Kramer importantly shifted the perspective of racial formations to the Philippines, showing how race there was not merely an export of American imperialism but was also a category created through struggles over the recognition of Philippine nationalism and American authority. This body of scholarship, however, takes the "nation-state" of the Philippines as a given, positioning it as a fully formed foil against US empire. In doing so, they neglect the disaggregations, negotiations, and violence that produced the Philippines and the stories of working-class and Indigenous subjects within these elite projects of state formation.[4]

Much can be (and continues to be) gleaned from the histories of elite people and institutions, particularly in volatile colonial states such as the early occupation of the Philippines.[5] However, due to the archival predominance of elite voices in the archive, scholars have taken this privileged sliver of Philippine colonial life as a synecdoche for the entire archipelago itself.[6] Rather than placing racialization at the feet of US administrators, such scholarship locates the origins of projects of racialization in an elite minority who, by and large, had nearly zero linguistic contact with the majority of the colonial population.[7] Furthermore, privileging this minority also disproportionately shifts how we understand experiences of racialization to the top.[8] While these studies problematize the idea that racism in the Philippines was an American export, they nonetheless limit themselves to American ideas that emerge from elite spaces rather than from the longer continuities of dispossession experienced by nonmetropolitan highlanders and lowlanders themselves.[9] It is Philippine elites who pass racial judgments of "uncivilized" people and from whom these judgments are pronounced; missing are the longer experiences of those who experienced these racisms themselves, the vast majority of whom hardly had any contact with these privileged spaces. By contrast, I supplement the histories of American and Philippine elites with those of working-class diasporas,

Indigenous people, and nonmetropolitan voices, particularly those found in Northern Luzon.

Problematically, this elite few comes to stand in for the (provisional) nation-state known as the Philippines and the imperial nation-state known as the United States. Put simply, there is a slippage between, on the one hand, the nationalist imaginary of the Philippines and the Filipino people and, on the other, the subsuming of nonmetropolitan people into a single ethno-national identity within an assumed single nation-state.[10] Effectively, a focus on the nation-state as the container of colonial history obfuscates the diffuse social and political relations that proliferated across the islands and its regional diversity. For example, Kramer often writes of the diversity of languages in the Philippines from the perspective of *mestizo* and American elites, but this range of distinct peoples is taken as an inconvenient problem of colonial rule or, more mundanely, as a unique feature of the archipelago.[11] I contend that a nation-to-nation historical account obfuscates the cosmologies and epistemologies of the majority of the islands' population who, by and large, experienced colonization in markedly different ways than their Manileño (let alone their Tagalog) counterparts and had responses to colonization all on their own. In the Northern Luzon lowlands, Tagalog nationalism figured less intensely in broad anticolonial movements than the reverberations of local struggles against plantation capitalism. In the Indigenous highlands, Igorot experiences with military occupation and an encroaching police state did not begin with the Philippine Commission but instead were experienced as a continuity of Spanish-era invasions that informed American practices after 1898. Thus, to account for these marginalized histories, neither a Philippine nor an American nationalist history can account for the diversity of a transnational Filipino condition, accounting for experiences across the lowlands and the highlands and across multiple islands and regions. Such a method must problematize the nation-state as the object of analysis as well as the nation-state as itself an actor of history.

Thus, recognizing that transnational and international history continue to privilege the nation-state, I move historical analysis into the bundok in order to advance a transimperial history of the native people in the northern Philippines and their experiences of dispossession. The transimperial takes into account the multiplicity of historical geographies and their connective tissues but points directly at the structures of power—imperialism—that enable them.[12] Studying the bundok brings into focus the heterogeneity of colonial terrain (and colonial history) and the continuities of violence in what comes to be known as the frontier. Despite its distance from the metropole, the bundok is intimately subject to state violence.[13] The state here is not necessarily the nation-state, demarcated by "Spanish" and "American" periods, but rather the coercive technology of domination that naturalizes itself through its civilizational histories. This transimperial critique does not separate between imperial occupations named after their respective nation-states but instead sutures their histories.[14] Recognizing how colonial states cannibalize extant forms of domination enables a counternationalist analysis of state violence and native life.[15] Moreover, while this story begins and ends in Northern Luzon, it does not remain bound there. The violence of the bundok also reverberates in the region's diaspora, loosely known in the United States as Filipino America. Therefore, I concordantly hold the liberal multicultural notion of ethnicity under transimperial inquiry.[16] This study roots Filipino America in the *longue durée* of transimperial violence and capitalist extraction of the long nineteenth century before and within what is formally known as the American period of colonization (1898–1942).[17]

The emergence of Filipino America, then, does not have to begin in 1898, when the United States invaded the Philippines. These stories begin at the aftermath of the Seven Years' War (1756–63) and Spanish Bourbon administrators' efforts to extract natural resources from the archipelago. The emergence then moves through the end of the Mexican War of Independence, when the new Mexican polity gained control of the Port of Acapulco, ending the centuries-long supremacy of the Manila galleons in transpacific trade. Finding itself in direct control of an archipelago at the other side of the world, Spain sought to repurpose the Philippines from a port to the Orient into a productive colony in its own right. Throughout the nineteenth century, Spain launched a campaign of knowledge production that the United States would later replicate in the early twentieth century. Botanists and geologists joined social scientists in accounting for the resources of their colony, and in doing so, as this study shows, reconfigured the colony and its natures (including human natures) as resources for competing in a global marketplace.[18]

Regarding the organizing logic of human nature in the archipelago, the human resource management of colonial peoples produced a body of knowledge that justified the military and agricultural dispossession of people from their land and their mobilization in global industries as labor commodities. In becoming human resources, the various groups of the Philippines entered into colonial knowledge according to their capacities to work in specific industries. For instance, the Igorot became the industrious savage, the rural Tagalog and Ilokano became the perpetual peasant, and the Chinese Filipino became the ideal domestic worker.[19] This colonial legacy has inadvertently bled into studies on Philippine labor migration. To provide depth in the study of transpacific migration, historians of Filipino America have specified their analyses toward distinct communities (e.g., Little Manilas in Stockton and Los Angeles) and particular occupations (e.g., nurses and agricultural workers).[20] As these scholars suggest, understanding patterns of labor migration requires a transpacific perspective, from empire and recruitment to global industry.

But how were these Filipinos understood as ideal cheap workers for specific industries in the first place? The production of race as industrial knowledge is a matter of how capitalism organizes labor through the classification of difference. In recognizing how Filipinos are made out to be ideal workers for specific industries in American empire (what we come to know as racial stereotypes of subservience, among others), this study turns to the material specificities of region and environment that produced the imagined Filipino peasant and savage in the first place. The historian's tool kit must then be equipped with the requisite tools to study race (and racism) as a history of industrialization and its environmental consequences. The production of race was intimately tied with the agricultural commodities that workers produced or were intended to produce. Savage laziness and indolence as well as industriousness and "essential qualities" for plantation work prevailed in racial discourse and were ably deployed for the purposes of accumulating and disciplining labor power. In turn, these labored archives of industry and empire provided the fabric of modern discourses of race.[21]

A region long known as an economic hinterland, Northern Luzon produced much of the stuff of Spanish and American industrial empire. Since the nineteenth century, Central Luzon's fertile plains produced the food provisions that fueled Manila's industries. Luzon agriculture orientated the island's food systems toward Manila, effectively acting as a microcosm of imperial commodity production within the larger Spanish and American empires. Rice, fruits, and livestock from the plains fortified the rise of Manila's economic growth and place in a capitalist world system through the nineteenth and twentieth centuries. On the other hand, from 1782 until the early twentieth century, Northern Luzon's chief economic export was a single crop: tobacco. Inaugurated as the region's primary monoculture by the Bourbon governor José Basco y Vargas, the tobacco monopoly in the Philippines reconfigured the island of Luzon from coastal and friar-dominated settlements into a large-scale industrial farm of Spain's commodity empire. Under the monopoly, local growers and cigar artisans were no longer permitted to sell their own goods. Instead, massive tobacco *haciendas* dominated the lowlands around the northern circumference of the Cordilleras.[22]

The Luzon highlands had long been an impediment to Spanish colonial administration, initially for the failed search for gold. However, by the nineteenth century, the Cordilleras and its people became obstacles to building transportation infrastructures that could connect the northeastern tobacco-rich regions of the Cagayan Valley to Manila. The regional warfare in the mountains during the nineteenth century, continuing into the American occupation of the early twentieth century, may have been justified as Christianization campaigns but were instead waged to subsume the region into industry. The Spanish and American empires invaded the region to clear space for roads, while prospecting for minerals and appropriating arable landscapes were tended to by highland peoples in the bundok.[23]

To tobacco and other crops, I add two other major exports from colonial Northern Luzon. The second export was a racialized labor force. From slavery to tributes, regimes of forced labor had long existed in the islands now known as the Philippines. Precolonial *datus* established power through enslavement and regular raiding between *barangay* (the basic unit of Philippine social life).[24] During the early modern Spanish occupation (1521–1762), churches imposed mandatory labor taxes on natives living in Catholic *barrios*. However, the rationalization of colonial extraction since the death of the last Hapsburg monarch in Spain (1700) and the Seven Years' War (1756–1763) effectively changed the character of colonial labor as well as the racialized modes of social difference that the Spanish used to manage the native population. In order to produce a nonedible crop in a region with poor soil, Spanish forces launched comprehensive military and education campaigns to coerce Luzon natives into industrial work. After the 1898 Treaty of Paris when the United States acquired the Philippines from Spain, American investors drew upon an already-mobilized labor force to recruit workers to Hawai'i and the continental West. Imperial spectacles too drew upon the ethnological materials of the nineteenth century conducted by European social scientists and, in some cases, the photography of Anglo-American naturalists from across the Pacific.[25] Therefore, the third mass export from colonial Northern Luzon was colonial knowledge and the vast array of multimedia materials from which to draw concepts of race and social difference in the Philippines.

The triumvirate of cash crops, cheap labor and colonial knowledge in Luzon's hinterland plantation industries subjected the region to a global market regime that, in the process of profiting from resource extraction and commodity production, intensified racial difference along the axis of populations' capacities to do industrial work. The development of racial difference happens at the onset of primitive accumulation, or the processes of expropriating subsistence economies into state-driven labor and resource extraction, namely under continuous and uneven processes of colonial dispossession.[26] Furthermore, primitive accumulation and the establishment of capitalist relations exhibits a distinctly racial character. By coercing people into labor the colonial state calcified the abstraction of native labor through the creation of social difference based on race. According to political scientist Cedric Robinson, the inauguration of racial capitalism begins at the moment of primitive accumulation, or specifically through a shift from the "parochialism of the town to the parochialism of the state."[27] This did not mean that the town went away; rather, through the processes of enclosure, colonial-capitalist states privatized native lands once held as commons and gathered native people into governable towns. In nineteenth-century Luzon, this enclosure took two forms. In the lowlands, the Spanish state subsumed Catholic barrios, supplanted priests who monopolized local rule, and expelled Chinese traders at the strongholds of interisland commercial life. In the highlands, the Spanish state launched campaigns of *reconquista* (reconquest) to *reducir* (enclose) Igorots into the lowland barrios, now under state rule, so as to clear the mountains for infrastructural development and coerce Igorots to work.[28]

As discussed above, the process of geographic and economic enclosure in Luzon depended on the sedimentation of early modern Catholic logics of race into capitalist logics, most predominantly through their rationalization and archiving. Through the development of the disciplines, the bourgeoisie-led state developed systems of knowledge to justify its expropriation of land and labor time. Some of these disciplines across national contexts include eugenics, history, literature, geography, and anthropology.[29] These state disciplines as well as the institutions that deploy them simultaneously articulate nationalism to solicit consent to be governed and extract resources from the very same governed people.[30] As the imperial successor to Spain and twentieth-century broker to transnational capital's extraction of Luzon's resources, the United States subsumed the racialized and gendered character of Luzon's nineteenth-century plantation economy.

The racial character of capitalism cannot simply exist ethereally and must be inscribed into the imperial repositories of knowledge production and domination. In other words, race must be archived. Migrant workers, capitalists, governments, Indigenous peoples, and social scientists all participated in—and competed over—the global economy of the racial archives. Through her study of colonial plunder and the imperial museum, cultural theorist Sarita See shows that the racialized notion of primitivity was used by American scientists to justify primitive accumulation, manifesting in the archiving and museumization of native peoples in the Philippines.[31] In turn, these scientists and other producers of knowledge, all working in the service of potential profit from resource extraction, cited older materials from Philippine racial archives to chart out their colonial plunder.

Therefore, I show how primitive accumulation in the colonial hinterlands haunts the racial archives of Filipino America and their production and circulation around the world. Furthermore, recognizing how native workers themselves have taken up the archiving project as well as contributed to the propagation of colonial-capitalist rule in Luzon, I examine how race manifested as archival conflict between different groups as they sought to define the terms of what it meant to be Filipino. The terrain of these archival conflicts do not take place only in the dwellings of historical materials. They emerge out of their production and circulation as well as their reception and reproduction. In this study, I give a term to this distributive character of racial archives: "racial economy."

Racial Archive, Racial Economy

On the physical nature of the Philippine colonial archives, one might map it quite simply: the Archivo General de Indias in Seville, the various national and private archives of Manila, the National Archives and Records Administration in Maryland, and the different institutions of the Midwest or, perhaps, in the contemporary moment, the "digital archive." On a practical level, "going to an archive" presents many gates (and gatekeepers) that stand between the researcher and the source: travel costs, reproduction and permissions, and the archival catalog. The dispersal of archival materials and the resources required to peruse these contents inevitably shape the historical scholarship that follows.[32]

Between the dwellings of archival materials, both physical and virtual, we are presented with the archive's circulation. Simply put, where do particular materials gather, and how does this shape knowledge production? Writing about Philippine photographic collections (many of which appear in this study), archival scholar Ricardo Punzalan posits the framework of an archival diaspora. The archival diaspora, Punzalan shows, accounts for the difficulty in consolidating analyses between groups of materials by virtue of the barriers erected through their distribution. Punzalan advances four modes of dispersion. The geographical dispersion of archives accounts for their locations and what institutional conditions (e.g., preservation facilities, wishes of donors) led to their final locations. The temporal dispersion of the archive accounts for when materials were accessioned, which shaped the patterns of dispersal over time. The provenancial dispersion identifies the creation and ownership of materials and the change between ownership, both public and private. Finally, the material dispersion investigates the specific forms, both physical and digital, through which sources may be investigated. These dispersions not only make the historical study of Philippine indigeneity and diaspora practically difficult but also impact how race itself historically emerged as knowledge producers across time themselves drew upon archival research to consolidate the intellectual corpus of imperial management.[33]

Archival diasporas underpin this study in a multimedia investigation of the following question: Why are materials on Philippine indigeneity understood to be more dispersed than Indigenous people themselves, and why are Philippine labor diasporas more dispersed than their archival materials? Furthermore, why are materials on indigeneity predominantly visual, while those on lowland workers are numerical or textual?

As chapter 1 argues, this archival discrepancy emerges from the geology and spatial politics of Luzon. It examines the *longue durée* of the tobacco monopoly in Luzon and its reorganization of native land and life through the production of racial archives. Between 1776 and 1882, the Spanish Bourbon monarchy launched a full-scale campaign in its dwindling colonies to liberalize their economies through the rationalization of agriculture in the northern frontier. The colonial state incorporated missionaries' ideas of race into their capitalist imperatives. As a result, the Catholic Church categories of *infiel* (highland non-Christian native; also *salvaje*, or savage) and *indio* (lowland Christianized peasant) also took on an expressly industrial character, which is examined in the state technocrats' racial archives.

Likewise, chapter 2 locates the aforementioned discrepancy to the differentiated circulation of Luzon's racial archives. The opening of the Suez Canal in 1869, the dominance of transoceanic steamships, and the advent of mechanically reproducible media circulated the infiel and the indio to scholarly and popular audiences. But because of ongoing difficulties in accessing the Luzon highlands, colonial officials continued to find lowland peoples easier to count statistically through barrios and plantations, while highland peoples were approximately accountable through ethnology and (eventually) photography.[34]

The act of counting takes place before the circulation of archival materials, through which the counter decides who is to be accounted for and by what means. The protomoment of archiving, the originary act of data collection prior to its taxonomization—as if it were an archival resource to be made ordered, if accounted for—remains in question. Both production and circulation (that is, the archival economy) are necessary for grappling with the disparity of media produced from Northern Luzon. As an experimental ground for Spanish and American Manila's economic development, Luzon's peoples and environments were beholden to comprehensive projects of data collection and knowledge production. We must understand the core impetus of archival productions in modern Philippine colonial history to account for their circulation abroad.[35]

To unpack the nature of race and the colonial archives, I turn first to the work of philosopher Jacques Derrida. In the last decade of his life, Derrida's thought shifted from the textual deconstruction of his career's zenith toward the more mundane and material aspects of text. On June 5, 1994, at the Freud Museum in London, Derrida delivered a lecture titled "Mal d'archive: Une impression freudienne" (Archival Fever: A Freudian Impression). Atop Sigmund Freud's archives, Derrida began not with the archival dwelling as colloquially understood but instead from the word "archive" itself. "Archive," Derrida reminds us, comes from the ancient Greek word *arkhē*, meaning at once "commencement" and "commandment." The discipline of history derives from the ontological (the nature of being) and the nomological (the nature of lawmaking) dimensions of arkhē—(1) From where does historical knowledge begin, and (2) from whom does the authority to declare that beginning come?—or, in simpler terms, between periodization and the historian or between the originary source of knowledge and the entity creating that document as knowledge.[36]

In Derrida's terms, the archive—the collection of that which is admissible by arkhē—constitutes civilization; those inadmissible to arkhē, or *anarkhē*, destroys the legitimacy of the archive. The archive as the dwelling from which authority springs (or the civilization's metropole) is constantly in danger of having its authority to consign order delegitimized. Anarkhē is that which is outside archival order, that which is without order, or that which is barbaric: "There is no archive without a place of consignation, without a technique of repetition, and without a certain exteriority. No archive without outside,"[37] or more commonly in English, "anarchy."

Order and chaos in the archives are more than a Manichean duality, between good and bad. They reflect practices of archival production, as civilizational projects of capitalist development in the Philippines sought to subsume environments and peoples into value regimes for commodification. Lowland natives, already incorporated into Church-centered labor regimes and living within domiciles visible to the colonial state, could be most easily counted through archiving practices such as statistics. Those deemed anarchist were accounted for through the sciences and arts of savagery—of the precivilization, or prearchival—in ethnology and photography.

Beyond the production of an archive, its circulation and reproduction call attention to how its authority is legitimized. According to Derrida, there is no archive without an ordered institution to claim authority to archive in the first place and without the means of reproducing its authority to be taken for granted. In Spain, the inauguration of the Archivo General de Indias corresponded with the Bourbonist reforms in the colonies, declaring Spain as the font of civilization to its colonial south. Meanwhile, records of specific private industries in the Philippines brokered by the Spanish and American states are stored in an archipelago of records, from Harvard University to the University of Hawai'i. In the continental United States, colonial archives of the Philippines are dispersed amid the various locales of imperial rule. Despite the entangled relationship between ethnology and policy making in the Philippines, anthropological materials are kept at the University of Michigan and the Newberry Library, while American colonial government documents are stored at the National Archives in College Park, Maryland. Finally, after the civil rights movement, the Filipino communities in Seattle and Stockton continue to collect archival materials on the Filipino American diaspora through the Filipino American National Historical Society.

The partitioned archives obscure the intersections between modern concepts of race and practices of colonial capitalism. Echoing Derrida, cultural anthropologist Ann Laura Stoler asserts that the colonial archive is a technology of power that, while serving as a repository to establish imperial domination, reproduced the problems of incoherence and uncertainty that archiving itself sought to eradicate in colonial management.[38] These archival inconsistencies do not just highlight what Stoler calls the "anxieties" of colonial governance but also point to the brutality of colonialism itself. Drawing from Stoler, literary theorist Lisa Lowe argues that these divisions reinforce the forgetting of colonial violence behind the archives of European liberalism itself. By recognizing these divisions and how they organize historical material, Lowe proposes reading practices that reveal how "the archive that mediates the imperatives of the state subsumes colonial violence within narratives of modern reason and progress."[39] The colonial archives' distribution severs our understandings of the underlying global connections behind European liberalism, transatlantic slavery, the "coolie," and Indigenous dispossession, which she calls the "intimacies of four continents."[40] Lowe contends that the distribution of colonial archives erases the revolutionary labor of historical freedoms between four continents while reifying a European notion of progress to obfuscate its constitutive violence. Race and social difference are traces of how archives have been distributed in order to obfuscate the mutuality of colonial violence and European liberalism, behind liberal notions of freedom and subjectivity.[41] In order to resist this systematized forgetting, the divisive organization of colonial archives demands reading practices that pay attention to the work behind the creation of modern racial categories by both imperial capitalism and the workers subject to its regimes.[42]

By situating race within the archive, I suggest that race itself should be studied in terms of its production, circulation, reproduction, and consumption. I give a term to this phenomenon: the racial economy. As scholars of racial capitalism have noted, race in the age of industry functions to maintain divisions of labor among potential human resources. I draw on the definition of economy as the allocation of resources from production and circulation to consumption. By extension, I posit that studying a racial economy compels the scholar to trace racial categories from their production during different political economy conditions to their circulation by means of various media and to their reception and reproduction within societies. Just as Lowe asserts that the production and distribution of "colonial archives [are] intrinsic to the archives of liberalism,"[43] the haphazard archives of colonial racial stereotypes must be rooted to the industrial labor regimes that reconfigured native populations' relationships to mobility and place. Since stereotypes of Philippine indigeneity and migrant labor appear in the same early twentieth-century American colonial moment, this study accounts for them and their relevant sources together, despite their apparent disparities. The racial economy attempts to account for this constellation of colonial images together and in doing so finds the common colonial capitalist roots of disparate racial formations during the early twentieth century.[44]

All this is not to say that race lives solely within the privileged structures of formal archives. Archiving can be—and has been—used by marginalized peoples to challenge the logics of social difference to which they were subject. This study explores how workers engaged with the racial economy through their participation in—or production of their own—colonial practices of archiving. Chapters 3 and 4 explore the visual cultures from the Philippine Cordilleras and their dissemination across the Pacific. Through dog eating and headhunting, two racial images of the Philippine savage, these chapters follow how Igorot labor and economies challenged American visions of imperial conquest. Likewise, chapters 5 and 6 explore Ilokano migrant workers' interactions with capitalist infrastructures, such as Hawai'i plantation banks and West Coast railroads, in producing various notions of the "Filipino" in the context of particular American labor regimes. Chapter 7 highlights how two writers actively challenge the racial economy of the Filipino condition through literary acts of solidarity between the lowlands and highlands.

An examination of the archival economies of race allows us to follow Philippine diasporas before and beyond their provincialization into an "American" diaspora or, for that matter, a product of the "Philippines."[45] This study attests to the assemblage of the "Filipino" itself as an ethno-racial archive in the context of Spanish and American imperialisms as well as by the workers differentially subjected to the archive's racializations. Furthermore, the racial economy enables scholars to account for flows of commodities across the Pacific not simply on American terms but also along the infrastructures that the United States appropriated from Spain or otherwise developed in tandem and in competition with other empires. For instance, while the boats that brought American soldiers to the Philippines followed the US military infrastructures, those that brought civilians to the islands and migrant workers to the United States were Canadian and Japanese boats. These infrastructural connections—the collaboration of shipping companies as well as the flexibility of migrant pathways—calls our attention to the interimperial and material dimensions of colonialism and diaspora.[46]

But from where do the building blocks of the "Filipino," let alone the "Filipino American," emerge? In the Philippines, as far as nonmetropolitan peoples were concerned, there was no Philippines from which to derive a Philippine diaspora in the first place.[47] Indeed, while they are entangled, the Philippines and the Filipino as well as the Filipino American exhibit diverse genealogies behind their modern formations.[48] An emergent field, Filipino studies (or Filipino diaspora studies), which centers diaspora and transnationalism in the study of Filipino people, further emphasizes the palimpsestic nature of ethnic subjectivity.[49]

However, I wish to add that creating such identities did not only depend on colonial migration or, for that matter, colonial migrant labor. Creating this subject out of the "immigrant" and the "colonized" necessitates excluding who was not such a subject. In the Philippine transnational context, these exclusions took many forms, most notably through the various Chinese exclusions throughout Philippine colonial history.[50] The so-called savages or infieles of the Philippines, as Igorots in the Cordillera highlands have been termed, have been studied as those constructed within a Philippine colonial and national ethic but who remained unincorporated into its visions of a modern subject.[51] To return to the reading practices put forth by Lisa Lowe, underpinning the analyses that the racial economy undertakes in Philippine transnational history, "the racial classifications in the archive arise . . . in [the] context of . . . colonial [administrators'] need to prevent [the] unspoken 'intimacies' of the colonized."[52] In other words, the intimacies between migrant work and Indigenous dispossession are not only across continents. In this book, we shall find these intimacies in the Philippine colonial nation-building project, between Ilocos shores and Cordillera highlands, severed through the archive.[53]

In sum, situating race within both the archival dwellings and the practices of archiving allows us to see how historical archiving accounts for cultural and industrial differences as racial characteristics. The racial economy accounts for racial stereotypes that arise from the racial archive's production, circulation, reception, and reproduction. Colonized people too participate in—and challenge—the racial economy of imperialism through their practices of counterarchiving, whether it be through their insurgent assertions of sovereignty against imperial rule or by producing materials themselves within community practices of memory and preservation. By approaching Philippine-US histories through the racial economy, this study unpacks the intimacies between the production of social difference from Northern Luzon to Filipino America.

Indigenous, Native, Settler

Racial economy allows us to think with archives and their institutions, from the production to the dissemination (and reproduction) of racial logics and images, to trace the material processes of racialization. However, there is a fundamental difference between racial economy as an insurgent reading practice and its implications for Indigenous people in Asia and across the Pacific. Racial economy does not mean that indigeneity, in its relations and subjectivities, should fall neatly within the critical study of race and ethnicity. Namely, though racialization acts upon indigeneity, indigeneity is not race. This is well established in the myriad fields of Native American and Indigenous studies, which refuse colonial logics of blood quantum (among other biosocial formations of race) and have advanced a theory of indigeneity as a genealogical and cosmological relationship to land and place, against colonial techniques of subjugation and dispossession. But as my study shows, as do other scholars of indigeneity and race, so much of racialization under empire emerged around Indigenous people and in erasure of Indigenous place making.[54]

To address this, I raise two problematics for us to consider. First, what are the contours of that which we call indigeneity, nativeness, autochthony, and the like especially in a context outside of North American academe, let alone North America and Oceania for that matter? Can a global Indigenous framework, that which begins from the constitutive outside of capital and its epistemes, enable us to rethink these categories and their relationships with one another? And second, are Filipino migrants, even as "native" or "US national" workers, settlers? What are the implications of settler colonialism on a population that has also been displaced of their native land though are read as "Asian migrants" in contemporary contexts?

As this study suggests, while all Indigenous people from the Philippines (Igorot, Lumad, and Aeta, among others) are native, so to speak, not all native people are Indigenous. From the late eighteenth century through the nineteenth century these relations were much more in flux, and the most fixed modes of this distinction take place between native peoples' associations with Christianity and Islam (i.e., "Christianized natives" and "Muslim Moros") and those beyond the purview of these racio-religious regimes (i.e., "non-Christianized" natives). As this study moves deeper into the twentieth century, I will distinguish between the Indigenous and the native with more clarity. Following Indigenous anthropologists and ethnohistorians of the Philippines and other Asian Indigenous contexts, I make this distinction to bring attention to the fact that in the contemporary context, lowland natives comprise the hegemonic groups that dictate nation-state formations and capitalist modes of relation.[55] As the conclusion shows, the dictatorship of Ferdinand Marcos, an Ilokano, was particularly brutal against Igorot people in the 1970s and 1980s, who mobilized against the president's vanity projects on their sacred sites. Furthermore, it was predominantly lowland natives who emigrated across the Pacific to work in industries built on stolen land. And in the United States, it is predominantly lowland diasporas, such as Tagalogs, who commodify and appropriate Indigenous cultures for the sake of their precolonial self-discovery. Despite their nativeness to the islands known as the Philippines, under this political economy of state and cultural violence, it must be said that such atavistic claims to indigeneity are nothing short of the dispossession of Indigenous people.[56]

This leads us to the question of settler colonialism and its related frameworks, such as Asian settler colonialism. Migrants from the bundok, both lowlands and highlands, are caught in a double bind: even if migrants do not settle per se on the stolen lands of Hawai'i and the continental United States upon which they work, they nonetheless benefit from infrastructures of capital that condition their livelihoods and mobilities even as they themselves were displaced from their native lands by the same imperial powers. Overseas labor, from its historical roots in the plantation to its contemporary modes of exploitation, is made possible through settler colonial capitalism. But as we will see in chapter 6, Ilokano men bring certain settler colonial ideologies into their travels and travails across the North American West. As Asian settlers and as colonized natives under Spanish and American imperialisms, migrant labor from the Philippines is inextricable from Indigenous dispossession across the Pacific, including within the Philippines itself.[57]

Despite the inherent limitations of racial economy, it nonetheless provides a means of bringing together the often differentiated categories of Asianness and indigeneity, complicating questions of settler colonialism, nativeness, migration, and racialization.[58] Racial economy does so by putting into conversation the archives created by imperialism with the counterarchives created by colonized people as well as the moments in which colonized people elude archival legibility altogether. As such, *Bundok* follows the severing of lowland and highland people in the wake of the plantation economy. But in doing so, I also wish to provide a blueprint for the suturing of these relations in the hope of charting a logic toward decolonization. Throughout the histories of the bundok, despite the constant severing of their ties under colonialism, lowland and highland peoples have been mobilizing together in the promise of anticolonial liberation. We will begin with one moment of suture and struggle, in the late eighteenth century, with the work of revolutionary northerners Gabriela and Diego Silang.

Part I

Building Luzon's Racial Economy

CHAPTER ONE

Rationalizing Race

In Vigan a century before Don Belong's birth, two northerners tossed the colonial city into political turmoil. On September 1762, a motley crew of 1,700 soldiers from Europe and the Indian Ocean region, flying under the British flag, quickly invaded Manila at the beginning of the year's monsoon season. The colonial administration was caught completely off guard as a Southeast Asian front to the global war, and Intramuros fell quickly to British firearms and naval might. While the British invaded Manila to the south, Gabriela (Ilokano and Itneg) and Diego (Ilokano and Pangasinense) Silang seized an opportunity to revolt against Spanish Catholic rule in Northern Luzon. By December 1762, 2,000 insurgents, led by Diego and Gabriela, established control over Vigan and imprisoned local friars and officials. Appealing to the invading British forces to the south, the Silang-led revolutionaries demanded substantial reforms to Catholic Church rule and peasants' rights. But the British aid that was promised never came.[1]

In response, the Spanish authorities enacted revenge. On May 28, 1763, two of Diego's friends, Miguel Vicos and Pedro Becbec, bribed by Bishop Fray Bernardo de Ustáriz, assassinated Diego in broad daylight. In response, Gabriela gathered approximately 9,000 rebel forces from Abra to invade Vigan but failed. On September 20, 1763, the Spanish forces captured Gabriela and approximately one hundred of her followers in Abra and sentenced them to death by hanging. Six months later, despite the orders having been signed over a year prior, the British finally withdrew from their occupation of Manila, and Luzon returned to full Spanish control. As a result of the Spanish victory and the swift extension of an inland penal system against rebellions, the agrarian region was quelled of major uprisings for four decades. In the colonial order after the Seven Years' War, the state saw fit to fine-tune its practices of controlling native peoples through discipline.[2]

The swift (though brief) efficacy of the Silang Uprising, and the Spanish state's failure to quell revolutionary fervor in the north reveals how tenuous colonial rule was in the northern hinterlands. After the Seven Years' War, the Spanish Empire regained political control over Manila and the archipelago. Influenced by a new wave of reformist Enlightenment-era thought from Europe, the Bourbon colonial government sought to implement reforms that could maximize the value of their far-flung colony. Through various schemes and economic ventures, the most successful reform ultimately came as an import from other ventures in colonial Latin America. For the next one hundred years the Spanish implemented a tobacco monopoly, which brought vast profits to Spain and foreign investors but completely devastated native life.[3]

The political history of the Silang Uprising exhibits two features of particular significance. First, the Silang revolt can be examined through the intimacies between Diego and Gabriela themselves and the swift power they had in amassing support for a formidable native insurgency. Under duress of famine and colonial violence, myriad peoples of the lowlands and highlands declared themselves *kailian* (the working masses, or literally "fellow townspeople") against the *babaknang* (the feudal warrior and merchant classes). The solidarities that Diego and Gabriela cultivated were interethnic among lowland tribes as well as through the valley streams and mountain slopes. By reclaiming the slopes as a commons against Christian colonial discipline and labor, the kailian elided the spatial regimes of the Catholic Church and organized a hinterland insurgency that struck fear into the Spanish Empire.[4]

Second, by demanding alternatives to the mandatory labor tax and tribute system, the revolts showed that early modern labor regimes in the Northern Luzon hinterlands already provided the seeds of a future plantation economy as well as the spatial strategies required for the state to put native people to work. By the time the tobacco monopoly and the Philippines' Sociedad Económica de los Amigos del País (Economic Society for the Friends of the Country) was established in the late eighteenth century, the leaders found that they did not have to reinvent the wheel to exploit native labor. Rather, the Bourbon state came to consolidate its power by magnifying the expressions of extant systems of colonial rule, including how local people were understood by the Church in terms of their social and religious difference. Thus, the Bourbon reforms in Luzon amounted to the development of a racial capitalist system, both globalizing and particular to Luzon, brought about by heterogeneous processes of primitive accumulation.

Accounting for Luzon's varied geographies and native peoples, we can see that primitive accumulation and the establishment of a racial capitalist plantation state on the island was not a teleological process. Instead, these economic reforms were enacted in piecemeal ways as the colonial state reckoned with difficult terrains, native economies, and social movements on the ground. Meanwhile, in the absence of centralized archives about its native subjects, the Bourbon state quickly developed techniques of producing knowledge about Luzon's land and people so that the state might ascertain strategies to extract value from the island. Between the violent establishment of a plantation state and the tenacity of regional economies, social movements, and native lifeways, a robust racial archive began to emerge. These archives formed the epistemic foundations of racial capitalist regimes in the Philippines.

The economic ventures of the Spanish Bourbon regime rationalized race in Luzon. By rationalization, I do not mean that the Bourbon government somehow ameliorated socioeconomic conditions through a regime of technocratic uplift. Rather, just as the Bourbon leaders launched economic campaigns to render the northern landscapes profitable, they did the same for its native people under those same economic logics. The rationalization of race suggests a secular codification of social difference for the purposes of extracting value from people under a capitalist order, from a Church-based set of racial archives to ones around the agricultural production of an export economy.[5] Rationalizing race depended on developing racial knowledge in order to discipline native peoples to work on establishing a plantation economy while concealing the violence done through colonial conquest through archival codification. This was enacted through enclosing and appropriating local economies as well as through extant modes of exploitation established by the Catholic Church. In sum, rationalizing race was the primitive accumulation of knowledge.[6]

Early Modern Indigenous-Colonial Interfaces

The racial grammars of the colonial Philippines begin with the spatial configurations of conquest and conversion. Even though the Philippines was an economic backwater of the Spanish Empire, the first two centuries of colonial rule fertilized the racial archiving practices of the tobacco monopoly. Spain's wealth extraction from the Philippines most significantly manifested through its position as a port of call for the Manila-Acapulco galleons. However, the most intimate form of extraction came through local labor forces of Christianized natives and the acquisition of colonial knowledge by means of the Catholic Church. Once highly mobile maritime polities, the native peoples of what would become the Philippines became fixated through spatial containment around a parish and its Christianized society.[7] For the most part, despite the weakness of the colonial state, initial efforts to contain and govern natives were successful, at least in the lowlands. The continuity of movement and kinship between lowland and highland peoples in the Amianan posed challenges to the state. Despite the expropriation of native land and labor in the north during early colonial rule, the north's persistent economies laid the foundations for the particular aggression of plantation establishment in the nineteenth century as well as the insurgencies that destabilized the Bourbon state's efforts at exercising its despotic power.

Precolonial Philippine societies anchored around units roughly called barangays, the most basic social unit. The term "barangay" also refers to a type of large outrigger boat through which *datus* (heads of barangays) and their warriors led expeditions for trade and raiding against other barangays. The locus of Philippine kinship and governance centered around the social unit and the maritime means of mobility. Barangays established land-based settlements but in response to regional conflict and economic opportunities could uproot themselves time and again through the barangay boat. Philippine archaeologists remark on the supremacy of mobile precolonial societies through the lack of fixed monuments and urban settlements. Instead, arts and rituals orbited around the social life of bodies and adornments, themselves not dependent on fixed space. Property, both necessary provisions and social luxuries, were essentially as movable as barangays themselves.[8] In Ilokano-speaking regions, native people called the barangay social unit the *ili* and the common townspeople kailian. While these townships could, for a time, be fixed, they were similarly bound together by social kinships. Thus, like the barangay, the ili was not a fixed unit but instead was highly mobile. This ethic of land-based barangay mobility is exemplified in the caravans that wandered Luzon and fled the Ilocos coast, eventually settling in the Cagayan Valley and the Central Luzon wetlands.

Beyond local barangays, other regional powers established maritime polities by way of the Indian Ocean and the West Philippine Sea. The Sultanate of Sulu was one of the most powerful maritime states in the region, posing challenges to the Spanish and early American colonial states for over three centuries. The sultanate was most likely founded by Sharif ul-Hashim of Johore (present-day constituent state of Malaysia) in 1405, capitalizing on Muslim proselytizing in the region since the late fourteenth century. The sultanate therefore manifested as a mixture of the barangay structure of social mobility—with trading and raiding economies—and the introduction of a governing sacred text: the Qur'an. The political innovation of the sultanate and other Muslim barangays centralized worship and authority toward Allah and his religious emissaries. Rather than dependence on a local datu, sovereignty instead became deferred to a higher power, and the locus of political-religious relations looked westward toward Mecca. Recognizing the increasing influence of Muslim maritime power, many datus of non-Muslin barangays renamed themselves as rajahs to facilitate the translation of their local power should they encounter conflicts with Muslims.[9]

During contact and conquest in the late sixteenth century, European expeditions in their small numbers might be considered as foreign yet nonetheless maritime participants in the archipelagic contests of power in Southeast Asia. Precolonial maritime polities themselves facilitated the first contact with Europeans in the Philippines. When Ferdinand Magellan's depleted expedition landed on the Central Philippine island of Homonhon on March 16, 1521, they disembarked on uninhabited land to find food supplies. Rajah Humabon of Cebu found them and led them ashore farther in the Visayas to his island settlement. Enrique, Magellan's Malaccan slave and interpreter, facilitated discussions between the crew and local rajahs and datus. Recognizing a potential ally against other datus in the Visayas, Rajah Humabon converted to Christianity in order to gain the allegiance of Magellan's fleet. However, the datu Lapu-Lapu refused conversion, and on April 27 Magellan waged war on Lapu-Lapu's barangay. Recognizing the threat of a Humabon-Magellan alliance, Lapu-Lapu commanded his *maharlika* (warriors) to wage war against the combined fleet. He killed Magellan and most of the Portuguese forces, forcing them to flee. In the process, the Italian chronicler Antonio Pigafetta (who had accompanied the expedition) not only recorded the flora and fauna of the Magellan travels but also jotted down different Bisaya-language vocabulary with rudimentary translations. Pigafetta, then, may be considered the first racial archivist of what would become *las islas Filipinas*.[10]

Pigafetta's account of the interbarangay wars became the foundations for the late sixteenth-century conquest of the Spanish East Indies. In 1529, the kingdoms of Spain and Portugal agreed on a partition of Southeast Asia between themselves, with Spain taking the Philippines. Seeking to gain an economic foothold into a China market, the conquistador Miguel López de Legazpi established the first successful Spanish settlement in Iloilo, in 1566. However, a 1565 voyage pressed the need for more strong-handed colonial occupation in the archipelago when the Basque sailor and friar Andrés de Urdaneta charted a safe nautical path between Manila and Acapulco. In 1570, the Battle of Manila (1570) was the death knell for Luzon barangay leadership and signaled the rapid rise of Spanish commerce and conquest in the region. Through the permanent colonial settlement of Manila, Spain established military rule and facilitated Catholic missionaries' expeditions inland. Furthermore, Manila became the port of call for the long-lived successor of the Urdaneta voyage and the boon for Spain's investments in the East Indies: the galleon trade.[11]

Unlike its larger administrative body to the east, the Viceroyalty of New Spain (now modern-day Mexico), the Philippines was too inaccessible from Spain to become a viable settler colony. But despite the weakness of direct colonial rule from Europe, Spanish authorities were nonetheless able to swiftly coerce barangay into fixed villages and labor regimes built to sustain a local church. Across the Spanish Empire, this process was called *reducción*. To *reducir* a native population, the colonial state forcibly moved people from dispersed villages into the spatial management of a parish. Furthermore, they were made to convert to Christianity and conduct mandatory labor for the local church. This colonial labor system was known as *polos y servicios*: hard labor in construction and military expeditions (polos) and domestic service for churches and religious orders (servicios). Furthermore, tributes were to be paid to the friars as in-kind tithes or as fees for religious rituals.[12]

Thus, reducción is a process of enclosure and dispossession but is marked by its chiefly Catholic (specifically friar) orientation. Through its theft of land and labor time, reducción inaugurated a highly localized form of racial capitalism. Vis-à-vis local churches, priests developed their own racial archives by organizing people according to their utility as *barrio* laborers, as economic contributors, and as Christian subjects. Under a locality that had undergone reducción, families did not possess legal titles to the land, since they were assumed to have no such hereditary rights, as natives were declared *ni rey ni roque* (without king nor castle). Instead, families were assigned to plots of land legally owned by the king of Spain and brokered by the local parish. Furthermore, since parish-led barrio life increased agricultural production, it also demanded sedentary life, and thus *indios* were generally banned from leaving town.[13]

However, the Church alone could not ensure the tenacity of its rule in the lowlands. Since native townspeople vastly outnumbered missionaries, the Church also maintained its hold on power through native elite collaboration. In particular, these native collaborators, who were designated *cabezas de barangay* (barangay heads), enforced the polos y servicios necessary to maintain colonial rule. The parish, in collaboration with these elites, maintained secular rule of law and Christianized life among barangays.[14] Without a Spanish settler population and a consistent flow of resources, reducción remained within lowland barrios and only then among the limited spatial jurisdictions of rural parishes. A result of this piecemeal reducción was the tenacity of Indigenous economy and sociopolitical sovereignty in the highlands. In the Cordilleras, archaeological evidence suggests that rather than being 2,000 years old, the rice terraces were only as old as Spanish colonization.

The terraces were thus built as a means of maintaining control over native political economies in the mountains and valleys against an encroaching colonial order.[15]

As a result of the retreat and construction of economy in the mountains, highland peoples creatively responded to lowlands colonization while maintaining strongholds against it. According to Oona Paredes, non-Christianized highland peoples such as the Lumads in Mindanao (and likewise the Ifugaos in Northern Luzon) exemplify a pericolonial condition. That is, while not directly colonized by Spanish missionaries, Indigenous peoples, their economies, and their oral traditions nonetheless formed out of such encounters with colonial forces.[16] The fledgling state thus relied on attempts at military recruitment among lowland indios for expeditions up the mountains in attempts to subdue highland peoples. Around the Cordilleras, cabezas de barangay and missionary priests mobilized their indio populations into military polos for such expeditions. This punitive technique of military enclosure finds its continued use during the nineteenth-century Spanish and the twentieth-century American colonial states.[17]

But despite the Church's best efforts to police native mobility and despite the state's periodic demand for military power around the mountains, native peoples moved and organized along the slopes of the Cordilleras. Political alliances between lowland and highland peoples, often the bane of the weak state's efforts to control the region, stemmed from well-integrated routes along the valleys and slopes. These trade routes also doubled as ways of developing kinship structures across regions, which proved fertile for the late eighteenth-century revolutions that struck the Amianan. For example, Anselmo Cariño, Gabriela Silang's father, made a living (as many others did) as a trader between Vigan and Abra. During Cariño's travels, he married an Itneg woman in Abra. They sent their daughter to the Ilocos coast to be educated in a parish. Through pastoral education, Gabriela learned Spanish and was able to navigate religious and civic leadership as well as Ilokano-speaking native life.[18]

The persistence of highlands-lowlands trade in the Amianan outside of the state also promoted the Ilokano language as the lingua franca of the region. Even though Ilokano was one of the native languages well documented by the Church, it allowed Christianized native life to maintain contact with the highlands beyond the purview of the parish. Thus, the tenacity of Ilokano as the lingua franca in Northern and Central Luzon fertilized the seeds of anticolonial organizing in and out of the Spanish state. It is not a surprise that insurgents called themselves kailian, or fellow townspeople, even if socioreligious rule had meant to divide and conquer native people in separate jurisdictions.[19]

On the eve of the British occupation of Manila, kailian had long expressed fervent dissatisfaction with the exploitative regimes of socioreligious colonial rule. Furthermore, in 1756 a smallpox epidemic killed 710 people in Vigan alone during its first six months and many more beyond the city.[20] Already suffering from depleted populations, indios were then subject to increased polos for expeditions in the Cordilleras. In 1759, the Spanish authorities ordered about 2,000 recruits to invade the Cordilleras. Seizing upon the tenuousness of Spanish rule during the British invasion and the frustration of native people, the Silang Uprising proved effective in destabilizing Spanish assumptions in its colonial strength. After the Seven Years' War, the Amianan became subject to some of the earliest state-led initiatives at increased police power and plantation capitalism. The robust organizing of the kailian in the Amianan thus made counterinsurgency and conquest a priority for the Spanish state.

Visions of the Plantation State

After the Seven Years' War, the Spanish Empire transformed extant forms of labor into new forms useful for a modernizing state. In turn, the establishment of a plantation-driven economic regime through a tobacco monopoly crystallized forms of race that mapped directly onto emerging capitalist modes of production. Racial archives, when organized around the barrio and its church, aggregated around the friar's technologies of colonial order: the confession box, attendance at mass, and barrio work.[21] Through polos y servicios, lowland indios became known as readily available farmworkers. As pericolonial people, highland natives since the sixteenth century stood in as the impediment for total control over Luzon as well as access to a possible Spanish gold rush in the Cordilleras.[22] But a new regime established more robust and sweeping techniques to collect knowledge and—in their view—render Luzon's land and people productive. Thus, this Bourbon plantation state imbued Luzon's racial archives with more explicitly economic logics, carrying forward Catholic racial forms into state-driven agrarian capitalist ones.

In 1700, the death of the Hapsburg monarch King Charles II of Spain triggered a war for succession for the throne. By 1813 in the Treaty of Utrecht, the French Bourbons lay claim to the Spanish Crown but maintained its sovereign independence from France. However, by the end of the war Britain rose to dominance as the chief commercial and naval power of Europe whose interests looked to expansion in Southeast Asia. Despite the new Bourbon monarchy's hold on the Spanish Empire in terms of military infrastructure and capital, the early eighteenth century marked the beginning of its slow decline on the world stage. The Bourbon monarchs' propensity for Enlightenment-influenced governance spread across the empire into the Americas and—slowly—to the East Indies. During the mid-eighteenth century, the Spanish colonial state increased its interests in extracting labor and land through the Church's land estates, or the barrios. In rudimentary efforts to participate in commodity production in the region, Spanish landowners increased sharecropping production. As a result, in lowlands Luzon increased colonial landownership and industry displaced peasants who became dependent on precarious livelihoods through commercial agriculture.[23]

While some local industrial production found success with the aid of parishes, the circulation of commodities—overland trade and transportation—proved difficult in practice. Bandits in the provinces endangered the circulation of small produce between barrios. Into the late eighteenth century, Philippine liberalization took off only in spurts, with piecemeal successes and much failure. And throughout, the immediate solutions were enacted through attempts at racial and labor management.[24]

The Seven Years' War revealed the precarity of Spanish colonization in the Philippines. The occupation of Manila (1762–64) perhaps encapsulated the tenuousness of the Spanish order in the archipelago. Immediately after the war, the Bourbon monarchs sought to invest in liberal economic reforms in the Spanish colonies. In 1765, King Carlos IV appointed his lawyer José de Gálvez as the *visitadór general* (chief inspector) of the colonies. Tasked with economic development in the Indies, de Gálvez prioritized two state-run or state-led industries in New Spain: tobacco monopolies and mining. In the Philippines, gold in the mountains had attracted conquistadores' efforts to invade the Cordilleras but to little success against well-organized Igorot warfare. In the archipelago, a commodity monopoly looked more favorable as an option to generate profit.[25]

Spain implemented economic reforms throughout its colonies in the eighteenth century, and these initiatives in the Philippines came under two *gobernadores-general* of *las islas Filipinas*: Don Simon de Anda (1709–76), a Basque official and lieutenant governor of Manila during the Seven Years' War, and José Basco y Vargas (1733–1805), from Andalusia. More than their other predecessors on the islands, Anda and Basco developed the most comprehensive plan to liberalize the Philippine economy and consolidate capitalist development. At the command of de Gálvez, Philippine governors were tasked to rationalize Spain's most remote and most precarious colony. Looking to the success and profits that de Gálvez had in Mexico, Spain mandated that the monopoly be established, despite the lack of local capital and land to establish it in the Philippine project at the scale of New Spain. Furthermore, Madrid urged that the monopoly be a peaceful enterprise. In response, Anda limited his economic experiments to Luzon so as to contain its implementation to a single manageable island.[26]

The liberalization of the Philippines required the following economic necessities. The Spanish government needed to wean the islands off of its dependence on the volatile galleon trade. Under Anda, the Philippines launched research into establishing a partial monopoly in the Philippines while finding ways to finance the scheme. Between 1785 and 1789 under Basco, Spain opened Manila to limited foreign commerce in an attempt to transition out of the galleon economy. Next, Basco founded the short-lived private Sociedad Económica de los Amigos del País in the Philippines in order to generate intellectual exchange between the Spanish colonies that had implemented a tobacco monopoly and other profit-driven ventures. Furthermore, the Sociedad was to take the intellectual helm of rational colonial government. In the founding documents of the organization, the group declared its vision for the islands they had deemed unproductive for far too long. First, the Sociedad aimed to maximize the use of productive time (*empleo del tiempo el uso más noble, y provechoso*). Second, the organization sought to introduce markers of civilized productivity in the islands through abundance, general prosperity, and decadence. Third, the organization aimed to instill a culture of study and observation and the application thereof for the good of economic development. These goals, the group envisioned, could be implemented if the colony was to be run as a commercial company (*empresa*) rather than in the "unawake lethargy of [their imperial] forebears [*Despertar el letargo de nuestros antepasados*]."[27]

The Sociedad with the aim of promoting economic development, implemented rigorous disciplinary study of various aspects of the colony. In order to extract natural resources, the organization promoted the research of natural history so that it might educate "general ignorance" and "foment" the industrial arts among natives. Consequently, the Sociedad also took upon itself the task of agricultural research, especially "rustic" practices as a means to educate subjects in the fundamentals of production. Rustic practices included fundamental climatology and knowledge of harvest seasons. Next, the organization researched manufacturing systems as well as the promotion of factory labor among native people. After this, the organization was to undertake research in internal and international commerce so that the Philippines would serve as a more robust market node rather than simply facilitating Chinese-European trade. Finally, the organization undertook research into industrial and popular education in the islands so as to promote the colonial economy and develop industrial uses of local populations. In effect, the Sociedad Económica de los Amigos del País immediately envisioned the islands as a self-sustaining production and distribution center rather than a port colony, from farm to factory.[28]

While the Filipinas' official mandates for economic development hinged on the tobacco monopoly, the Sociedad expressed its desire to diversify the production portfolio of the colony. In Cagayan, which became a central production site for tobacco in the nineteenth century, members of the organization looked to produce cotton as well. A 1783 correspondence delivered by José de Galvez suggests that state agents had been researching smaller plots of cotton to ascertain the sustainability of mass cultivation. Furthermore, agents had gathered samples of local dyes and textile production with the possibility of stimulating production in other parts of the islands. The perpetual problem for these massive projects was a lack of labor. The colonial regime needed to fashion native people into workers of the empire's image.[29]

Through the economic research facilitated by the Sociedad Económica de los Amigos del País, Basco's Luzon administration became a site for economic research and deeper practices of archiving. The practical and philosophical aims of the organization, facilitated by the state and its military, allowed the Spanish Empire to penetrate into native life by means of language training, production surveillance, and various other methods. As a part of its efforts to maximize internal commerce, the Sociedad promoted military and civilian expeditions such that the inland provinces could be better mapped and connected through better communication infrastructures in the name of "prosperity."[30] The organization also acted as a de facto advisory board for Basco's leadership. Basco's own hesitation to implement an immediate monopoly emerged from his subordinates' reports of the limitations of state-led production. He would need to finance resources to mapping the terrain of Luzon while also noting the differentiated ways in which indios and *infieles* used tobacco. In turn, Basco's state could theoretically find self-sustaining markets for its product.[31]

To facilitate the smooth development of commodity production, Basco needed to suppress all forms of dissent. Since Madrid mandated that the monopoly not be established in a state of warfare, Basco's administration coupled economic development with counterinsurgency. In particular, opposing the tobacco monopoly branded one as a sinner, because the monopoly was exercised through the divine right of kings that emanated from Spain to the Philippine colony. The most prominent inland threat to the monopoly was smuggling, from which developed different gradations of punishment with increasing harshness for repeat offenders. Smuggling occurred at three points: production (through unregistered fields), circulation (through banditry, stealing high-grade crop, or unsanctioned pathways of transport), and sale (through the black market). In order to bring counterinsurgency into village life, the administration established the Resguardo, the tobacco revenue police. Not wanting to stoke rebellions and local conflict, Basco warned the Resguardo of the importance of gathering evidence on townsfolk before embarking on a full-fledged investigation for contraband. Furthermore, Basco mandated that every barrio should have a tobacco warehouse in order to centralize farmers' deposit of crops and to develop accounting records of production and distribution. The native overseers, or *caudillos*, were chosen for their cooperation with the state and their proficiency in Spanish. They were tasked with reporting all dissent to officials based on their local relationships with other farmers. Therefore, economic policing served as a technology to produce racial archive.[32]

Therefore, the tobacco monopoly's production and circulation inaugurated a Luzon-wide system of carceral capitalism. The monopoly's administrators criminalized alternative economies against the plantation and punished nonproductive activity as laziness. In particular, Basco and the Sociedad Económica de los Amigos del País called those resistant to work *vagos* (tramp, slacker, loafer), and urged state troops to keep accounts on anyone who refused to work. To extract economic value from nature and people while suppressing nonindustrial activities, the colonial state practiced economic archiving. Through a robust project of ongoing knowledge production, all potential resources were orientated toward the monopoly in a cash-strapped distant colony. The colonial state's techniques of knowledge production would be put in place well into the nineteenth century and taken up in earnest by the American occupation in the early twentieth century: militarized (proto) ethnological expeditions, statistical data collection, and counterinsurgency against dissent.[33]

In practice, racial archiving and economic development were uneven processes in Luzon. The state could cultivate lowland areas closer to Manila with minimal investment but instead opted to strike deals with local *principalías* or auction the rights to land or commerce among monied *mestizos*. During the monopoly's first decade, Basco and later administrations focused their efforts on Central Luzon, the most accessible expanse of fertile land in proximity to Manila.[34] After centuries of friar-led conquest, repurposing the environment inland for cultivation amounted to a new type of conquest but this time akin to counterinsurgency. In a 1787 letter on the difficulty of establishing *renta de tabaco* (tobacco revenue sites), Basco noted that tobacco officials faced "outlaws, vagabonds, and contrabandists" in the immediate provinces around Manila, who took to insulting the work of the state's forces and robbing them of their wares before they could establish the *rentas*. Despite the risk of skirmishes in the countryside, Basco emphasized the importance of the "public peace, security and righteous value" of the monopoly, carried out in the name of the Spanish king. Those quickly subjugated became known as *dociles*: pacified and loyal vassals of the empire.[35] In the process of establishing tobacco production in the countryside, the state bore the responsibility of recording and managing obstructions to the project by means of local surveillance and subjugating people to more direct means of colonial rule.[36]

The industrial conquest of Northern Luzon was the crown jewel of the tobacco project. The state expanded the monopoly northward in 1785, first into Pangasinan and the Ilocos and then swiftly into the Cagayan Valley to the northeast. The soils of the Cagayan Valley and the Ilocos coast in the northwest proved favorable for the crop's cultivation. Prior to the monopoly, tobacco had been cultivated on small plots of land and used in diverse ways around the islands. It could grow highland or lowland, and indeed the crop quickly took hold as a comestible drug in the Philippines even before formal Spanish settlement in Manila. The Spanish ground it into snuff, while indios and Igorots used tobacco primarily as leaves and cigars. The finest-grade tobacco, if not ground into snuff for *criollo* consumption, was to be rolled into cigars for sale around the world. Low-grade tobacco was distributed instead among indios, who could only buy cigarettes directly from the state. Through the monopoly and its exploitation of extant tobacco consumption, the Spanish colonial state found a ready market among native people.[37]

But despite the Spanish *cortes generales*' wishes, the monopoly was not a peaceful affair. As quickly as 1788—three years after the economic conquest of Northern Luzon—authorities in the Ilocos and Manila received word of an uprising to take place immediately after the harvest season. Colonial police moved swiftly across the coast to arrest those rumored to be leaders, but into the nineteenth century the area percolated with social unrest. Furthermore, this period marked the mass caravan emigrations from the Amianan (Northern

Luzon) Ilokano homelands toward the forests and marshes of Central Luzon. As the historian Grace Mateo argued, lowland natives did not simply flee an oppressive order but instead actively rebelled against colonial violence by uprooting their ties to specific plots of land and bringing their labor power elsewhere around Luzon. In the nineteenth century they reinvoked the barangay—the moveable social unit—to protest the fixed exploitative space of the colonial barrio.[38]

While the upheavals and mass emigrations in the Ilocos coast posed immediate challenges to the swift Spanish order, the state's economic development nonetheless benefited from the violent displacement of Ilokanos from their coastal homelands. Mobile Ilokanos, without the economic livelihoods of the coast, could be coerced into working wage jobs or into sharecropping schemes in tobacco plantations in the Cagayan Valley. For those who traveled *idiay abagatan* (to the south, into Central Luzon), they provided free labor power for clearing the forests and planting rice and for other tobacco farms.[39]

Through the monopoly, the concentration of capital in Manila became less dependent on maritime trade and prospered through inland agricultural production. By the 1840s, Manila's financial strength rose due to the upsurge in its cigar factories. Furthermore, the rise of foreign settlements and cigar factories in Manila brought about a wave of women's labor and feminized work into the city. The gendering of tobacco work was a direct import of the monopoly's Mexican counterpart, wherein women were believed to have better coordination to roll cigars, while men had the vigor to work in the fields. Therefore, the lowland indios who were seen in the fields were, in the vast majority, men. From the masculinization of those racial archives, state administrators and later ethnologists developed ideas of who was a worker.[40]

With easier access to the Philippines by steamship, European and American trading firms set up shop in Manila by the mid-nineteenth century. While the Spanish formally denounced the threat of the foreign, in practice they encouraged foreign merchants into the colony, with the advantage that Spanish finances could be conserved while economic development came from the outside. These trading houses opened up employment for indios and mestizos from the lower middle class, with some measures of literacy from a widening public educational system. The major US investors were from New England, such as the Boston-based Russell & Sturgis firm, while from Germany firms included E. Kloepfer & Co. Among these economic travelers several stayed in the Philippines, reading both the friars' local studies and emerging works in Southeast Asian anthropology. Through their own economic data collection and ethnological pursuits, they further developed a racial archive of the nineteenth-century Philippines.[41]

Between Northern Luzon and Manila—a prominent tobacco monopoly circuit—the racialization of three broad groups emerged in their modern forms, according to their relationship with the production and circulation of the Philippines' most profitable crop. At the nexus points of commerce (e.g., marketplaces and middlemen), repatriated Chinese were necessary to the distribution of tobacco but with the caveat that they become easier to archive by the state: they, like other subjects, were forced to standardize their names into romanized script to make them more manageable by state officials. In the fields of Northern and Central Luzon, Ilokano indios who emigrated from their homelands became migrant peasants, ready for plantation labor. In the mountains, infieles who smuggled tobacco were seen as a danger to the colonial economy but with the potential for economic benefit for the state. I chart some of their aspects below.

Cordillera Contraband

Through the tobacco monopoly, colonial officials in the Philippines steered criminal penalties toward offenses against state profit. The monopoly criminalized alternate economies of distribution as contraband and equivalent to treason against the colonial state. The infiel, initially signifying the myriad peoples beyond the purview of the Catholic order, became offensive to God and the king as disruptions to colonial profit. Through the nineteenth century in Luzon, the most predominant overland offender was the Igorot.

For the Spanish state, the Cordilleras' primary impediment to tobacco cultivation was not just the undulating terrain. The Spanish feared Indigenous geographies of circulation, long practiced between highland and lowland peoples, that took place along uncharted rivers and valleys beyond the purview of the colonial state. For Ilokano tobacco smokers who lost their local supplies to the monopoly, Igorot mountain cultivation and trade offered them an alternative source to buy goods. In 1800 Joaquín Martínez de Zúñiga (1760–1818), a Spanish government chronicler, observed that the premade cigars sold in Ilocos (through official government *sari-sari*, or variety stores) were so deplorable that Ilokanos boycotted purchasing them altogether.[42] Igorot economic prospectors, in response to lowlands demand at the implementation of the monopoly, increased cigar production from local craft quantities toward distribution in a Luzon market. From tobacco cultivation and pericolonial trade, an Igorot elite emerged in the western and southern slopes of the Cordilleras who controlled distribution to Ilokanos and Pangasinenses.[43]

For Basco, a provisional means of patrolling infieles in Luzon resistant to state rule would be to charge every individual in the island's population an *impuesto de capitación*: a poll tax. In a 1779 letter that proposed ways to discipline native people into "tranquility" (*tranquilidad*) and to "foment industry," Basco posited the reestablishment of reducción paired with a racially stratified tax, at six pesos per Christianized indio and twelve for "the infidels that live in San Fernando [La Union]." The location, in the southern Ilocos coast, ascertains that Basco particularly targeted Nabaloi, Ifugao, and Kankanaey Igorots, all of whom had easy valley access to the lowlands by means of modern-day Baguio. Reducción and the *capitación* as Basco imagined it had the goal of bringing unconquered peoples into state surveillance by means of a poll.[44]

Unfortunately for the Spanish state, the people of Luzon did not consent to the *impuesto de capitación* easily, despite renewed efforts at reducción. Dociles, as indios complicit with agricultural projects came to be known, were frequently valorized as loyal subjects (*vasallos leales*). In 1837 in order to patrol contraband economies, the state declared the Cordilleras a *comandancia politico-militar* (a political-military command). Through military occupation, policing contraband became synonymous with colonial counterinsurgency. In practice, the colonial government purchased contraband tobacco from Igorot traders in times of economic dearth around Luzon in order to sell to indio purchasers as official state goods. The Spanish still managed to extract wealth from the Cordilleras by allowing contraband as long as it was sold to the state.[45]

Indeed, over the course of the monopoly, *alcaldes mayor* (district mayors) in tobacco-cultivating areas observed, with considerable jealousy, the skill of highlands tobacco cultivation in the mountains beyond the purview of the colonial state. In an 1860 industrial manual noting the inconsistent quality of colonial tobacco, Don Rafael Garcia Lopez of the Cagayan rebuked the monopoly for its poor cultivation practices. In contrast to the indios working in plantations, Lopez noted that the "wild natives [*los indios salvajes*] . . . who plant tobacco in the woods" do so "with much more care" than lowland cultivators. Mountain tobacco, planted by Cordilleran peoples, produced higher-quality yields "not infrequently [*no pocas veces*]."[46] Lopez's jurisdiction, a major producer of Philippine tobacco, lies between two major mountain chains (the Sierra Madre and the Cordilleras) and their intersection. While Lopez may not have gone up there in extended trips—especially during vola-

Throughout the Philippines' modern history, the ambivalent nature of the Spanish toward chinos shifted ostensibly in the direction of modern capitalist logics. During the British occupation of Manila, while many ethnic groups rebelled against the Spanish at signs of their vulnerability, the Chinese were particularly vulnerable targets against racist cries of treason against the colonial state. Immediately after signing the 1764 Treaty of Paris, Don Simon de Anda instructed all Spanish officials to deny pardon to any Chinese left in the islands. Unlike previous expulsions, wherein businessmen in Manila defended the Chinese as critical to their operations, wartime spurred on complete anti-Chinese legislation and racist attitudes among officials. On July 17, 1767, a royal decree from the *cortes generales* declared that all Chinese were to be expelled except a select few who were to remain in remote agricultural towns. In the process of rounding up Chinese people in the islands, the Spanish military documented their numbers and any indio allies who might have conspired to hide them from officials.[53]

Mestizos (of both Spanish and Chinese descent) filled the economic void left by the expulsion of the Chinese from the Philippines. In particular, they entered into points of sale and distribution as well as into printing. At the helm of the Philippines' burgeoning literate cultures, their descendants would benefit from new wealth to study in European universities as the *ilustrados* (enlightened ones). Furthermore, this rising mestizo bourgeoisie, with control over nineteenth-century print capitalism, was well positioned to foment the rise of Philippine nationalism.[54]

However, many Spanish and criollo elites quickly expressed regret over expelling Chinese from the Philippines on the charge that indios were unsuitable to take up the work of handling money in which the Chinese were supposedly proficient. In 1772 Pedro de Calderon, a well-respected member of the Council of the Indies in Spain and a public servant in Manila, testified that barrios with Chinese residents were quantifiably more prosperous than those without, since they stimulated local exchange for necessary goods without demanding the compensation that Spanish merchants earned. From these economic testaments, Manila began to make concessions to allow reentry for select populations. On July 27, 1778, the Spanish government issued a decree to readmit Chinese farmers and artisans into the Philippines at a hard quota ceiling of 4,000 immigrants. But many of the old artisans and businessmen were too old to return, leaving the mestizos to run the vacancies they had filled since the post–Seven Years' War expulsions. In response, Basco sent emissaries to Guangdong to actively recruit younger entrepreneurs to the islands.[55]

Under a Bourbon state, the Chinese would need to be accounted for in more efficient ways. In 1779 just as he had proposed with infieles, Basco proposed the *impuesto de capitación* on approximately 10,000 *sangleyes cristianos*, or the Christianized Chinese who converted to do business on the islands on behalf of the Spanish.[56] However, for the trickle of newer Chinese migrants as well as outstanding Chinese families on the islands, naming practices proved to be an obstacle to comprehensive state archiving. In 1849, in order to account for their subjects, the government proclaimed that all people in the Philippines would need to register with their barrio parishes under a Hispanized name. As historian Richard T. Chu argues, name standardization was meant to fix Chinese people in the Philippines into a colonial surveillance system, subjecting them to the racial archives of the state. Since many southern Chinese merchants changed their names at different stages in life, Spanish administrators maintained that they could elude the watch of the state and exploit a different identity to profit from smuggling and contraband economies. Nonetheless, many maintained use of both names, further fueling anti-Chinese sentiments among the islands' elites.[57]

In its early work to establish commodity production on the archipelago, the Sociedad Económica de los Amigos del País kept watch of the shifting roles of the Chinese in Philippine industry. In a 1783 letter, Ariaco Gonzalez Carvajal, a director of the organization, warned of the vulnerability of the islands' developing industry. He claimed that the predecessors of the Bourbon administration had adhered far too long to old and corrupt commercial ties, particularly to a peculiar "fanaticism" (*fanatismo*) for the Chinese as well as for Malabars (from South Asia). Consequently, the Sociedad saw commercial education as part of its projects of "industrial fomentation" of natives: teach indios how to become self-sustaining market subjects, preferably with Spanish-language instruction, so that the state could wean itself off of its reliance on Chinese distribution. Nonetheless, these fears attest to the tenacity of non-European maritime trade within the South China Sea, the Indian Ocean, and the northeastern archipelagoes. In practice, the colonial state needed to draw upon the deep fabric of Chinese commercial life in Luzon in order to make headway into inland markets for tobacco and other future state goods.[58]

Through their roles as economic middlemen, Chinese merchants developed flexible social structures to navigate the hostility of Spanish colonial rule. What Calderon noted as a frugal lifestyle and economic propensity emerged from long-standing negotiations that Chinese businesspeople made with their communities. Despite periods of brutal exclusion in the Philippines, they nonetheless made headway in Philippine commerce in the unevenly enforced weak state of the nineteenth-century Spanish regime. When European and American trading houses began to dominate Manila commerce, Chinese businessmen adopted flexible economies of trust to profit as conduits in exchange for selling foreign goods at their sari-sari in the rural provinces.[59]

As conduits of capital from Manila to the provinces, the Chinese were simultaneously coveted for their economic utility and denigrated for their racial status. *Mestizos de sangley* (mixed-race Chinese), descended from Chinese merchants in the eighteenth century, replicated the anti-Chinese racisms of the nineteenth century. Through their colonial education, mestizos de sangley in the nineteenth century desired the racial economic position of Spaniard criollos and Spanish-blooded mestizos. Perhaps the most infamous case of this ancestral hatred was the intellectual and *filibustero* (dissident) José Rizal, whose Fujianese ancestry can be traced to Binondo-dwelling merchants from the late seventeenth century who converted to Catholicism. In his revolutionary novels, Rizal frequently expressed disdain for Chinese merchants' lowly civilizational status while disavowing his own ancestry as he incubated in European higher education. These legacies of cultural and economic racisms have carried over in other manifestations of arts and quotidian culture in the Filipino diaspora today.[60]

As embodiments of abstract capital, the Chinese in the Philippines were simultaneously vilified and desired for their economic uses. In practice, they facilitated the flow of goods and finance between Manila and the provinces while continuing to operate in more remote regions through maritime economies. In European, elite Philippine, and American observations, Chinese merchants stood in as the infrastructures of capitalist exchange and commodity circulation. They are racialized as embodiments of alien capital, as ethnic studies scholar Iyko Day argues in North American contexts, but not as abstract labor. In the Philippine context, abstract labor became embodied by the lowlands native, or the indio.

Industrious Indios

A single supreme crop required a singular homogenous cheap worker. To propagate the tobacco monopoly's production, this worker was to be precarious enough to depend on plantation labor for livelihood but with enough income to purchase the final product from a single seller. In practice, implementing the monopoly saw many cases of violent clashes and other means of protest. For example, in Bicol (the southeast peninsula of Luzon), Bikolano peasants protested the swift action of the state monopoly by giving up tobacco, despite the drug's popularity as a recreational substance and as a gift or barter item. Basco refused the prospect of deregulating tobacco economies because the state could not govern gift and barter, which are noncapitalist modes of exchange. In Bataan, an infamous 1787 incident saw *resguardos* clash with rebels, leading to a swift but brutal response from the state. Resguardos burned illegal fields, and rebels killed the forces with arrows. In response, Manila sent police forces, a judge, and a hangman. Prior to the monopoly, justice would have been doled out by individual barrios or *hacenderos*.[61] But because the state claimed ownership over production, Manila moved quickly to extend penal sovereignty over the Bataan hinterlands. Coercing indios into industry, it seemed, could not be done without violent action but in the process extended state power into rural areas faster than the friars had allowed Manila to do.[62]

Like infieles, indios as workers were conceived to be a constant project of civilization and labor. The state feared that if indios lost their work animals (such as the *kalabaw*), they would resort to reverting back into vagabond lives, uncentered around a barrio, in informal settlements. Furthermore, without industrial labor, Bourbon administrators feared, indios would resort into becoming *ladrones*, or bandits who preyed upon the circulation of commodities and capital along rudimentary roadways outside Manila. Around Manila, the Spanish did indeed report "epidemics" of banditry in the city's outskirts and used peasant economic resistance as justification to extend penal systems beyond major municipalities.[63]

In the late eighteenth century, Spanish officials did not immediately conceptualize the indio as inherently skilled for industrial labor. For Basco, in order to promote basic levels of labor power, indios were to be rationed rice, their racially suitable carbohydrate.[64] For Sociedad member Patricio Daruin, the abundance of Philippine soils could also translate to the fecundity of its workers. For "*indios sin arte*," the state would need to cultivate a sustainable work ethic. Indios would need "intelligence and practice," developed in a suitable environment for work. Feeding indios could be a start to awakening a labor force and "fomenting industry," but the organization would need to target more intimate aspects of native culture in order to do so.[65]

According to the Sociedad Económica de los Amigos del País, one of the obstacles to forging an indio was family life itself. Indio women, according to Daruin, held too many responsibilities at home, which limited the ready labor supply for cigar manufacturing. Furthermore, family life itself focused the energy of labor at home and remained unproductive to the reinvigoration of the Filipinas that the organization imagined. Indio life, including the distribution of men and women among social kinships, would need to be organized around state commercial activities.[66]

To maximize the productivity of men and women in their agricultural projects, the Spanish administration implemented a gendered division of labor to facilitate cigar manufacturing. The men in the fields, overseen by forepersons (*sobrestantes*), labored over the raw resource, far removed from the feminized industrial labor of the Manila factory. But around the management of tobacco plantations, men became the primary resources for the racial archiving of indios in rural Luzon. In Manila as in other monopolies of the Spanish Empire, administrators established separate women's offices, specifically mandated to oversee the production of cigarettes. As with the foremen in the fields, tobacco factories were overseen by forewomen. In the Mexico monopoly, women were believed to have the innate ability to delicately roll cigars. Women's labor in cigar factories was used to advertise an effeminate quality of Spanish colonial cigars for which monied men in the Global North developed tastes.[67]

Like the crop itself, the tobacco monopoly's imagined indio was not cultivated peacefully. As elsewhere in Luzon, the late eighteenth-century Ilocos coast was a hotbed for uprisings against a waning Spanish order. Four decades after the Silang Rebellion, the Basi Revolt fomented years of dissatisfaction with Spanish economic reforms in the agrarian coast. While the Spanish monopolized the production and circulation of tobacco, they also shaved off profits from *basi* (sugarcane wine) private production. In 1807 in the Ilocos Norte town of Piddig, Ilokanos revolted against the Spanish sari-sari distribution centers. The fighting spread for weeks around the region until it was pacified by Spanish military response in September 1807.[68] Under the collaborative power of officials, friars, and principalías (native and mestizo economic elites), the northwest coast of Luzon became a politically unstable region amid the state's desire to cultivate tobacco there. Ilokanos in the coast maintained an uneasy and often violent relationship with mestizo and indio elites. Certainly, rural Ilokanos may have had the numbers to overwhelm plantation elites, as the region experienced a population boom in the early nineteenth century. But unable to sustain larger family numbers in the absence of subsistence farmland, many Ilokanos left to farm elsewhere in the northeast or to the south.[69]

Ilokano emigration responded to the alienating fixity of tobacco labor on expropriated land, but state and other foreign ethnologists nonetheless attempted to harness Ilokano mobility for profit. The monopoly's implementation in the Ilocos disrupted the small-plot cultivation of Ilokano farmers along the northwest coast and mountain slopes. Whereas local Ilokano tobacco had been sold by artisans in robust local markets, the monopoly diverted all grown tobacco to Manila for rolling. If farming families did not outright rebel against the state, they packed their belongings and traveled *abagatan* (south) to Central Luzon.[70]

Through their mobilities, Ilokano emigrants to the Cagayan Valley and the Abagatan (Central Luzon) could overturn the spatial fixation of the Catholic order and relocate the loci of indio life beyond the Church. From the north through Ilokano emigration, Central Luzon became famed as the Philippines' rice granary. The inland Ilokano diaspora cleared the swamps and forests of this region, tilling the land for more diverse commodity production after the monopoly.[71]

The state's racial archiving accounted for emigration in ways that could be potentially beneficial for the monopoly and its agricultural afterlives. For the Spanish state, the mobile indio peasant could be a potential settler into areas they deemed cultivable. European social scientists and other investors decontextualized the emigrations and labor of the Ilokano as essential racial characteristics, noting the state's desire to harness them for resettlement projects and other regions in need of cultivation. Therefore, the industrious indio crystallized as an abstract migratory peasant suitable for plantation work, certainly in Luzon. It would not be long before the colonial state would look specifically to Ilokanos as settler colonial human resources in places such as Palawan, Mindanao, and later Hawai'i.[72]

A CENTURY AFTER THE TOBACCO MONOPOLY was first implemented, it became clear to Spanish administrators that the monopoly was unsustainable as a state project. Out of fear of growing insurgency and concerns of corruption, Spaniards campaigned to abolish the monopoly but not to halt its profit-generating activities. When the *cortes generales* abolished the monopoly in 1882, the industry was sold to a Spanish entrepreneur, the Marquis de Comillas Antonio Lopez y Lopez. Lopez managed its operations through the Compañia General de Tabacos de Filipinas, or Tabacalera. Witnessing the lucrative potential of the Philippines, private investors magnified production and dissemination of other tropical crops.[73]

Between Northern Luzon's tobacco and Manila's cigars, the state needed to build efficient ways to transport crops and distribute the final products.

This endeavor was more easily achieved in lowland plains, but the mountain terrain of Luzon posed a threat to the circulation of capital. In the 1880s in a last attempt to render the Cordilleras accessible to colonial industry, the Spanish invaded the mountain range with more force. More aggressive invasions, especially from recruited Ilokano soldiers in the lowlands under Spanish command, rendered the Cordilleras a war zone. In the process, the Spanish built horse-cart paths to facilitate easier transit of commodities through the mountains but nonetheless maintained maritime modes of circulation. Well into the early twentieth century, Tabacalera continued to use company steamers to ship harvests to Manila for processing rather than rudimentary overland roads.[74]

Overall, the tobacco monopoly rendered the island of Luzon an industrial plantation.[75] Witnessing the monopoly's success, prospectors launched research expeditions to ascertain the viability of other crops, such as sugar and tropical seeds. Agricultural products funneled into Manila for processing, to be sold throughout the islands or for a global market. No longer a port colony and a religious borderland, Luzon became imagined as a fecund tropical producer for colonial industry, with native workers in need of civilization through labor regimes. Through tobacco and its managers' racial archives, nature, including human nature, became commodified as resources for capitalist production.[76]

In the process, colonized peoples, already subject to coerced labor systems in precolonial and early modern societies, effectively became a Philippine proletariat. Highland peoples at the periphery of colonial rule flourished through the insurgent economies and trading routes that took advantage of Northern Luzon's mountainous geographies. Through alternative trade routes and production schemes, Igorots carved out economic niches in response to Spanish colonial occupation, responding as well as shaping imperial commodity regimes. But these economies targeted the Cordilleras as a renewed cite of conquest for the Spanish military and, later, the United States.[77]

The Luzon plantation generated knowledge commodities, in tandem with (and in the service of) the acquisition of capital. The knowledge cultivated and manufactured in the long nineteenth century decontextualized the social and economic upheavals of the late eighteenth century, rendering multiethnic responses to capitalism as racial characteristics. Racial archiving throughout this period became material that needed sorting for future research. In 1778, José de Gálvez founded an actual archive, the Archivo General de Indias in Seville, the epicenter of Spanish colonial research for historians. From its economic cultures of archiving, Bourbon Spain amassed a glut of papers from correspondence and observations that needed an institutional home from which future interpreters could study the empire through the documents of economic development.

Philippine visual commodities as well as tobacco and other tropical goods found in markets around the world. The Suez Canal and rapid steamship travel facilitated the velocity of exchange. Furthermore, the mechanical reproducibility of print and pictures made racial archiving more accessible to audiences far distance from the Philippines and allowed them to participate in racial formations as well. In the late nineteenth century, the Spanish Empire brought racial spectacles onto the continent through its expositions. Philippine writers and artists sought to exploit the ease of access to printing and reproduction. Through capitalist circulation, the racial economy of Luzon not only industrialized through the monopoly but also crystallized into its modern forms—as racial images and as labor commodities—through exhibition around the world.

CHAPTER TWO

The Work of the Filipino in the Age of Mechanical Reproduction

In Two Parts

I want a History of Looking.

—Roland Barthes, *Camera Lucida: Reflections on Photography* (1981), 12

During the first two centuries of Spanish rule, the Philippines was an economic backwater in Spain's transpacific empire. General knowledge of Philippine peoples was restricted to conquistadores and missionaries who lived among native populations. In the first eighty years of the tobacco monopoly, global access to the Philippines remained limited except for regional powers in Southeast and Northeast Asia. The distribution of knowledge circulated for regional investment, local development, and friars in the islands or otherwise recently expelled. However, by the 1870s, the visual and print cultures of the Philippines exploded with prolific creativity. Arts education, photography, popular newspapers, and books found voracious reception in the Philippines, produced both within the islands and from abroad. Furthermore, with the opening of the Suez Canal in 1869, the Philippine literate middle-class gained access to educational opportunities and European texts, while Europeans acquired popular materials from Southeast Asia.[1]

From upper-middle-class literate cultures to the democratization of popular art, especially in Manila and other urban centers, the media revolution in the Philippines fertilized how elites and nationalists created imagined communities for themselves. Within accelerated circulation of print and visual cultures and the colonial state's failed efforts to contain the rates of circulation, cosmopolitan ideas of the Filipino emerged. But for *indios* and *infieles* in resource hinterlands, only a few local elites could indulge in the mobility afforded by the late nineteenth century's infrastructures. In the early twentieth century, Christianized peasants and non-Christian highland peoples found ways to travel en masse but as precarious workers in the US empire. Instead, cultural productions circulated independent of them in novels, maps, travelogues, photographs, and film.[2]

Commodity production and colonial economic thought inflected industrial aspects of race in Luzon. However, production alone does not a racial economy make; cultural products circulated with and against the movement of the people from which they were drawn. The nature of knowledge and racial archiving between 1869 (the opening of the Suez Canal) and 1914 (the beginning of World War I) can be understood with respect to the circulation of stereotypes produced through the nineteenth century in relation to structures of capital in Luzon. As chapter 1 showed, by the nineteenth century the lowland indios no longer centered around missionaries but instead around commodity production in the Philippine lowlands. Likewise, the highland infieles became reconfigured according to their resistance to industrialization through contraband economies and counterimperial warfare. The US invasion and early occupation did not necessarily shift categories produced by the nineteenth-century racial economy but instead translated and fixated them for American markets. Through these circulations of ideas and archives, the indio became the cheap and flexible worker sought by American agricultural corporations, and the infiel became the savage dog eater and headhunter for the cultural consumption of the American middle class.

This chapter blueprints a geography of multimedia racial economies in Luzon between 1869 and 1914. Modern notions of race crystallized out of the Industrial Revolutions of the nineteenth century and the mobility of ideas, media, workers, and their observers that it enabled. Filipino subjectivities emerged in circulation through two technologies of circulation: transportation infrastructure, such as steamships and canals, and mechanically reproducible print and images. However, this chapter focuses on not solely academic racial thought but also the global conditions that allowed the Philippines to be observed as a site to cultivate racial ideas. In particular, racial economies from Luzon developed in the formal spheres of racial knowledge and discourse as well as in how the islands' visual interlocutors looked—and were looked at—in an age of globalized circulation.[3] Before the absorption of the Philippines into American popular photography—or the Kodak Zone, as I explore in chapter 3—Luzon became a racial theater to behold, out of context, the social upheavals that plantation capitalism and commercialization wrought. Between the opening of the Suez Canal and the end of the Philippine Commission's direct rule, the fertile ground of Luzon's racial economy set the stage for the cultural productions of the Filipino in the American imperial context.

The first half of this chapter surveys steamship development through the late nineteenth and early twentieth centuries that connected Luzon to Europe and the United States at accelerated rates. Simultaneously, we consider the various knowledge producers (such as botanists and polemicists) who traversed through Luzon and the various media of print capitalism that traveled with and independent of them.[4] Together, I show how the production and circulation of ideas about Luzon around the world simultaneously fixed visions of race. Using the histories of circulation as a launch pad, the second half of this chapter theorizes how Luzon's incorporation into a global market, through myriad manifestations of circulation, crystallized into the bifurcation of the migrant peasant and the savage. In opposition to the mobile lifeways of lowland and highland peoples, this process renders images of peasants and savages in dialectical tension with each other. While the archiving practices of people from Northern Luzon likely existed in various forms, whether through textual and visual production or vernacular collections, this section blueprints the circulatory infrastructures of imperial archives against which such vernacular practices existed.

I. Archiving in Transit

Suez Crossings

Philippine knowledge production in the nineteenth century as well as the *ilustrado* nationalist fervor that percolated in Europe could not have been possible without the steamship and its transoceanic routes. Until the last Manila galleon sailed in 1815, the Philippines connected Asian goods to Europe via the Pacific and the Caribbean. The tobacco monopoly localized profitable industries toward Spanish military investment in Southeast Asia while siphoning wealth to Spain and its heavily reduced empire. The steamship accelerated the flow of capital in and out of (but mostly away from) the Philippines, but without new channels to connect bullion and raw materials to Spain efficiently, the flow of capital nonetheless remained provincial to Southeast Asia.[5]

However, in 1869 the Suez Canal connected the Philippines anew to the colonial metropole. The new passage reduced travel from Spain to Manila from several months to a few weeks. With new access to Europe, the sons of the nineteenth-century *mestizo* bourgeoisie in the Philippine urban centers began to take up various vocations at European universities. The Suez Canal, then, briefly reoriented Philippine economic and elite civic life from a Spanish Pacific toward the Indian Ocean. These students became politicized through their studies in European literature and thought. The ilustrados noted a discrepancy between the professed liberalism of Europe and the social inequities in the Philippines as well as among the European working class. As literary historian Resil Mojares argues, they were ilustrado—enlightened—because they saw fit to awaken Spain to the Philippines' plight and awaken the Philippines to modernity.[6]

These students also participated in the transnational culture of spectatorship in the Philippines. Writers such as Pedro Paterno and José Rizal sought to create histories and ethnologies of their imagined homeland. Drawing from both in-depth and surface-level fieldwork, they watched indios and infieles, giving themselves legitimacy to translate the Philippine community to a global audience. Turning to the masses, the ilustrados constructed various notions of nationhood out of their descriptions of natives, positioning themselves as the colony's race men. Furthermore, while some continental ethnologists enjoyed the thrill of Indian Ocean travel to the Philippines, other notable ones enjoyed the luxury of having ilustrado friends communicate the islands back to Europe. Ferdinand Blumentritt (1853–1913), a Bohemian teacher and ethnologist, befriended José Rizal through frequent correspondence. Blumentritt benefited, so he thought, from diasporic native informants with authentic experiences from their homeland. But Rizal himself was an expatriate of his homeland, traveling the world on the steamships and railroads that imbued his thought with a cosmopolitan ethic.[7]

Ilustrados themselves became new spectators of the Philippines, commodifying the islands of their ancestry into comestible images for translation to European audiences. Unfortunately for them, grotesque images of their homeland clashed with the respectable images they wanted to convey to their European contemporaries. For expatriate students and nationalist scholars such as José Rizal and T. H. Pardo de Tavera, the 1887 Madrid Exposition popularized in Europe the images of Igorots that were anathema to their nationalisms. A Filipino Enlightenment did not just necessitate a vision of modernity; for ilustrados, the Enlightenment implied being seen as modern as well. This project began with responding to what they and their audiences imagined as the premodern: the infiel tribes of the Philippines.[8]

Not all Indian Ocean Filipino intellectuals were ilustrados in the sense of being overseas students. Nonetheless, the ability for people and media to cross at accelerated rates produced literature important to this burgeoning intellectual movement. As an Ilokano provincial journalist, Isabelo de los Reyes's writing drew upon his own middle-class spectatorship of Northern Luzon but with the advantage of knowing the local languages of the region, unlike his intellectual contemporaries. He was also well read in European ethnology and Philippine nationalist texts of his period and frequently drew upon contemporary social sciences to write subversive—even satirical— versions of ethnology as a provincial denizen. De los Reyes took advantage of print capitalism in the nineteenth century to disseminate his works among European and metropolitan Philippine readerships. For his anticolonial writings—or for his status as a *filibustero* (subversive) under Spanish rule—he was imprisoned in Barcelona. Through prison guards and allies outside the prison, de los Reyes managed to have his writing smuggled out toward a wider audience.[9]

For German entrepreneurs, steamships gave access to the archipelago's industries and opened opportunities for traders in Manila. Otto Scheerer, a German tobacco entrepreneur, started his prospecting business in Manila and Baguio in 1882. He became one of the founding ethnologists of Cordillera anthropology. Citing Scheerer's treatises on the Igorots of Benguet, among whom he lived in the late nineteenth century, the American colonial administration developed their differential policies of military and civilian governance in the different non-Christian areas of the archipelago. Social sciences, especially anthropology and linguistics, drew upon Scheerer's work in the Cordilleras. Therefore, the mobilities afforded by the Suez Canal and trans–Indian Ocean steamships underpinned the genealogies of ethnological knowledge in the Philippines.[10]

The Philippines' orientation to the Suez Canal did not just facilitate the flow of money and commodities toward Europe but also beheld the islands toward a transnational community of spectatorship. People from abroad could see the Philippines, while people from the islands could look outward. Within this transnational exchange, ilustrados staked their claims on becoming Filipino by reclaiming the term from its exclusive use among Spain-born Manila denizens. In constructing that nationalist identity, the ilustrados presented themselves as respectable citizens of modernity through their literature and scholarship as well as in how they dressed and conducted themselves.[11] However, the ilustrados composed these visions along the lines of measuring those who were premodern against those who were supposedly enlightened. While the modern Filipino was to be constructed along Indian Ocean routes, the increasing Pacific invasions churned the maelstrom of racial economies at the turn of the century.

Pacific Notions

While the Indian Ocean fomented Philippine nationalist thought and European capital, the Pacific Ocean underwent its own steamship revolutions. Other empires competed for maritime supremacy in the mid-nineteenth century. Through the Opium Wars in China, the British Empire subjected the Qing dynasty to a series of unequal treaties that favored the commercial and military power of European powers in Asia. Through naval warfare, the port cities of East Asia became nodes for the transit of people, weapons, drugs, commodity goods, and cultural artifacts. Using the port cities and maritime routes that warships used, Canadian and Japanese shipping companies facilitated the flow of commodities and people from colonies to imperial metropoles. Nineteenth-century imperial wars rendered the Pacific Ocean into an infrastructural space, propelled by coal-powered ships and reinforced by colonial occupations in port cities.[12]

The availability of ships made transpacific tourism a feasible pursuit, at least for those who could afford them. For example, Charles Longfellow, the son of the Anglo-American poet Henry Wadsworth Longfellow, was one such wealthy traveler. Charles Longfellow inherited fortunes from his grandfather and mother, which he used to sail all over Asia and the Pacific. From his voyages, he amassed a personal archive of photographs and journals and adorned his body with tattoos to distinguish himself as a well-traveled individual. As visual historian David Brody argues, transpacific tourism went hand in hand with the aesthetic rise of American Orientalism, and wealthy spectators in the United States amassed petty archives through the access to travel. On the home front, designers drew upon this circulation of images from the Orient in visual arts and interior design. Once the United States purchased the Philippines from Spain, the archipelago would then be consumed in this transpacific culture of voyeurism.[13]

Some of the most prominent voyeurs of the Philippines were zoologists from the University of Michigan. Joseph Beal Steere (1842–1940), an 1868 graduate of the university, was enlisted by the University Museum to collect natural specimens for the institution's collections. Steere began his career in the Amazon and the Andes but soon after took advantage of transpacific steamships to collect specimens from Asia, especially in Formosa. In 1887, he brought a group of his students to the Philippines, with the liaison of Alex Webb, the American Consul to the Spanish colony. The trip bore considerable scientific fruit: the team collected over 300 specimens and brought them back to the University of Michigan. For Steere, the trips to the Philippines also presented an economic opportunity to sell American seeds to the Philippines, where a global famine spiked the prices of produce.[14]

Among the graduate students Steere brought to the Philippines was a young zoologist and photography enthusiast from Vermont, Dean Conant Worcester. With his fellow photographers, Worcester snapped pictures of wildlife and native industries while collecting specimens for the Steere expedition. In English, Worcester compiled a travelogue and ethnological treatise on the Philippines but because of a lack of an interested readership held off on publishing it. In 1898 soon after the American invasion into the Philippines, he published the treatise and was appointed as a commissioner to the Philippines by President William McKinley. Having first traveled to the islands as a graduate student and specimen collector, Worcester turned his attention toward colonial governance and private investments in the islands. Through his photographs, he collected visual specimens of the various ethnic groups of the Philippines and sold his prints around the world. Worcester served as US secretary of the interior for one and a half decades and was one of the Philippines' most notorious American profiteers.[15]

These travelers, while powerful in the long run (certainly in the case of Worcester), were a select few from the American upper middle class. These individuals could either afford the trips independently or had funding to do so. Like Otto Scheerer from Europe, who began as a tobacco sales representative, American ethnologists and ethnolinguists were cut from a higher echelon than the average American citizen and thus were able to traverse imperial spaces with the independence they enjoyed.[16]

Artillery and Archive

While ethnological spectators of the Philippines produced large visual archives, war brought an influx of new voyeurs to the Pacific. Unlike the entrepreneurial scientists, soldiers, many of whom were among the white working class, proved to be voracious tourists in the new US colonial acquisitions. The Spanish-American War and the Philippine-American War brought more American eyes to the islands by steamship but along military routes rather than the civilian voyages that scientists and early photographers followed. In the wake of 1898, soldiers produced travelogues abundantly, recounting their experiences from the continental interior, sailing to Hawai'i and Guam, and waging military campaigns in the Philippines.[17]

Accompanied by gunboats and rifles, Spanish-American War soldiers brought cameras and notebooks. To reinforce the wartime military government in the Philippines, many soldiers stayed behind as teachers and administrators. In the meantime, they wrote about their experiences to publish later as memoirs. Some soldiers' memoirs described the transpacific voyage vividly, from California disembarking to Hawai'i, the "Ladrone Islands" (the Mariana Islands, especially Guam), and then the Philippine warfront. Upon return to the United States, soldiers pitched these memoirs to trade presses for popular consumption in the early twentieth century cultural market.[18]

Soldiers who brought cameras often found two primary outlets for their work. For some, Dean Worcester's administration purchased their prints, to be added to Worcester's massive collection of Philippine photographs. More often, however, soldiers kept private albums to join the archives of travel paraphernalia they kept in their homes. Private albums such as those of the Ifugao governor Owen Tomlinson, kept at the Bentley Historical Library in the University of Michigan, stayed with the Tomlinson family until the 1970s, when the Bentley acquired them. Today, the six albums remain largely understudied but offer rich insights into more quotidian aspects of American imperialism in the Cordilleras.[19]

Formal soldiering too drew upon the circulation of ethnological knowledge while simultaneously serving as a conduit for the production of race. For example, Robert R. Rudd, an African American carpenter from Kentucky, first served in the Ohio National Guard in 1875. He was promoted to captain in 1881 and was commissioned by Congress in 1899. In the Spanish-American War and the Philippine-American War, he commanded the all-Black I Company of the 48th Regiment. From 1900 to 1901, the company was tasked with counterinsurgency measures in the Cordilleras in regions that would become the Baguio hill station.

Because Rudd's troops primarily operated within Benguet, they served as the primary interface between the United States and non-Philippine residents who held considerable influence in the region. One of those residents, over whom Rudd's troops were tasked with keeping surveillance records, was the German ethnologist Otto Scheerer. Since the revolutionary leader Emilio Aguinaldo was rumored to have escaped to Benguet under Scheerer's care, Rudd's command branded him as a person of interest. But despite his regiment's suspicion of Scheerer, Rudd nonetheless compiled fundamental ethnological information from the Bohemian in order to instruct his soldiers on how to liaise with potential Nabaloi allies in Benguet. Among his small library was a draft of Scheerer's *The Igorrotes of Benguet* (1900), which the civilian government would also study in its efforts to pacify the archipelago.[20] Through Rudd's company, the subsequent civilian government in the Philippines had access to a colonial archive amassed through military occupation.

Military archiving, made more accessible by the transpacific steamships, would also inaugurate colonial engineering projects. In Benguet, Rudd's company was tasked with surveying the landscape for future development on behalf of the Office of the Chief Engineer in Manila. Their surveys in the Cordilleras took into account climate and topography as well as the "adaptability of country for military operations and camps." Beyond building infra-

through the regional shipping routes of East Asia. These travel routes that facilitated conquest and tourism made possible new sites and sights of fieldwork. That interface has continued to fascinate Western anthropologists, albeit those who can travel by plane. As recently as 2013, ethnolinguists recapitulated the "Negrito" language question, following the same Luzon-Formosa ties that turn-of-the-century ethnologists cultivated.[28]

II. The Filipino as Commodity

As Manila became the financial and distribution center of the Philippines, Luzon's commodities found interest among markets across the Pacific and in Europe. Likewise, knowledge produced by and about the Philippines' native peoples took hold among imperial travelers from Europe and across the Pacific. Economic prospectors in transit through Luzon eagerly found themselves in the global enterprise of ethnology and its allied technologies of photography, travel writing, and folklore collecting.[29] Despite the epistemic anxieties of documenting the heterogeneous landscapes of the island, the multimedia archives that emerged from this late nineteenth- and early twentieth-century milieu became a knowledge base for later uses during different periods of colonial conquest.[30]

The incorporation of Luzon into a global market also brought ideas and images of native racialization into the market exchange. From the opening of the Suez Canal through the early twentieth century, colonial interest in the Philippines rose outside of the Spanish Empire and Catholic friars. European and American audiences came to know the Philippines through fairs, expeditions, photography, cinema, and museums. Meanwhile, in order to facilitate the influx of new investors in the region and quell counterinsurgency, Spain bolstered its military presence in hinterland areas such as Central and Northern Luzon, which the United States continued into its period of colonial occupation. In the process, more parties tapped into the stores of archival data about Luzon in order to forge knowledge structures useful to the myriad projects of capital: road building, plantation management, labor recruitment, visual cultures, and tourism. In the process, these parties modified the racial archives of Luzon.

However, racial archives of lowland and highland peoples did not circulate in the same way. Ethnologies and images produced in the highlands took hold predominantly in popular culture, World's Fairs, and academic ethnology. Meanwhile, data produced in the lowlands found its most active readership among labor recruiters for American colonial industries, such as the

Hawaiian Sugar Planters Association. The circulation of the savage and the peasant took on entangled yet distinct trajectories. Furthermore, they did not circulate parallel to each other but more often than not were in dialectical tension with each other. For colonial observers, the savage, as an outsider to the labor regimes of capital and as an undesired occupant of frontier resources, hinders the desired productivity of a plantation regime, embodied by the peasant. Furthermore, what appears among Philippine ilustrados (and later among Filipino American intellectuals) as ideas of respectability politics against the supposed "savagery" of the Filipino can be understood as an aspiration toward the European liberal working subject, to which the peasant (as a mobile worker) is closer in proximity. Historian Paul Kramer calls this "calibrated colonialism," through which Filipino colonial subjects were measured according to their proximity to civilization under American tutelage.[31] Transnational intellectuals and workers themselves aspired to civilized subjectivity but predicated on their potential as economically viable subjects through their agrarian labor and contributions to local and national economy.

Therefore, calibrated colonialism and other civilizational imperatives cannot be understood without capitalist logics at their core. The dialectical nature of the savage and the peasant points to the economic and belabored nature of the racial archives of the Filipino and therefore the economic logics that belie the nature of colonial conquest, labor mobilization, and ethno-racial formation across the Pacific. Whether for visual or agricultural production (and consumption), Filipino subjectivity took hold in places such as the United States and Hawai'i as an exportable resource for performance entertainment or agrarian labor. Thus, this genealogy of the "Filipino" as a racial category, insofar as it can be exported and circulated, takes the form of a commodity.

We already know that the savage and the peasant are in their own rights knowledge commodities produced out of tobacco monopoly–era archiving. In the late nineteenth and early twentieth centuries, the tumultuous colonial state was not the only party invested in reactivating racial archives to account for native peoples and put them to work. As we have seen, foreign parties from Europe and the United States—and later the US colonial regime—came to Luzon to extract value on their own rights through their scientific and economic investments. These prospectors produced knowledge in the Philippines for their own personal and institutional racial archives in order to ascertain how they might proceed to take advantage of their tenure in the islands. To do that, they needed to amass data about people they could take advantage of, collaborate with, or otherwise subvert to gain access to resources. Thus, native people, both lowland workers and highland peoples resistant to colonial rule needed to be counted.

The Problem of Native Countability

Between 1869 and 1914, Luzon was opened to new foreign eyes, and new modes of global comparison. During this period of prolonged warfare and capitalist development, Spanish and American colonial officials accounted for the masses they coveted to work in industrial production. At the same time, nationalists debated on whom should count as a Filipino in the new revolutionary and colonial orders. Without access to colonial institutions to vote and run for office, indios and infieles presented both a challenge for governance and endless opportunity for potential workers. The industrial cultures of racial archiving from the Bourbon Reforms in the Philippines subjected indios and infieles to economically oriented observation.[32]

For the colonial state, watching Philippine peoples doubled as a means to account for its subjects through two genres of knowledge production: statistics and ethnology. Through statistics, Philippine groups became compiled as numbers through whom characteristics could be ascertained en masse. Through ethnology, Philippine groups became rendered as types—and, through reproduction, stereotypes—for intellectual and popular consumption. The products of these branches of colonial knowledge production became the multimedia archives of Philippine studies today. I stress the archive's multimedia nature to account for their circulation but also for the types of presentation each artifact bestows on the researcher.

Through statistics, the state counts people through arithmetic means. Arithmetic counting gathers what is given, that is, population counts through the censuses of the colonial state from which to gather quantitative data to manage the masses.[33] Under civilian government, the Philippine Commission conducted expeditions across the islands to gather knowledge and count their new subjects. However, crises of locust plagues and rinderpest (hoof-and-mouth disease) made census gathering double as a way to mobilize lowland populations in agricultural maintenance.[34] The 1906 census furthermore attempted to account for the new US subjects and found its most success among lowland populations, wherein there were *barrio cabecillas* (town leaders).[35] In areas of continued warfare into the 1910s—or what the colonial state called counterinsurgency—Americans accounted for encounters with insurgents (with rough estimates) as well as casualties among Philippine Constabulary soldiers.[36]

Like statistical evidence and textual narratives, many visual sources, such as maps and paintings, record data after the fact or are otherwise products of the imagination. In the process of conducting expeditions in the islands, Americans produced maps of their new territory, but different practices of mapping needed to be gathered in areas that were less explored. In the Cordilleras, the maps produced took the form of blueprints, produced out of hand-drawn sketches by the Philippine Constabulary and mass distributed from Manila.[37]

While visual sources such as maps and cartoons exhibited the same temporal lag between observation and media creation, one significant exception exists among the visual archives of the Philippines: photography. Photographs are indexical; that is, each photograph points to a moment around a camera that actually happened and the subjects whose bodies are registered on the film of the apparatus. In the nineteenth century, photography gave a sense of objectivity to ethnological data collection and inaugurated a visual nature to knowledge claims and evidence.[38] People who dictated knowledge claims from photographic evidence could only make them by means of visual metonyms. Ethnologists inferred insights from photographs from a sliver of any population or environment. Military censuses, such as the Benguet surveys under Robert Rudd's regiment, could account most effectively the Ilokano towns down the slopes in the region or otherwise only estimate by means of counting houses.[39] The 1906 American census, like Spanish censuses before it, merely estimated the populations of mountainous regions by counting how many houses observers could spot in the barrios along slopes and valleys.[40] The thousands of photographs thus transformed the mountains into scenes from which observers could infer racial conditions or append images to their generalized writings about the region's cultures and landscapes.

Ethnology, bolstered by photography, thus represented geometric counting to police Philippine subjects. Geometric counting involves ascertaining common features toward imagining a community and accounting for a larger community through metonyms of the whole. In the absence of being able to account for every single subject as a statistical data point, photographs gave credence to ethnologists who sought to generalize claims of phenotypic and cultural features across different groups. In ethnological discourses from the colonial Philippines, they register as types: one example for a homogenous tribe, such as a Kalinga or an Ifugao. The type—as in the phenotype, the racial type—in the racial archives of ethnology in the Philippines signifies geometric counting when conditions of warfare and obscure terrain make statistics impossible to carry out.[41]

Two modes of counting thus marked colonial knowledge productions in the Philippines, all derived from ways of watching indios and infieles. These modes reflected the different terrains, implicit in which are empires' limitations to conduct comprehensive expeditions in undulating mountains and forests. As anthropologist James C. Scott argues, colonialism operated easiest on flat land through plantations and other modes of spatial and racial capitalism. On highlands, empires turned to other media to render the Cordilleras into circulatable scenes or phenotypic examples in the impossibility of accounting for all subjects, especially when these subjects refused subjugation as anarchist groups.[42] The terrain discrepancy of counting Filipinos inflects the different media and circulation trends of the Philippine racial archives.

Exhibition Values

Early photographic images of the Philippines in the nineteenth century provided the colony with a new visibility that circulated readily around the world. The Suez Canal accelerated the circulation of ideas and images between colonial and metropolitan people. By virtue of the ease of transportation across the Indian Ocean, the Suez Canal also inaugurated a culture of colonial spectatorship that rendered the Philippines into a spectacle for tourist pleasure and professional knowledge production. Through revolutionary literature, colonial lithographs, and industrial expositions, the Philippines became aestheticized for the purposes of Spanish colonial rule.

In particular, the Cordilleras and other "non-Christian" regions of the Philippines became most readily aestheticized for mechanical reproduction. The market for popular pictures and literature rendered the Philippine Cordilleras a mechanically reproducible work of art. Travelogues and pictures from the Philippines attracted audiences from Europe and the United States to capture their own cultural products for distribution, and to establish themselves as the authority over having explored a foreign land.[43] According to the cultural theorist Walter Benjamin, mechanical reproduction allowed artworks to be replicated but also gained a currency of its own as artistic process itself.[44] Photography in particular gave the Philippine Cordilleras the character of a source of spectacle.

As an aesthetic site, visual sources from the Cordilleras bestowed upon the mountains the nature of a commodity under capitalism. According to Benjamin, the value of mechanically reproducible art takes on a dialectical value: cult value and exhibition value. Mechanical reproduction, through circulation, increases exhibition value. The cult value of the image harkens to the image's originality, or uniqueness. On the other hand, the exhibition value, through the image's circulation, allows an image to be recontextualized in circulation, heightening its political uses. Mechanical reproduction skews images toward exhibition. In ethnological practice, photographs allowed colonial officials and scientists to make claims to legitimize their rule in the Philippines.[45]

However, if the face is present in the image, the cult value of the image presents itself over exhibition value. The face in the image allows one to keep it as memento or, specifically, as *memento mori*. In different colonial contexts such as India, chromolithographs of Hindu gods provide popular faces for lower-caste Indians to bring upper-caste devotion into their own households. This fact, of the face in the image, underpins how we might grapple with the proliferation of human faces in the Cordillera archives in both highly circulated collections (e.g., Worcester) and private albums (e.g., Tomlinson). As philosopher Emmanuel Levinas argues, the human face compels an ethical responsibility to the Other. In the photograph, this manifests as one asking who subject was and what happened to the subject. Through his consideration of the photograph's ontology (especially in his infamous "Winter Garden" image, which he never reveals), photography theorist Roland Barthes identifies a *punctum* common to every photograph. The punctum is that which fills a photograph with unexpected meaning beyond the purview of the discourses the spectator imparts upon it or the operator intends the image to take.[46] Even without such a unique feature, every photograph's punctum is that the subjects in front of the camera will die or will have died. In other words, the human face of the photograph compels an ethical response that has the potential to reach beyond the alienating discourses of ethnology.[47]

The ethical conundrum of the human face in ethnological photographs challenges the exhibition of the Philippines in global audiences. As later chapters demonstrate, faces challenge the removed ethnological voice ever present in the archives' index captions. While captions attempt to dictate meaning over the photograph, faces posed challenges to the ethical nature of colonial development in the Philippines. Americans such as Worcester sought to profit off of ethnological types by selling photographs to different collectors. However, those ethnological photographs became his undoing among Filipino critics in newspapers. In 1913 *El Renacimiento*, a Manila-based newspaper, rebuked Worcester's visual industries in the Philippines, calling him a "vampire" that sucked the soul of the islands through his photographs. While Worcester successfully sued the paper for libel, that "vampire" label never dissipated. He resigned unceremoniously the following year, reaping his profits but never again gaining the same influence that he had enjoyed in the Philippines.[48]

Recently, human faces in photographs have been deployed by anthropologists to take advantage of their cult value once they are brought back to the subjects' communities of origin. At the University of the Philippines Baguio, Igorot anthropologist Analyn "Ikin" Salvador-Amores brought the prints of Worcester's images to different peoples in the Cordilleras for their perusal and identification. Townsfolk were able to identify the subjects through their tattoos, despite a century's difference, and traced their ancestries to the photographic subjects. These surplus activities, far beyond the alienating ethnological purposes of the original photographs, were made possible through the human face in the images.[49]

Nonetheless, the aesthetics of the colonial Philippines in the global circulations of racial archives are, for the most part, faceless. These include depictions of tropical commodities, landscape photographs, and statistical data sets. Abstract images of the colonial Philippines increase its exhibition value; that is, without the faces of colonial subjects, abstract images in circulation allow colonial officials and Philippine elites to more easily impart their own meanings on the image. Taking into account the multimedia nature of Luzon's racial archives expands visual scholars' notions of the economies of image circulation. Images do not just appear in visual sources but are also produced through textual and numerical ones. These various sources thus form an assemblage from which the racialization of the modern Filipino—the indio, the infiel, and those who respond to them—is derived. Because race is seen, envisioned, imagined, and replicated in multimedia archives, the multimedia nature of racialization beckons to a racial economy within which different economies of the archive operate.[50]

In circulation, racial images and imaginaries are not only decontextualized; they also gain new contexts wherever they land. Altogether, they crystallize into the various vocabularies through which metropolitan people came to know the colonial Other. The World's Fairs and the midway "Igorrote village" performances that followed offer an example of these localized rubrics of race. As chapter 3 shows, these performances are themselves moments of photography. They offer scenes to publics who might themselves carry cameras or otherwise purchase images as souvenirs of an imperial encounter. However, as in the photographs with human faces, the presence of native labor in the World's Fairs allowed men and women to stake their claims as workers by influencing the images captured in the popular racial archives of the United States.

At the wane of World's Fairs and midway village performances in the 1910s, film became a way to maximize the Philippines' exhibition value. While Worcester and his team planned out films all over the islands, both lowland and highland, production companies only expressed interest in those that could create thrilling narratives. There is a corresponding film outline for almost every tribe the Americans recognized in Luzon: Negritos, Ifugaos, Ilongots, Tingians, Lepanto and Bontoc Igorots, and Kalingas.[51]

The conflict over the film plans reveals the conflict over two types of filmic gazes: an ethnological gaze and a popular gaze. Both commodify the subjects whose movements are narrated through commentary accompanying the film, whether in captions or in lectures. Both the ethnological and popular gazes are orientated toward acquiring profit from the Philippines but with capital flowing in two different directions. Considering potential popular audiences suggests the notion of maximizing commercial value through exhibition, because film time (the immediate product of film production and distribution) is measured literally in the materiality of film length, by feet. Furthermore, film time for these producers indicates a potential measurement for audience attention spans, or the optimal time to show a film and maximize exhibition value. Because these films were silent, "the pictures 'must do the talking.'"[52]

Worcester's ethnological gaze, through his films, sought to profit based off of his financial stakes in the distribution of the films of his subjects. However, the film companies with which he communicated considered how to profit based off of audiences' attention spans and how they might take to exciting sensational narratives with their admission fees.[53] Two ways of filmic narration competed in the Philippines, between the scientific-objective and the sensational-popular. Nonetheless, both film styles suggest that extracting visuals from the Philippines is to extract exhibition value and control the profits from its circulation. Because film immediately orients performances toward exhibition, it decontextualizes the Indigenous contexts of lifeways and performances onscreen, opening them up to reinterpretation through display. In Worcester's film plans, Igorot performances became ornaments to sensational narratives in the Philippines, or assemblages of different aspects of Indigenous life.[54]

Photographs, village shows, and films are circulating media through which Europeans and Americans sought to extract the exhibition value of the Philippines. In what journalist Frank Millet called the Kodak Zone in 1899, the US colonies became spectacles for American eyes. However, as with every commodity—even visual ones—their production and circulation are labored spaces.[55]

"Civilized Tribes"

The most prolific and public visual archive of Luzon comes from Dean Worcester's photographic collections, distributed across the museums and libraries of the United States. Other collections exist but primarily in private albums that did not circulate in the same way that Worcester's photographs did. But as Worcester himself admitted, the wealth of certain representations made for the dearth of others: "I did not realize how little we had showing types of the civilized tribes, their methods of life, their industries, etc. I shall have attention given to these subjects in the near future."[56]

This archival discrepancy warrants some pause. What made lowland peoples less photogenic than their highland counterparts? What diverted the photographer-ethnologist's attention from—or what bored them about—the peasant farmer? Chapter 5 explores how the Ilokano indio became an abstract migrant peasant in the Spanish and American corporate imagination, from Luzon to Hawai'i. However, all these racializations are derived from the nature of the sources that circulated about them. Imperial sources account for indio workers in two ways: through their abstract (arithmetic) count in statistics and through the products of their labor. In other words, the indio became a faceless statistic, an abstract worker in colonial industry.

Counting lowland peoples allowed the state to distribute commands across the archipelago, especially at a time when industry was precarious. Despite the diversity of Luzon's products, Philippine agriculture at the turn of the twentieth century constantly faced the threat of ruination. To ward off locust plagues and maintain crops, the Philippine Commission ordered local cabecillas to enforce town labor to gather locusts and keep them off of the fields. In doing so, the early Philippine Commission reports developed robust statistical archives that combined environmental and local population data.[57]

Despite colonial efforts to promote tropical goods, the El Niño–Southern Oscillation famines of the nineteenth century ravaged the Philippines and its industries. As historian Mike Davis argues, the making of the third world emerged through mass agriculture and resource extraction at a time of environmental dearth and destruction. Colonial agriculture exacerbated the impoverishment of the masses of the Global South, including the Philippines.

However, colonial Luzon nonetheless needed to maintain the production of goods. Popular publications on America's new colonies highlighted tropical goods of potential value to American distribution and consumption. By showcasing tropicality and its potential industrial abundance, the Philippines became a spectacle for agricultural industry. These single-crop industries emerged when foreign investors noted the success of the tobacco monopoly and its swift profits.[58]

In the late nineteenth- and early twentieth-century industrial fairs, empires occupying the Philippines advertised the colony by means of its tropical products. Despite the popularity of savage shows on midways, colonial investors organized industrial fairs to showcase the economic value and potential benefits of maintaining investments in the islands. In the 1887 Madrid Exposition on the Philippines, organizers displayed crafts and natural resources from the islands. In the 1904 St. Louis World's Fair, organizers commissioned pavilions for each major commodity industry of the Philippines, including native lumber, tropical produce, and minerals. The thousands of Philippine workers at the World's Fairs were the obvious labor force for the enterprise. But behind every commodity was concealed the proletariat in the Philippines mobilized to produce commodities through the nineteenth century.[59]

When Philippine exhibits waned, American colonial officials saw cinema as a potential means of showcasing the colony's value. However, unlike the fairs, the production process would require Luzon's workers to be visible on-screen. When Dean Worcester laid out plans to create films of Philippine industries, the handwritten outlines focused on portraying an industrial production method, following the commodity from raw material to valuable commodity. The plans begin with "preparing the seed buds" and the various ways of "cultivating tobacco" to its "arrival . . . from the north" and the Tabacalera company's infrastructures to move it to Manila. Bringing the viewer to Manila's factories, the film's projected scenes showcase the sorting, stemming, cigar rolling, and packing for distribution. The penultimate scene displays the annual profits of the enterprise. The only time the film explicitly focuses on people are in two cases: the board of directors and the "employees leaving factory."[60] By focusing on the production of the commodity in the film, the labor regimes of Luzon are taken for granted. But if the film had ever been produced, we would have indexical visual evidence of an Ilokano and Gaddang masculine labor force that grows the tobacco and a women-run factory floor in Manila cigar production. Perhaps this evidence will not have been candid, as the scenes will have taken several takes to accomplish. However, the filmic imagination nonetheless reifies a peasant labor force readily mobilized to produce the annual profits of the Tabacalera under American stewardship.

In the absence of a large photographic archive, lowland peasants were archived for utilitarian purposes among industry elite. But while images of their highland counterparts circulated far more widely, emigrants soon followed on the *Empress*-class steamships across the Pacific or as seamen on US Navy vessels. In the United States, lowland Philippine migrant men became a "third Asiatic invasion," considered by white Americans as a racial threat to jobs and white women. Traveling on the *Empress of Canada* by steerage, they themselves would become Philippine visual interlocutors in diaspora.[61]

THE "FILIPINO" EMERGED from colonial work and was worked out in the colonial imagination. Sorting and managing populations' relationships with agricultural infrastructures shifted extant vocabularies of race toward industrial logics. Furthermore, commodity production rendered provinces outside of Luzon into impoverished hinterlands, spurring Indigenous strategies that sought to counteract the colonial flow of wealth and escalating colonial efforts at policing them. Finally, the rise of the social sciences, American empire, and mass culture displayed a voracious appetite for exotic new races.

How did particular ethnic groups in the Philippines engage with the racial economy, given that they were differentially subject to its cultural technologies? Due to its proximity to Manila and the tobacco monopoly, rural Luzon presents a case study to elaborate on the intersections of imperial labor and culture. Lowland and highland tribes did not equally engage with a metropolitan Filipino identity in the wellspring of the Philippine Revolution of the 1890s. However, in the US colonial imagination, the ways in which lowland and highland peoples were subject to racialization and labor mobilization disproportionately produced notions of the transpacific Filipino in the early twentieth century. They are variously known as follows: headhunters, dog eaters, migrant workers, Pinoys, and Filipino Americans.

Part II
Highlands

CHAPTER THREE

No Dog, No Work

Benguet, 1902. As the United States waged brutal warfare in the Tagalog regions of Luzon, representatives of the Philippine Commission set out from Manila to survey the mountain range of Northern Luzon known as the Cordilleras. Bringing food and supplies and accompanied by American soldiers and Filipino guides, they made their way from sweltering tropical heat to higher elevations in search of a temperate microclimate for the health of their troops. The rugged terrain proved to be a challenge to navigate, aided somewhat by horse and cart paths built under Spanish military occupation just decades earlier. And in response to an ongoing guerrilla war against freedom fighters whom they called insurgents—or *ladrones*, from the Spanish colonial term for "thieves"—the commission brought ample firepower.

Colonial occupation brought something else besides guns with which to shoot Philippine bodies: cameras. Handheld film cameras were all the rage in Europe and North America at the turn of the twentieth century, and soldiers found much opportunity to shoot with both gun and shutter. Colonial surveyors preferred larger mounted cameras in the pursuit of optimal clarity. Through photography, US imperialism brought the Cordilleras from relative obscurity into popular visibility. Commissioners photographed Igorots (the collective term for groups living in the highlands of Northern Luzon) for documentation, classification, and commodification.[1] Across the Pacific, American viewers became enamored by photographs of their new "head-hunting, dog-eating" "little brown brothers." In St. Louis (1904) and other small midway shows across the United States, audiences brought their eyes, pens, dollars, and cameras to consume performances of their conquered possessions. In 1899, American artist Frank D. Millet lamented that unlike Hawai'i and other tropical imperial acquisitions, the Philippines was unfamiliar to Americans and "remained outside the kodak zone." Within five years, the Philippines was engulfed by the Kodak Zone.[2]

Photography reorganized the Philippines into a source of disciplinary knowledge and colonial experimentation. In order to turn the islands into a source of commodities, knowledge, and imperial might, Americans converted—in ideology and practice—their colonial possession into a readymade studio.[3] However, the studio is never a totalizing space, no matter how hegemonic or teleological the narratives around its products—photographs—turn out to be. Studios are spaces of posing, negotiating, bartering, and laboring. The workers most obviously include the camera operator or his assistants. But the subjects in front of the camera are workers too. Some Cordilleran communities found measures of opportunity for income and adventure in the colonial studios at home and abroad. While the power relations were highly unequal in the American visual regime, Igorots in front of and around the camera recognized photography not just as production of knowledge about them but also as a set of labor relations that could be negotiated, contested, and protested from employee to employer. The results of these contestations left their traces all over the visual archives of the US-Philippine colonial encounter.

This chapter traces the labor history of colonial photography and the visual production of race in the Philippine Cordilleras as well as its diasporic performances abroad. Scholars have investigated the limits of American racial formations by means of interelite contests or otherwise by the cultural formations within what Amy Kaplan has called "the anarchy of empire."[4] Acknowledging the importance of imperial and local elite politics as well as the tools provided to us by the cultural study of American imperialism, this study tempers the production of culture—especially race in the early twentieth century—with attention to the labor behind it. In recognizing the difficulty that official and mass culture productions found in representing Cordilleran subjects, these visual and discursive contradictions also involved the active negotiation and conduct of Igorots themselves. What registers variously as the "ig/noble savage" or the dog-eating subject of American civilization appears in part as a result of workers' assertions for fair wages, good working conditions, and individual and collective dignity in visual representation. Igorot subjects who worked in the visual economy of American imperialism seized upon photography as both an economic opportunity and a bargaining chip.

This chapter anchors itself with three photographs of cooking dogs—a prominent element of US-Philippine iconography in the early twentieth century. They manifest as an instance of visual abjection of empire, as Philippine scholars Vicente Rafael and Nerissa Balce might call them.[5] These photographs are a part of what visual anthropologist Deborah Poole calls the "visual economy," synthesizing the production, consumption, and circulation of visuality. The visual economy connects photography in the Philippines to events of photography—including World's Fairs—in the United States.[6] Not to foreclose the individual and collective actions enabled by the visual economy, I then blueprint the systems of migrant labor opened up through the visual economy of colonial photography and follow Igorots who participated in this industry by means of recognizing their negotiations with photographers and World's Fair recruiters. Finally, as an example of how labor relations precisely manifest in visual understandings of race, we follow depictions of dog eating to explore the intersections of Igorot workers' actions, political responses against "misrepresentation," and the media ecologies of dog-eating photography.

Three photographs, kept and cataloged in the American Historical Collection at the Ateneo de Manila University, show the entire process through which a small group of Igorots slaughtered their canines. Taken in 1902, these photographs are products of the Benguet expeditions undertaken by the First Philippine Commission. The expedition included Dean C. Worcester, a zoologist and the secretary of the interior, accompanied by his photographer, Chas Martin. Unlike most soldiers who occupied the Philippines, many of whom brought handheld cameras with cheap film, both Worcester and Martin worked with glass and cellulite nitrate plates on heavy tripod cameras. The depth of quality and some minimal motion blur in these photographs attests to their status as ethnological works rather than handheld camera snapshots.

In the first picture, "Dog Killing," a domestic scene depicts a group of Igorots outside of their abode slaughtering dogs against a backdrop of pines. In the doorway of the nipa hut, a dark figure with a buttoned jacket leans against the frame. In the figure's right hand, a leash holds a white dog in place, the rope tied around its neck. The dog is rather skinny, and its rib cage is visible through its now-translucent skin. It is looking away from the slaughter scene as if it expects its fate. In front of this dog another squatted individual, on a thick plank, holds two other dogs in place and also safeguards two kindling torches for singeing the dogs. In front of the dog is a black dog, hardly visible and its head turned slightly toward the slaughter scene. A second white dog looks directly to our right, the compositional focus of the picture: four men slicing the neck of a third white dog and draining its blood into a white bowl below. Two of the men look directly at the camera, while the other two prepare to slice the dog's neck. No blood drips into the bowl, and as of yet no incision is made, even though the dog's joints have been tied and broken.

The second picture, "Igorottes preparing a repast," shows the aftermath of the slaughter and blood draining. The plank on which the man from the first picture squatted is used as a table for presenting the four dogs. The camera's aperture here is open wider for a shallow depth of field, the focus of which is the black dog. One of the slaughterers from the first photograph—the young man holding the feet—crouches behind the table, shirtless now, his *bolo* (short sword) dipped into the incision of the white dog in front of him.

FIGURE 3.1 "Dog Killing, Benguet, P.I." American Historical Collection, Rizal Library, Ateneo de Manila University, Quezon City.

FIGURE 3.2 "Igorrotes preparing a repast, Benguet, P.I." American Historical Collection, Rizal Library, Ateneo de Manila University, Quezon City.

FIGURE 3.3 "Singeing a Dog, Benguet, P.I." American Historical Collection, Rizal Library, Ateneo de Manila University, Quezon City.

Behind him is the nipa hut, and his companions' legs are visible as the two men look on. The young man looks directly at the camera.

The third picture, "Singeing a Dog," takes place in the woods. Smoke fills the scene, obscuring much of the center of the photo. The man on the left holds a singeing rod to the carcass of the black dog, having been hung by the front paws by a second young man. This black dog is barely visible against the dark shades of grass and against the underexposed legs and coat of the young man. The three other dogs' carcasses are on the ground, still visibly white but singed, the heads semidismembered. The two young men on the right hold the singeing rods against the white dogs. All four young men wear what look like military coats, one with a scarf, but no one wears pants. At the extreme right of the photograph is a much taller figure, the face not visible, wearing a sharp black coat, black pants, and rubber boots. The figures, removed enough from the smoky area but a looming presence among the grasses and pines, looks over the scene.

The Cordilleras in Archival Transit

These three photographs are a sliver of the massive visual archive of Philippine photographs, but they appear in sequence, cataloged together. For historians who have worked with these visual archives, the sheer amount of material is immediately overwhelming. Negatives and prints of the ethnology projects have been disseminated all over the Philippines and the United States, to be found in research libraries such as the Field Museum and the Newberry Library, and in collections held by universities such as the University of Michigan. Colonial administrators such as Dean Conant Worcester, who scattered their photographic seeds across the imperial archive, are well known to historians of this period, and their names magisterially adorn collections and photographs. Colloquially, they are "Worcester," "Charles Martin," or "Sherman" photographs, depending on their photographer or their commissioner. Likewise, historical treatments of American colonial photography in the Philippines have for the most part rested on the use of photography as a technique of power to legitimize American rule on the islands. The vast quantities of photographs in the global archive of the Philippines have tended to reduce histories of photography as technological (re)production of Foucauldian power,[7] as otherwise fractured products of the imperial gaze,[8] or as a broader part of American colonial visuality.[9] Histories of photography and imperial visual culture are excised from the people in front of the gaze.[10]

To bring together photographs with the practice of taking them as well as the colonial practice of sorting them for ethnology and archival records, I draw upon Deborah Poole's concept of the "visual economy" to broaden critical approaches to colonial photography in the Philippines.[11] In Northern Luzon, photography is the primary technology of the visual production of race. The ethnological surveys conducted by the Philippine Commission carried with it both guns and cameras. As Filipina/o bodies were massacred during the Philippine-American War, bodies (both living and dead) were petrified onto glass plates and photographic film and disseminated as visualizations of the new US colonial wards. Through photography, race in the Philippines came to be seen and contested together by Americans and Filipina/os. To understand the production, consumption, and dissemination of how race is seen, it is necessary to begin with that first layer of the visual economy: holding the individuals, technologies, and subjects accountable for their presence in front of and around a camera even if we do not have the photographs themselves in hand.[12]

Not having access to certain photographs also requires that we question how archives—those accumulated collections of materials from which historians execute their craft—construct a particular visual field in favor of particular power relations. As historian Kevin Coleman reminds us, we have a responsibility to consider how photographs might both reinforce and disrupt the visual field of (neo)colonialism and reveal modes of counterconduct that take place in front of the camera and around it.[13] By taking into account the complexity of the subjectivities of the photograph's subjects—quotidian working people—the historian as the beholder of the photograph is held accountable to the civil contract of photography. The visual archives of Igorots in the early twentieth century are both disproportionately plenty (with prints numbering in the tens of thousands) and devoid of Indigenous production, at least behind the camera. In front of the camera, however, scholars have access to the work of photography: posing, negotiating (and refusing) poses, clothing (and unclothing), and bartering in exchange for compensation and some measure of self-representation. Through photography, as Kevin Coleman argues, workers can "make themselves with others," their fellow subjects (and later performers), their employers, and their audiences.[14]

How do we write a labor history of Igorots in performances and in front of cameras, whose activities and politics were documented more through visual means than through extant written and oral ways? Visual culture theorist Ariella Azoulay posits a definition of photography as an event and an "apparatus of power . . . [bringing together] an ensemble of diverse actions that contain the production, distribution, and consumption of the photographic image."[15] Furthermore, "the photographic event makes use of a direct and an indirect force—taking someone's portrait, for example, or looking at someone's portrait." Following the logics of the photographic event as laid out by Azoulay, I contend that photography, taken within the context of its concomitant rise with imperialism in the early twentieth century, is itself a manifestation of social relations under industrial capitalism. Defined by Sven Beckert as the accelerated spatial conversion of natural resources, land, and people into units of commodity exchange, industrial capitalist practices in the nineteenth century integrated colonial borderlands through extensive "administrative, political, and military penetration."[16] Likewise, colonial photography seized upon borderlands spaces and peoples as decontextualized scenes, made manifest through photographs that circulate as commodities. Photography and capitalism are equally apparatuses of power, irreducible to their components or their individual lines of processes (e.g., production, consumption, negotiation). In the age of empires, photography and industrial capitalism both involved the violent seizure of commodities and working lives through force both overt and covert, both "formal" and "informal."[17] Both photography and capitalism, through their internal contradictions and ruptures, produce the heterotopic spaces necessary for responses to its otherwise overwhelming but uneven power. To consider a labor history of visuality,

Igorot workers navigated through, appropriated, and resisted imperial visuality means to recognize them under the aegis of both photography and capitalism. The visual economy of colonial photography served to taxonomize Cordilleran bodies into racial categories for the purposes of their exploitation but also offered specific instances through which the means of production could be seized, even for a moment.[18]

Photography as Extractive Technology

In the Cordilleras, photography did not only make visible a region that had—by virtue of its geological difficulty and its people's political resiliency—remained obscure throughout most of Spanish rule. By producing large quantities of colonial images for dissemination, consumption, and profit, photography incorporated the Philippines into the Kodak Zone by entangling the visual commodification of bodies as human resources into a larger context of the commodification of land, agriculture, and mineral resources in the Cordilleras.

The visual economy does not simply broaden our discussions of photographic productions of American imperialism but also draws attention to the uses of visuality in reorganizing ways of seeing mountainous terrain or, generally, terrains that are difficult to penetrate. For Spaniards in Northern Luzon and other colonial mountain ranges, rugged terrain signaled both danger and economic opportunity. Through photography and other visual arts, produced by empire and kept in check by Indigenous productions, race in mountainous colonial spaces came to be seen and entered into a modern visual economy through the global circulation of its pictures.[19]

In Northern Luzon, similar logics of making the mountains and its resources productive for empire were at play but with different results. Spanish occupation both in the Andes and in the Philippines was oriented around extracting value from production and establishing ports for global trade rather than the settlement of European bodies. In the Cordilleras, the Spanish struggled to make much headway for over three centuries. The impenetrable terrain posed challenges, as did the success of Cordilleran groups in consolidating their sovereignty through mountain warfare. In the Spanish colonial imagination, Igorots appeared first and foremost as the guardians of the wealth of the colonies or, specifically, gold. The Spanish conquistadores who explored the mountains in the late 1590s wrote of headhunters in rugged mountains who worked their own gold mines in order to trade with the lowlands for rice, worker animals, and meat. The "Ygolote" gold mines were noted to be the best in the archipelago, and Spanish writers such as Juan Manuel de la Vega noted that Igorots possessed an essential racial character of being able to pan gold in difficult weather conditions.[20] After several unsuccessful Spanish-led invasions, the Cordilleras were left relatively untouched by settlement and economic colonialism, though Igorots nonetheless responded through economic, political, and spatial practices.[21]

In the nineteenth century after the Mexican War of Independence and the subsequent reduction of Spanish colonial holdings in the Americas, the Spanish government doubled down on direct control in the Philippines. These efforts to consolidate control and reorient the islands toward a global market stepped up the need to escalate Spanish efforts into the Cordilleras. Under paradigms of making the consolidated land productive, Spanish colonial officials debated what to do with the region. Military forces had launched an occupation in a last attempt to penetrate an Indigenous stronghold that had eluded them for three centuries. Accompanying the nearly two-decade military occupation were two groups: missionaries and anthropologists. The former group pushed for the effective continuation of *reducción* policies that would gather Igorots into manageable *barangays* (townships) for Christianization and development; however, this proved to be difficult for Igorots in the Cordilleras, who responded by means of negotiation, warfare, and fleeing into more inaccessible mountains. Anthropologists treated the Cordilleras as laboratories and collected Igorot crafts for exposition. Spanish military occupation sought to put the terrain to work by building roads over cleared Cordilleran land, made barren through missionary and military reducción, which involved both Christian conversion and the expulsion of highland populations by means of destroying houses and trees for cultivation. Spanish officials also debated over continuing the religious mission of reducción while emphasizing the need to make them "useful to society and fit to receive religion."[22] Anthropologists and military occupiers alike emphasized the importance of forging alliances with Igorots, with similar goals: to make the mountains more visible for the purposes of putting Igorots to work.[23]

Continuing the work of social scientists in the Cordilleras, Americans surveyed and governed the Philippines' "non-Christian tribes" but refined the dispossession of the Cordilleras through photography. By capturing them as posed stills and writing on their "primitive industries" such as crafts, these various Americans in the Philippines oriented Igorots toward a global market for not only development but also mobilizing their labor and their commodities as goods. As far as my own research and the previous work of scholars have found, photographers avoided producing images of Igorots at work in gold mines. Instead, colonial photography sought to capture nude photographs of Igorots performing "primitive industries" to show evidence of industriousness but still within the terrain of savage cultures. Photography, supplementing the work of cultural anthropology, wedged culture and economy apart by visually (through photographs) and discursively (through supplementary writings) dispossessing Igorots from their political economies of trade, local production, and regional politics. Like natural resources, Igorot bodies in front of the camera—and, by extension, people in the mountains—were understood in terms of their utility for employment in mining. The racialization of Igorots as human resources in the extractive economy of the Cordilleras is not only present in the visual archives; this racialization also created the structure of the archives and the knowledge derived from it. In Dean Worcester's photograph index of the Newberry Library, he notes that "[the Lepanto Igorrotes] are quite expert miners and find ready employment at the hands of the American mine owners in this vicinity."[24] Of Benguet, he writes that "[many] of the men are quite expert miners, but decline to work for themselves gold ores in which free gold cannot be seen with the naked eye."[25] Worcester did not have to put Igorots to work on the mines to make money off of them, although his American-Philippine Corporation would later continue profiting off of his holdings in the Philippines. He was effective as a photographer and an ethnologist as he was a profiteering huckster of the visual economy of empire. From these prints, Worcester received $5,340 ($141,070 in 2017 dollars, adjusted for inflation), at $1 per print.[26]

Dean Worcester and others behind the camera sought to render Igorots into ethnological types and their historically contingent practices into timeless cross sections of savagery. Photography reinforced visions of a productive mountain range and natives as natural resources that came part of the Philippine mountainous landscape.[27] The visual production of racial difference does not only, as historians Benito Vergara and Paul Kramer argue, serve to delegitimize Philippine nationalism and Indigenous self-rule.[28] By dominating how race was seen in both the colonies and the metropole's colonial culture, photography contributed to the production of racial difference, indexed on racialized capacities to work.[29]

Seizing the Means of Mechanical Reproduction

While photography extracted and mobilized Igorots as human resources, the racialized subjects in front of the cameras were far from disempowered in this industry. Decontextualized photographs, their subjects, and their circulation were not the chief province of colonial officials. The contexts grafted onto the photographs by means of their circulation could also be manipulated by the subjects themselves.[30] These negotiations and manipulations can be read against the aforementioned purpose of colonial photography in the Cordilleras, which seeks to separate culture from economy and thus deny to Igorots political economy and sovereignty claims to their land. By developing reading practices that recognize small-scale negotiations around the camera, we can observe emergent labor politics that take place within this visual economy.

Consider the dog-eating photographs again (figures 3.1, 3.2, and 3.3). These photographs are posed, but their posture does not make the event "false." The viewer is invited to rethink the ontology of the pose: as self-representation, as forging of identity, and as labor. I follow Ariella Azoulay's invitation to not simply sort photographs as objects of contemplation ("in which all movements have been eliminated") but instead recognize that photographs are active, "[attesting] to action and [continuing] to take part in it, always engaged in an ongoing present that challenges the very distinction between contemplation and action."[31] Photographs, and by extension, poses, must be watched. What negotiations must have taken place such that the subjects in front of the camera would have "agreed" to hold their bodies still, or been coerced to do, and surrender their posture and image to the capture of the camera? To surmise these exchanges—civil contracts, perhaps—involves watching the photograph and then placing it subject to inquiring about what is captured in front of the camera.

To return to what I have called the "dog-eating sequence," together these three photographs depict a labor-intensive process of dog killing, presumably for consumption. I say presumably because two important scenes are not seen, at least in this sequence: the moment of slaughter and the moment of consumption. The acts of killing and eating remain off-scene. While they are implied (but denied from our seeing), the fact that photographers and subjects were present throughout this whole process suggests that the event of photography will have taken place even if we do not have access to the picture. Furthermore, the dogs are denied from the culinary act of expert consumption, while the subjects are present at the moments of production. In fact, the process of preparing dog meat appears explicitly as work. In taking photographs of Igorots at the various stages of slaughter and preparation, the photographer captured a highly organized process of labor. The process takes several people to execute in tandem and in precise ways. Evidenced in these photographs is the skill of knowing how to navigate canine anatomy and therefore hygienic practice: the dog's blood is drained through a single incision in a designated bowl. The use of tools for cutting and cooking and the evidence of collective labor also gesture to hard work, made visible despite the ethnographic gaze. Furthermore, each step in the process of preparation was photographed as steps in a sequential process but not as American corporate photographers later deployed as motion studies.[32] This photographed sequence was not judged in terms of timing and efficiency—as laborers were—but showed instead an essential propensity for organized labor.

In the third picture, the clothing attests to some incongruences with the Igorots' supposed savagery. The coats are clearly too large for all four of them, and the shoulder seams hang low on the arms. The heft of the collars and fabric and the presence of breast pockets suggest that these may have originally been meant for soldiers, perhaps gifted to the Igorots in exchange for being guides. Since the Igorots typically photographed by the Philippine Commission were generally almost naked, these jackets seem a strange addition. The man on the left has a coat more to his size, but the two on the right are almost certainly in military khakis. In other words, they are dressed like potential soldiers. Little brown brother soldiers, preparing dogs, under the watchful gaze of the American photographer and the onlooking commissioner.

These scenes gesture to later expositions of the strangeness of a dog-eating people, as certainly the onlookers of later World's Fairs have remarked, but reading the composition of these photographs reveals other matters. In two of the first three photos, the Igorots are not only deliberately posed but also aesthetically composed. "Dog Killing" follows the rule of thirds, a classic technique in European visual arts, and at the four intersects are, from top left going clockwise, (1) the figure in the doorway looking at the camera; (2) the man on the far right, holding the slaughtered dog's face and looking at the camera; (3) the slaughtered dog; and (4) the white dog looking at the slaughtered dog. At the center of the photograph is the young man holding the slaughtered dog by the ankles. He looks straight at the camera and, like the man holding the dog's face, looks at the photographer as if searching for approval over a pose. The four men holding the dog for blood draining are spread out in favor of a layout that can be easily photographed. This layout is not necessarily the most efficient, then, but the most presentable to the fascination of the photographer. The identifier of the photograph—"Dog Killing"—further suggests an ethnographic gaze for dissemination to a larger audience. This is an already-developed photograph, with the caption cut directly into the emulsion, and this was almost certainly intended for consumption by a wider

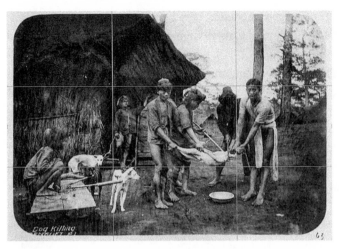

FIGURE 3.4 The "Dog Killing" photograph, diagrammed with the rule of thirds lines. American Historical Collection, Rizal Library, Ateneo de Manila University, Quezon City. Modified by the author.

audience. Furthermore, bringing out four dogs and enlisting six individuals to carry out the labor suggests that this preparation was meant for a feast. Off-scene, were there more households that could benefit from these prepared dogs? Perhaps, and the several people preparing the meat probably came from different parts of the community. But the gaze from the slaughterers in the first picture and the young man in the second picture still strongly suggests the presence of negotiated relationships that took shape at these photographic events. The subjects look directly at the camera, in visual dialogue with the photographers as well as future spectators.

While the captions of the photographs attempt to petrify the scenes as strange cultural practices of a savage people, the optical unconscious of the photographs lead us to some countermeasures against the wedging between economy and culture, which was integral to the American colonial project of the Philippines. As outlined above, the act of posing is itself a form of labor to be taken seriously as such, and within the larger industry of producing the visual archives, posing opened up some opportunities. The materials present in the photograph also point to some evidence of negotiation and economy that are effaced (but present, albeit unconsciously) in photography. The subjects' military khakis are especially incongruous to the "savage scene." Perhaps these subjects have been recruited into what would become the Philippine Constabulary in the region, but these uniforms nevertheless seem too large for all four of them.[33] It is likely that these coats and other objects not captured in front of the camera may have been part of the bartering economy into which the Philippine Commission and Cordilleran locals entered with each other.

Evidence of gift and barter economies between Americans and Igorots can be found before the 1902 Benguet trips. On February 6, 1901, Truman Hunt and P. L. Sherman, a former soldier and a photographer, respectively, accompanied a delegation of five individuals from Bontoc to Manila. Sherman was a prominent photographer for the Philippine Commission and by the third year of the American occupation would have been familiar with not only the political conditions of the Cordilleras but also how to navigate that community. Truman Hunt, the former soldier, would go on to lead one of two infamous Igorot village troupes that` made their way around North America after the 1904 Louisiana Purchase Exposition.[34]

In Manila, Dean Worcester "had a short talk with them [the Bontoc delegation] and took them in to meet the Commission informally." This delegation was brought down to Manila to discuss conditions in the Cordilleras, in preparation for occupation and ethnological surveying, but not before Worcester captured their images: "Took the Igorrotes home, fed them up and photographed them. The tattoo marks barely visible in best negatives and quite invisible in prints when negatives are made without ray filter. Experimented with rapid plates, wide-open diaphragm and with ray filter and got results sufficient to convince me that the tattooing can be photographed in this way. Gave nine seconds exposure with wide-open diaphragm and still had underexposure, using ray filter, when one-half second with same plates and 32 diaphragm was ample time without ray filter."[35] In the first instance, Worcester reduces the moment of hospitality into simply feeding and photographing Igorot bodies. The process of experimenting between plates, apertures, and filters on a large format camera (as ethnological-quality glass plates required) took all morning on February 6, which meant that the time of negotiating for poses and visual representation must have taken hours as well. What was available to prepare for food, and was there some dialogue as to the Bontoc delegation's preferences? How did the conversations take place that led the Bontoc subjects to undress for Worcester's photography? How many poses were taken, and how long were the poses and experimental trials held as Worcester experimented with different camera settings? Was there an interpreter present? I conjecture that these interactions were not as silent as Worcester's notes make them out to be; flicking the camera shutter takes only a moment, but around that image capture is the evidence of negotiation and interlocution.

On February 8, the last day the Bontoc delegation stayed in Manila, Worcester made prints of these negatives to give to the members of the delegation, "who were much pleased with them." Before they parted, a gift exchange took place: "Found the Bontoc Igorrotes and Hunt at my house on my return.... After lunch made up a list of questions for Hunt to take with him, made memorandum as to selling of Government property by the ex-Presidente of Bontoc and gave the Igorrotes all canes and Francisco an army blanket. Brought them all down to the Ayuntamiento [town hall], where I got from Branagan twenty-five dollars gold to turn over to Hunt for the purchase of arms and other products of the Igorrotes."[36] Perhaps for well-wishes and the promise of continued collaboration, Worcester and the Philippine Commission offered some gifts in order to assure future political and material exchanges in the name of American occupation. The products to be purchased may have been for personal collections or for display in industrial fairs in the United States. "Francisco" indicates the presence of Don Francisco Muro, a community leader in Bontoc and a former performer at the 1887 Philippine Exhibit in Madrid who may have also been a translator between the different parties.[37] In giving Muro the army blanket, the commission recognized that he held particular seniority among the delegation and possessed considerable influence in the Cordilleras to which they needed to cater. At some moments, Muro and the rest of the delegation were political interlocutors. At other times, they were workers in front of the camera. These encounters foreshadow the everyday encounters and exchanges that would mark the expeditions to Benguet and the development of the massive visual archive of the Cordilleras.[38]

In his analysis of the same stretch of time in 1901, American studies scholar Mark Rice argues that Worcester's expertise in photography was made possible by the Igorot delegation's knowledge of Western customs of dress and body aesthetics, evidenced by their wearing of clothes and their trimmed facial hair. He notes that "the Bontoc men had traveled to Manila clothed, aware of, and respecting Western conventions of attire while on their political mission." I am not completely convinced of this observation, insofar as this claim frames nudity as the counterpoint of being clothed for political purposes. Perhaps the Bontoc men wore different attire from their usual fabrics or simply wore the clothing they had available. (Rice notes that a pile of clothing can be seen at the edge of the nude photographs.) Nevertheless, what Rice observes and what Worcester's notes attest to is the material aspects of political and visual negotiation: the microeconomics of the colonial visual economy.[39]

While not made overt, the negotiation and bartering economies of photography were made well known to Americans who sought to make a heading in bringing their cameras to the Cordilleras. On one hand, as a technique of extracting human resources, colonial photography did not capture Cordillerans "at work" in the industries legible as wage labor: mining, road building, and plantations.[40] On the other hand, the photographic production and mechanical reproduction of images in the mountains meant economic opportunity, certainly for Dean Worcester and later photographers who took interest in the region.[41] However, these productions needed to reckon with the Igorots who worked behind, around, and in front of the camera lens. In some instances, they could seize the means of visual production and mechanical reproduction.

From Exposure to Exposition

The Worcester photographs (and others like it in the Philippine Commission's ethnology projects) taken by Americans in the Philippines were not the first time that Igorot subjects and scenes were captured for mechanical reproduction. In 1887, Igorot scenes were also displayed at the Exposición General de las Islas Filipinas. Much as later Igorots in the United States, the troupes in Madrid performed dances for fairgoers' delights in the service of a colonial display that organizers considered the last desperate attempts at portraying the Spanish-Philippine relationship as a modern one.[42] Concomitant with Spanish military occupation, officials coordinated the recruitment of Igorots for the Ranchería de los Igorrotes in Madrid by means of collaborating with local, well-educated, and multilingual leaders.[43]

Similar techniques of military invasion and the visual technologies of surveying mark the Spanish and American occupations of the Cordilleras. What differentiates the American visual economy of empire from the earlier Spanish cases, however, is the growing middle-class consumer group of the early twentieth century, which inevitably forged the visual economy into which the Igorot villages entered. From 1883 to 1913, Buffalo Bill's Wild West traveling shows captured audiences for their spectacular performances of military conquest over the Plains Indians. Riding the wake of interests in exposition, the fairs in Buffalo, St. Louis, and other cities also exhibited slices of supposedly preindustrial life in America's colonial acquisitions in order to highlight the technological achievements that they celebrated just paces away from these exhibits. All the while, large throngs of spectators paid admission fees, bringing cash for souvenirs and handheld cameras. In the expanding American empire across the continent and overseas, the economies of spectacle sought to legitimize the US acquisition of territory, natural resources, and labor through violent means.[44]

By contrast, the organizers of the Madrid Exposition sought to legitimize Spanish overseas empire even though it had been on the decline. The mechanical reproduction of images from the Madrid Exposition made pictures easily printable in illustrated books, increasingly in demand in the late nineteenth century. For Americans in the early twentieth century, the Igorot village displays built on a larger visual culture established by late nineteenth-century anthropology and photography and the improved capacity (and economic viability) of mass-producing photographs, complete with captions, forming a visual and discursive narrative of the US triumph as a growing empire. Soldiers and colonial officials brought cameras of all sorts with them, and in the wake of the new empire, government and popular writers rushed to the resultant photographs to produce new literature on America's new "island possessions."[45]

However, this differentiation between the Spanish and American exposition treatments of the Philippines does not preclude their connections. First of all, while American audiences were generally unaware of the late Spanish imperial expositions' Philippine visual tropes, organizers and workers had taken their cues from these earlier shows.[46] Furthermore, both the Spanish and American imperial fairs sought to visually domesticate knowledge production of a faraway colony for metropolitan audiences. Especially in the context of the Cordilleras—with difficult terrain and with a militarized imaginary of obscurity and always-hidden danger in the jungles—mechanically reproducible images of empire flattened the landscape and trivialized imperial occupation for those who could not travel to Madrid to see the exposition. But just as the Spanish and American impulses to exhibit their empires shared an interest in Philippine savagery and Western civilization, both exhibition projects unconsciously captured ways in which—at least in and around the camera—Western supremacy was tenuous and negotiated at best.[47]

When taken into the larger context of industrialization and photography, the imperial expositions—as grandiose forms of colonial display and as interimperial competition of progress and civilization—must be considered within the larger visual economy enabled by photography. The various expositions, in an attempt to paint grand pictures of Euro-American supremacy over technology, nature, and the colonial world, were actually fragmented and negotiated instances of display between organizers, transnational colonialists, performers, and audiences. Reminding ourselves of Ariella Azoulay's blueprints of the event of photography—as a visual apparatus of power that cannot be reduced to its component parts—these events can also be scaled at the microlevel (i.e., photographic encounters around the camera) and at the macrolevel (i.e., the visual economy of empire).[48] While earlier Buffalo Bill shows and other traveling circuses depended on extravagant storytelling for their success, the anthropologist joined the photographer (often the same individual) in turning exhibits into laboratories of social engineering and reform. While the scientist faded from the exposition scene (complaining of the lack of authenticity among the racial types brought to the fairs), photographs spread virally among the colonial imagination. As anthropologist Elizabeth Edwards notes, by virtue of photographs' indexicality—that the subject of the photograph was actually physically there at a particular moment in time—photography underpinned the visual economy of imperial spectacle with an air of objectivity. Photographs effectively vulgarized the scientific study of racial difference for a popular middle-class audience.[49] Furthermore, the Igorot village performances appeared within a global economy of increasingly accessible visual technologies, already oriented toward a mass market.[50] To incorporate the Philippines into the Kodak Zone for a middle-class consumerist empire, the midway was the most fitting place for empire to be.

The visual economy of American empire was predicated on pose, performance, and spectacle for large consumer audiences. While its products are aesthetic, its productions were labored and thus negotiated. Philippine exhibits generated a veritable migrant labor economy that presented measures of economic opportunity and adventure. Some Bontoc men learned clever ways to board ships to work in the United States: they descended from the mountains toward Ilocos port cities and presented themselves to recruiters in nothing but loincloths. After the St. Louis World's Fair, Bontoc mediators (and assistants to troupe businessmen) recruited local people into the performance industry while providing them some measure of legal safety by teaching them about contracts and litigation as well as other aspects of becoming workers in the United States.[51]

On the midway, performers could sell crafts while earning a living performing with the troupes of former soldiers Truman Hunt and Richard Schneidewind. The troupes performed decontextualized versions of *cañao* feasts for American audiences, with mock fights and dog-eating spectacles. On "domestic" soil in the United States, Americans consumed the spectacle of empire, providing impetus for commodity capitalism through imperialism.

As ethnic studies scholar Vernadette Vicuña Gonzalez suggests, the savage Igorot—as headhunter and dog eater—made the perfect Other for the justification of colonial consumption and conquest. Advertising the colonial project occurred in the form of the variety shows consumed by the public, feeding into the visions of race.[52]

The Canine and the Camera

Following the dog across the American-Philippine visual economy allows us to tease out labor histories of display and spectacle that complicate well-documented studies of US imperialism in the Philippines. Performers recognized the visual economy around the dog and capitalized on its shifting meanings in order to assert their rights to fair working conditions.

The dog-eating spectacles reveal the limits of American cultural consumption. Official descriptions and historical scholarship alike on the Igorot village shows have highlighted the variety of the performances.[53] After the Louisiana Purchase Exposition of 1904, advertising for one troupe that toured around the United States and Canada highlighted the main attraction as the "head-hunting, dog-eating Igorrotes" from the Philippines. This duality is not circumstantial; both descriptions render the Igorots visually and discursively abject in attempts to depict them savage. Neither photographers nor fair midway staff furnished them bodies for beheading. However, they were furnished dogs. From early colonial photographic encounters to the World's Fairs and smaller midway shows, Americans who sought out the spectacle of the dog-eating Igorot mobilized local economies that brought dog commodities in front of the camera and onto fairgrounds. Producing and consuming Philippine savagery meant reckoning with the cultural meanings and material realities of dogs in Benguet and American cities. For American and lowland Philippine publics, it seems that these productions of savagery were not only unpalatable to middle-class sensibilities but also rendered the entire colonial project distasteful.

The "Igorrote village" shows, led by former soldiers Truman Hunt and Richard Schneidewind, capitalized on an established social structure that connected the Cordilleras to a world of ideas, performances, and tongues, perhaps not through directly colonial means but nevertheless providing some local Bontoc men and women with means to enter into a global, multilingual world, accessible through schools and other institutions set up in the nineteenth century.[54] One difference between Spanish and American performance economies was the place of dogs; whereas the Spanish and earlier American expositions made dog eating circumstantial, later midway performances placed it at the center of the attraction, capitalizing on the fascination of audiences in the World's Fairs.[55]

Dog eating was recognized as a particular Igorot practice under Spanish military occupation of the Cordilleras but does not seem to have taken particular precedence as something for spectacle. Surveyors remarked that Cordilleran workers' diets were typical "to the *indio*: rice and *camote*, and only in major solemnities or in case of sickness do they make use of hens, eggs, water buffalos and dog-meat . . . to such an extent that many subjects in the military districts of Bontoc, Lepanto, and Benguet, who go to work for Christians [in the lowlands], demand in their contracts these foods once or twice a week."[56] Dog meat, as a part of Igorot migrant workers' diets in the lowlands, was both food staple and commodity wage, provisioned in exchange for labor power. Surmising from the earlier problems that Spaniards had in bringing workers down from the mountains, it is likely that the commodity wages in these workers' contracts were negotiated. The place of dog meat in these labor economies was as wage as well as important cultural provision. For Cordilleran workers in the lowlands, their negotiations with employers ensured the simultaneous place of cultural foods (especially community feasts, called cañao) within the social relations of commodity wage labor.[57]

What was the material economy that colonial photography captured? Returning to the "Dog Killing" photograph (see figure 3.1), notice the physical condition of the four dogs. The white dog on the left is particularly thin, with hardly any meat on its bones, its rib cage visible through its translucent skin. At least for that dog, this is not as much of a wholesome repast as the American-carved captions might suggest. In Baguio, the Daniel Burnham–designed colonial hill station in Benguet, Americans built a colonial marketplace to attract local commerce while subjecting these economies to colonial governmentality through sanitation and surveillance. Since the Spanish colonial period, the mountain-lowlands trade networks in the Cordilleras have been well known, and colonial powers wanted their own slice of the pie. As historian Rebecca Tinio McKenna notes, "free" market in a colonial built environment came with some unexpected consequences: Igorots sold dogs for food. Here, like the dogs of the 1902 photographs, they have been noted as rather scrawny but were sold in large quantities, to the delight and disgust of Western spectators.[58]

The photographed dogs of Benguet in 1902 and the market dogs that made their way to Worcester's *National Geographic* publications in look famished.[59] Two considerations might warrant some thought: first, a rinderpest epidemic

FIGURE 3.5 "The Sunday Dog-Market at Baguio." From Dean Worcester, "Non-Christian Peoples of Philippine Islands," *National Geographic*, 1913.

ravaged the Philippines' water buffalos and decimated its crops, especially rice. The better dogs may have been put to work, if they were around at all; local dogs may have been provisioned with less food during famine conditions.[60] Second, dogs of lower quality may have been selected for sale in the regional market, perhaps those not muscular enough for work or fattened enough for a local cañao but something to sell nonetheless as food. With both of these possibilities, we nonetheless see an economy of dog eating with which American colonial photographers—and later troupe businessmen touring in the United States—needed to reckon.

The sale of dogs in Baguio might have been provincialized to the Philippines—as something curious to the overseas colony—by means of Worcester's publications. However, American colonial officials as well as midway businessmen occupied a tenuous position as (disavowed) merchants and purchasers of dogs themselves. In early twentieth-century American (and English) cities, the social stratification of dogs also brought local urban economies of dog trade into which midway businessmen delved to provision their performances with sufficient meat. For example, a local paper in Sandusky, Ohio, reported that one Schneidewind performance could not proceed because evil spirits in the area required the sacrifice of a dog in order for construction to continue. Upon noting that no dogs were roaming around the area, the Igorots supposedly reneged on their position and continued their work until the "proper kind of chow dog" was provisioned.[61]

Whether or not this narrative is completely true, it attests to two features of the shows in the early twentieth century. First, this story may have been spun in order to sensationalize what was otherwise an instance of labor unrest and negotiation; setting up the village may have indeed been delayed, losing Schneidewind his income. Second, the cleanliness of the fairgrounds at Cedar Point (near Sandusky) attests to the active efforts of local officials to maintain a clean area by clearing out mongrels and tramps. Perhaps shows in other areas could more easily draw on local strays and mongrel hucksters to derive their supply of performance dogs. In trying to maintain the stereotypes of Igorot savagery, this story nonetheless recognized the performers as both construction workers and performance workers with the capacity to strike. Furthermore, it endangered the racial standing of Americans by recognizing them as workers, rendering Americans complacent in the illicit urban trades of dogs.[62]

Recognizing the tenuous positions that dogs occupied in the American imagination—or at least recognizing the centrality of dogs to the profits of their employers—it appears that performers on the Schneidewind troupe found other instances to mobilize. Just as in the Northern Luzon lowlands of Christian landowners, Igorot workers in the midways seized upon the dog, misread by popular media as commodity wages, to express some measure of control over the production of the midway spectacles. To be sure, they were supposed to be paid in cash; one contract for the Schneidewind shows with Felingao (a young Bontoc multilingual interpreter who lived with the American anthropologist Albert Ernest Jenks) guaranteed a monthly salary of "Ten Pesos, Philippines Currency, or its equivalent in United States Currency," with half of that salary paid back to his home.[63] However, dogs occupied the place of commodity wages in reports on the Schneidewind shows rather than financial compensation. The misreading by local media in Sandusky, Ohio, however humorous the piece was, is telling of the possible worker's movements on the midway. Other shows were not exempt from threats of strikes around dog eating; an exhibit in Fort Wayne, Indiana, was said to have been delayed because the manager had not delivered on his promise to provision for dogs before construction. Through the visual economy of empire, centered around the spectacular delight and disgust of dog eating, Igorot village performers struck.[64]

In the early twentieth-century United States, enough fascination over the goings-on "over there" in "our" new acquisitions brought the Igorot village shows to American shores and brought a transnational spectatorship to the dog markets of Baguio. But the visual contradictions were too great to overcome, and various measures of censure came about as quickly as they landed in the American gaze. Even as dog-eating images proliferated in American imaginations, physical photographs of abject moments could not make their

AN EXPECTANT MOMENT—Igorrotes singeing a dog, preparatory to enjoying a bow-wow stew. Although they burn the hair from the carcass, their simple natures rebel at the thought of dressing the animal quite as much as at the idea of dressing themselves. The Igorrotes at the fair attracted general and intense interest.

FIGURE 3.6 "An Expectant Moment." A sketched-over moment of a dog cooking at the Louisiana Purchase Exposition in a commemoration album. Source: *The Complete Portfolio of Photographs of the World's Fair, St. Louis, 1904* (Chicago: Educational Company, 1904).

way into American households. In commemorative photo albums of the 1904 World's Fair, the dog on the grill (or alternative animal, for we do not know which animal was actually slaughtered for the photograph) was not depicted directly and instead was crudely drawn over with a pencil sketch.[65] We have seen its analog in 1902, with the smells of dog cooking permeating the nostrils of the Americans around that Benguet clearing. Just two years later, the Igorot spectacle of singeing dogs arrived on American shores and then continued for several years after in midway shows. Audiences came into close contact with burning canine flesh, which may have smelled quite good, to the ire of fair organizers and certainly antianimal abuse activists of the time.

Photographic Filipinization

Under US-Philippine law in the early twentieth century, performers were recognized as workers. As early as 1907, Manileño elites lobbied the Philippine Commission to prohibit emigration of Philippine subjects but primarily in discussions about Igorot performers abroad. Citing the contemporary emigration of seamen to the US Navy and agricultural workers to Hawai'i sugar plantations, the commission and its lower house drew upon the language of "personal liberty" and contractual freedom to continue exhibition labor. Personal liberty under American law in 1907 included the "power of locomotion,

of changing situation, of removing one's person to whatever place one's incli-
nations may direct, without imprisonment or restraint unless by due course of
law." According to the attorney general's office, the Philippine Commission
had no authority to forbid the emigration of Filipinos, which, as exhibition
workers, included Igorots. As Philippine subjects were considered US "nationals" under American imperial law, they were afforded this sort of freedom to
move and work despite their lack of property rights and voting powers. However, emigration agents and recruiters such as Schneidewind could be fined
and taxed, and the attorney general made this recommendation instead. In
1908, an act by the Philippine Commission implemented a formal definition
for laborer but insofar as that which governed Schneidewind as an emigration
agent: "the term 'laborer,' for the purposes of this Act, shall, in addition to its
usual signification, include all persons who may be employed in any capacity
with any permanent or temporary exposition, and any traveling show, exhibition, or entertainment."[66] However, under the Philippine Commission, enforcement lay in the hands of a handful of American elites, the longest tenured
of whom was Dean Worcester himself. Since the Mountain Province was under
his jurisdiction, Worcester simply let Schneidewind recruit as he pleased and
continued to take cuts from the exhibition profits.[67]

However, for Philippine elites, the burdens of the Cordillera visual economy that proliferated abroad stymied their efforts. By 1914, due to protest
from Filipino elites as well as Igorot leaders, the Philippine Assembly (under
the Filipinization measures of President Woodrow Wilson) banned photography, exposition recruitment, and nudity in the Cordilleras. Newly empow-
ered by a Filipino political majority and new legislative powers, the assembly
moved swiftly to out-compete Worcester and the legacies of his photographic
enterprise. Manila-based reports noted that these laws were enacted to pro-
tect the dignity of the Philippines' vulnerable non-Christian tribes. A *Cable-
news* report on February 26, 1914, described the new legislation as explicitly
drawing ties between pictures and exhibitions under the unified rubric of
photography: "Assembly passes bill making it illegal to exhibit [Igorots and
Negritos]. DIGNITY PROTECTED. Lower House of Legislature Would
Put Stop to Circulation of Pictures of Nude and Semi-Nude Peoples. Woe
betide the amateur or professional photographer who dares to take a picture
of . . . any member of any non or semi-civilized tribe of the Philippines."[68]
The 1914 acts were against the visual economy around the camera and its
products but insofar as those cameras and their subjects were in the Philippines. However, banning photography of non-Christian tribes was not sufficient for the assembly to out-compete with a voracious American appetite for

Filipino savagery. While the punishment in the 1914 acts within the Philippines itself would be a fine or imprisonment, the assembly could not enforce this law abroad. Lawmakers initially banned cameras and their products but quickly needed to legislate the labor of photography abroad, which included potential camera subjects in midways. To legally shape who would constitute a Filipino in the eyes of a transnational audience, the assembly recognized the labor regimes behind the visual economy of photography.

Therefore, in 1915, out of the continued wave of protests against the visual economy of colonial photography, the Philippine Assembly passed an act that effectively banned exhibition labor migration, and thus the photography of Igorots—considered to be a metonymous "Filipino" abroad by means of performance—was banned in America and Europe. Act No. 2486 partitioned the categories of labor allowed and banned stemming from the Philippines. The act endorsed the emigration of seamen, servants, and agricultural workers (who continue to comprise Philippine emigration in the twenty-first century) while explicitly disallowing recruitment and labor migration for the purposes of exhibition.[69] While denied the legal or cultural status to be called Filipino among Manileño elites, the imagined Igorot became the metric through which elites crafted the respectability politics of nationalism under US occupation. Filipinization was not simply an export of the Wilson administration. Through the visual economy of colonial photography, Filipinization was a photographic endeavor at the interstices of imperial culture, elite nationalism, and Indigenous labor.

By the 1920s the dog market was banned as well, despite the popularity of the space as an attraction. Igorot nudity, the other controversy of the shows and photographs, could be addressed simply by being clothed. The savage spectacle of dog eating, on the other hand, did not only need to be made invisible; it needed to be excluded and pushed out "over there" in non-American geography. This spatialization of modernity percolates because of the politics of how one is represented or how one is seen, how one "looks" modern or otherwise. Furthermore, the visual economy of empire, as seen through dog-eating photography, gestures to the shift from logics of assimilation (in dressing the savage naked natives in Western attire) to the logics of exclusion (in sterilizing the American visual field from dog eating) around which US imperialism in the Philippines took shape.[70] Seeing and managing race and modernity, propagated through photographs and the geopolitics of American empire, manifested through the politics of photography.

In the twenty-first century Igorot performances have made a comeback—not in the midways of St. Louis and Nashville but rather back in the

Cordilleras—for local and overseas tourists alike.[71] Likewise, there have been movements to "reclaim" Worcester-era Igorot representations by Filipina/o artist-activists.[72] By and large, these countermeasures to colonial visuality have tended to shy away from its more "repugnant" aspects, opting instead for measures that straddle between respectability and self-representation. As anthropologist Patricia Afable and historian Paul Kramer note, the "dog-eating" stereotype—particular to the histories of the Igorots of Northern Luzon—were taken up by cosmopolitan Filipinos as the mongrel counterpoint to "proper representations" of Philippine culture.[73] Scholars' focus on this counterpoint have shied away from exploring the layers of that "stereotype," itself a result of the decontextualized visuality of race in the colonial Philippines. In 1998 the Philippine government passed the Animal Welfare Act (Republic Act No. 8485), which forbids the killing of pet animals except in the case of "religious rituals of an established religion or sect or ritual required by the ethnic custom of Indigenous cultural communities: however, leaders shall keep records in cooperation with the Committee of Animal Welfare."[74] Sequestered as "ethnic custom" or ritual, once again dog eating has been decontextualized as simply culture (to be reported—surveilled, made visible—to the government), disavowing the still-vibrant local economies of dog meat and many uses of dogs (other than as pets). Just as elsewhere in modern East Asia, such as Korea and China, the "dog-eating Asian" stereotype becomes a measure against which to judge modernity. These judgments are made through the visibility of dog eating, made hypervisible, decontextualized, commodified, and abhorred through colonial photography.

AS I WAS COMPLETING THIS CHAPTER, I entered into a Facebook discussion with Philippine scholars and writers about the Filipino movie *Oro* (2016), which raised some controversy about dogs that were actually slaughtered on camera. After offering some thoughts with other discussants in the comments section based on my observations that led to this chapter, a senior scholar was curious that I was working on a study on dog eating. The senior scholar mentioned that he recalled having a photograph sent to him that depicted Igorots slaughtering four dogs in front of a nipa hut. As this sounded awfully similar to the first photograph of that initial sequence (see figure 3.1), I asked him if he could send me his copy of the image: four individuals holding a white dog with its neck over the bowl in front of a nipa hut, with two others keeping three other dogs (two white, one black) company. It was the exact same location as that initial photograph after all except that an incision had been made across the dog's throat. Blood and viscera spill out of the throat into the bowl. On the left side, the individual crouching on the plank looks at the camera, grinning. Two of the remaining dogs stare at the camera as well. These three parties look as if they are responding to reactions of the individuals behind the camera, perhaps winces or yelps of disgust. That implied photograph of the dog slaughter—around which the event of photography existed—had found me.

It seems that this photograph has been spread around among scholars without archival location being traced.[75] In some instances, photographs are claimed by the photographer or by the institution of the archive itself. The ghosts of Worcester and other colonial photographers remain the gatekeepers to the use and distribution of these pictures, effectively as checks and controls to the visual economy of colonial photography. However, the mere presence of photographers at that scene suggests the picture's existence and circulation, and this is evidence enough of the negotiated relationships that took place around the camera.

Photographs are not didactic; they are dialectical.[76] Furthermore, as I hoped to suggest, photographs are conversational. As historians, we are invited to speak with them not just as token pieces of a social history puzzle but also as materials that invite us to think in alternative ways about the practice of writing and research. In speaking with photography, we might find small details—a khaki jacket, signs of a long exposure time, or a dog's visible rib cage—that rupture how we might write histories of people in front of the camera lens.

CHAPTER FOUR

They Are by Nature and Custom Head Hunters

The US popular imagination encountered Cordilleran people as the "head-hunting, dog-eating Igorrotes." In advertisements and exposition performances, American publics consumed the Philippines through the Kodak Zone. However, whereas dog eating was performed on carnival midways, headhunting could only be performed implicitly, and imagined headhunting artifacts could be bought as carnival souvenirs.[1] For the Philippine Commission, headhunting had a different use not only as a topic of knowledge production but also as a justifier for military occupation and development. According to David P. Barrows, the first director of the Bureau of Non-Christian Tribes, in the seasonal absence of agricultural labor—potentially useful to the American occupation—the Banaue Ifugao instead engaged in a season of headhunting. Even if the United States found Ifugao farming favorable to their development endeavors, "they are by nature and custom head hunters."[2]

Cultivating this racial signifier took place in a region where headhunting was practiced, as in much of Southeast Asia. However, as anthropologist Renato Rosaldo has shown, headhunting historically magnified in the mountains of Luzon at moments of colonial warfare in the modern period. From the 1880s through the early American occupation, economies of violence magnified as a response to increased military occupation of the Cordilleras as Spain and the United States sought to develop infrastructures in order to facilitate commodity flows across the mountain range.[3] A colonial community of spectators accompanied guns with pens, notebooks, and cameras, remarking on headhunting as an essential custom for various tribes collectively called the Igorots. Ethnology and popular visual cultures effectively decontextualized conditions of violence and grief under imperial occupation. Through the circulation of the imagined headhunter among popular audiences, with or without direct visual evidence, the colonial occupation became fueled by consumers' imperium.[4]

Whereas scholars of US imperialism in the Philippines have positioned the Igorot as an imagined "little brown brother" for civilization, I hesitate to universalize the rhetorical politics of racial uplift in practice. While the Filipino—by way of the visual archive of the Igorot—was imagined as a colonial ward of the United States, the actual practices of civilization involved more differential processes that were attuned to the everyday conditions of colonial occupation.[5] The ethnological archive of the Bureau of Insular Affairs was produced and circulated in order to discursively justify the coercion of a native labor force.

This chapter dwells on the ethnologies of Northern Luzon conducted by the Bureau of Insular Affairs. By investigating the contradictions between discourses of pacification and martial culture among described "wild tribes," I argue that the colonial state deployed ethnology that criminalized Indigenous peoples in Northern Luzon as impediments to capitalist progress, taking advantage of a voracious popular appetite for racial signifiers of savagery. This chapter shows that the term "headhunter" itself, as an imagined classifier, was deployed for the purposes of coercing Cordillera peoples into industrial labor. The discourse of headhunting during the rule of the Philippine Commission (1898–1914) served as a visual tool deployed by the United States in order to delegitimize Cordilleran claims to sovereignty in the mountains and establish a commercial order under American jurisdiction. However, that discourse was also forced to respond to various economies on the ground: warfare and violence, local bartering and trade, and native practices of cultivation. Headhunting in the colonial imagination consolidated in syncretic ways at the intersection of three factors: cultural techniques of colonial statecraft, Cordilleran lifeways under imperial duress, and the American appetite for visual spectacle.

From Warfare to "Warlike"

According to different terrains, Spain and the United States deployed various colonial tactics in the Philippines to maintain the population's subjugation to imperial rule; as a result, differentiated practices of conquest produced equally diverse calibrations of colonialism.[6] Civil and military governments kept in place the labor regimes of the tobacco monopoly, which favored commodity production on expropriated land. In the Christianized lowlands civil government remained, while in the highlands Spanish and American governments maintained military rule. While Ilokano, Gaddang, Ibanag, and other lowland peoples had long been coveted by *hacenderos* as readily available rural peasants, Spanish and Americans regarded highland peoples as prospective resources yet to be extracted.[7] In the temperate climates of Luzon's mountain ranges, Americans found native peoples at work, uncorrupted by tropical indolence. Colonial expeditions in the Cordilleras found in the mountains an "industrious savage."[8] Climatology may have supported the American case for human resource extraction, but material factors in the Cordilleras crept into these racial discourses. In particular, two Indigenous economies, both contemporary to industrial development in the mountains, wove together American racial formations of the Igorot as an industrious savage. The "industrious worker" crystallized out of Cordilleran production and economic systems extant to Igorot lifeways, including native trade and agriculture. The "savage" not only harkened to a premodern anthropological state but, in the Cordilleras, also emerged out of economies of violence and warfare contemporary to imperial invasions. In their mountain regimes, the American colonial imagination pit the industrious Igorot worker at odds with the headhunting savage.[9]

The steep verticality of mountainous Luzon lifeways offered two potential uses for Spanish and American imperialisms: connective roads and industrial workers. In particular to Luzon's rural hinterlands, colonial governors at the local level desired prospective agricultural labor, a work ethic that could be instilled through *reducción* into Christianized *barrios* and plantations. Furthermore, late Spanish and early American officials viewed reducción as an effective technique to clear the mountains for transportation infrastructures. Those views carried into the private sector, which took control of Spanish industry in the late nineteenth century. In 1882, the Spanish Empire sold the tobacco monopoly to the Compañia General de Tabacos de Filipinas (later renamed La Tabacalera). Antonio Lopez y López, the Marques de Comillas (a purchased title), purchased the monopoly's assets, including control over tobacco plantations in Northern Luzon and cigar factories in Manila. Unlike the colonial government's version of the monopoly, Lopez's company could focus purely on profit qua profit. Separated from the joint responsibility of income generation and governance, the Spanish colonial state instead brokered the development of private enterprise through its extant institutions of rule in the Philippines. Utilizing both the missionary corps and the military, Spain launched a *reconquista* (reconquest) campaign to industrialize the Cordilleras, the Caraballo Mountains, and the Sierra Madre chain. Spain invoked the language of a racialized crusade against non-Christian peoples and marched into the Cordilleras in an effort to subdue its peoples into the rule of industry.[10]

By the 1880s, the Cordilleras became a war zone for industry. For foreign investors—private entrepreneurs and colonial empires alike—warfare facilitated infrastructural development in the mountains in order to connect the Cagayan Valley and the Ilocos coast to other parts of Luzon. Even though the United States initially had different purposes for warring in the mountains, it nonetheless maintained the state of warfare in the region.[11] The formal end of the Philippine-American War arrived with the passage of the 1902 Organic Act, which inaugurated a civil government throughout most of the islands. Once war was officially declared over, Americans launched an information-gathering campaign in order to ascertain how to govern the islands as a colony. President William McKinley established the Philippine Commission to study the Philippines and ascertain the next steps in colonial management. In one year, the commission amassed a large archive of knowledge from which it made its recommendations to Congress. The commission members interviewed former Spanish officials and missionaries, Philippine barrio leaders across the islands, and European social scientists. Despite grandiose claims of improving Philippine colonial government, the United States replicated many of the late nineteenth-century structures that the Spanish had put in place.[12]

Among the governing technologies of the Spanish, the Philippine Commission carried over martial law and native policing in the Cordilleras. Colonial policy shifted from that of declared warfare to one of counterinsurgency. The United States established the Philippine Constabulary, composed of a white leadership and native recruits, in order to reconfigure an ongoing war in the rural Philippines into a colonial policing project. The constabulary waged war against tribes on behalf of the American government and disarmed guerrilla fighters by confiscating firearms and taking prisoners. Furthermore, in the Cordilleras, military invasions continued in the form of colonial expeditions, accompanied by native police and military forces. Dean Worcester, the Secretary of the Interior, in an American innovation enlisted the constabulary to carry out ethnological and geographical surveys in the Cordilleras. Worcester himself made yearly trips into the mountains but regularly commissioned the constabulary to compile reports and draw maps of road development.[13]

The dual role of the Philippine Constabulary, as native police force and industrial prospector, came out of the recommendations of the German self-taught ethnologist and governor Otto Scheerer. Scheerer lived in Luzon for two decades before the United States purchased the Philippines. Born on August 13, 1858, he arrived in Manila in 1882 as a businessman with a German trading firm, later founding La Minerva Cigar Company after Spain abolished the tobacco monopoly. Scheerer moved to Baguio, then a modest Ibaloi barrio in 1896, while the Philippine Revolution waged in Manila. Ethnology and travel began as a hobby for Scheerer, but he always had an eye toward acquiring wealth through business, and his writings on culture and linguistics paid attention to industry and development. Furthermore, he settled in Baguio in the middle of the Spanish military occupation and Cordillera-wide war-fare.[14] Because of Scheerer's long tenure in the archipelago and his inti-mate relationships with Igorot communities, the Philippine Commission was suspicious of him even as it relied on his information to compile its recommendations.[15]

Nevertheless, as Scheerer's comprehensive 1900 report to the Philippine Commission attests, his testament proved fundamental to the American co-lonial enterprise.[16] The Scheerer report described, in authoritative ethnolog-ical language, a landscape marred with industrial warfare. The report provided a political lay of the land in the Cordilleras with a focus on Benguet, framed as recommendations for colonial governance over the region's peoples and terrain. Scheerer recognized the Spanish in regard to industrial efforts of reducción in the late nineteenth century and encouraged Americans to con-tinue "the work of gradual civilization . . . avoiding [Spanish] errors and faults."[17] In particular, he envisioned bringing Igorots into the agricultural and economic order that underpinned lowlands Philippine life, revolving around crop cultivation, disciplined wage labor, and the circulation of money. This can be evidenced by his peculiar choice to trace the etymology of "Ig-orot" not to its Tagalog cognate (*I-golot*, meaning "from the mountains") but instead to an Ilokano one (*ag-urut*), which he cites as meaning "to tear out, to unroot." The Tagalog (itself coming from *taga-ilog*, or "from the river") ety-mology of Igorot indicates the geopolitical location of people in the Cordil-leras as those who retreated to the mountains in the face of colonialism and warfare. More likely the Tagalog etymology is valid, because the words for "to uproot" in Ilokano are *amurot* or *baguten*. However, Scheerer's Ilokano ety-mology of Igorot conceals a political motive to reroot mountain peoples from their vagrant states to a productive life of peasantry, or, more commonly put, reducción.[18]

The first series of steps that Scheerer proposed for the American version of reducción was to promote the fertility of land while directing local labor energies to its cultivation. He urged the "fomentation of agriculture" where possible to maintain some subsistence at first but with enough development for "money afterwards." Furthermore, just as the Spanish established churches to fix natives to governable barrios, Scheerer encouraged the building of schools to teach Igorots industrial skills such as agriculture and hygiene. For areas without fertile land, these schools could prove valuable to industrial re-ducción, as it would supposedly educate Igorots with a skill set to serve colo-nial development in other areas of the Cordilleras.[19]

This latter point, on the footloose nature of Igorots on infertile lands, may have been a decontextualization of swidden agriculture practiced across the Cordilleras in areas without rice paddies.[20] The "fomentation of agriculture" (as Scheerer put it) and the "preservation of woods" may seem like a matter of natural subsistence, but used against mountain tribes who used swidden agriculture, these colonial strategies were meant to coerce them into industrial agricultural labor.[21] To support his case, Scheerer reframed swidden agriculture and hunter-gatherer lifestyles as examples of "great poverty [among] the vast majority of the Igorrotes," which "if numerically expressed, may not be very much greater than that of the poor class of natives in the lowlands." Only by the fortune of an "abundant nature," he theorized, could these groups subsist, and it would be better to educate them in ideas and practices that promoted the acquisition of capital.[22] To maximize on potential human resources in the Cordilleras and reproduce a culture conducive to a capitalist order, Scheerer recommended the "circulation of small coin."[23]

As a potential risk to the colonial project, Scheerer emphasized the continuity of the *cuadrillas* (constabularies) and *gobierno politico-militar* (military government) systems under the Spanish. Military control was important, Scheerer noted, in order to insulate the violent tendencies of mountain peoples unto themselves until such time that they could be pacified into productive agricultural and infrastructural labor. In particular, he claimed that the high rates of headhunting posed a danger to the productive Christianized natives working on farms in the lowlands.[24] Furthermore, if poverty was not addressed and if order was not to be established in the mountains, people would "[swell] the hords [sic] of head-hunters, into whose savage life [the Igorots] fall back; thus . . . the work of long years of civilizing is undone."[25]

The quantitative logics of how Scheerer conceptualized Igorots as formless and disparate masses whose numbers and energies could be consolidated or otherwise surrendered to the wild "horde." Civilizing natives required that they be counted first, which then required the invasion of unexplored terrains in order to develop a comprehensive geography of the Cordilleras. If accounting for the land and its people did not take place, Indigenous geographies could challenge the colonial projects of road building and labor mobilization. As for the people, they would remain formless masses whose numbers could quickly overwhelm the project of civilization. Efficient colonialism quantified natives arithmetically. Through censuses and expeditions, the United States could enumerate everything from the mountain contours to colonial subjects and the value of their property. Colonial knowledge in the Philippines accounted not only for the raw materials of the Cordilleras but also their value and potential uses, to be harnessed and tested by state scientific means.[26]

However, as anthropologist James Scott argues, while such enumerative colonial state projects claimed to be pan-inclusive in their endeavors, its optics (i.e., the ways in which the state came to see) narrowed.[27] Arithmetic surveys did not make visible instances when Cordillerans eluded the state and retreated to the mountains or otherwise found new places to live as hunter-gatherers.[28] The inverse of accounting subjects for civilization projects were, as above, the feared hordes of headhunters in the obscurest fastnesses of the Cordilleras. Unable to be accounted for arithmetically and residing outside of the purview of the progressive state, hordes could instead be accounted for in terms of some common feature that they expressed. In the Scheerer report and as fortified by later ethnologists' accounts of the region, one observed feature was common enough across mountain tribes and worthy to stand as metonymic for the Igorots of the early twentieth-century colonial imagination: headhunting.[29]

At the core of the Scheerer report, much of which the United States implemented through the Philippine Commission, was a racial capitalist order in the mountains in opposition to an imagined "warlike" people. Rather than jail all Igorots outright for killings and warfare (although many were incarcerated into prisons under different subprovincial regimes), the colonial regime deemed it prudent instead to imprison Igorots within their own "mountain fastnesses" and racial stereotypes.[30] Scheerer and the Philippine Commission continued to call Igorots non-Christians, but these tribes were not merely infidels against a Catholic God. They were dangerous but potentially useful resources for a new deity: capitalism. The civilizing project in the Cordilleras would require the United States to refashion its colonial wards in the image of industry.

In the Image of Industry

Indeed, the image may have been one of the most potent US weapons in mountain colonial development. With the Scheerer report in hand, the Philippine Commission continued its military and civil invasion into the Cordilleras but to mixed results. The commission encountered impenetrable terrain in the Sierra Madre and Caraballo Sur (Ilongot land) and breathtaking rice terraces in the Cordillera Central that filled every corner of cultivable slope (especially in Ifugao land). When the commission launched a census across the colony in 1906, it could not count Igorots directly and instead had to esti-mate by counting barrio households from afar.[31] Furthermore, the commis-sion did not only face headhunting and ambush warfare but did encounter warring Cordillerans with Western guns.[32] Colonial development on the ground confronted Americans with the material realities of counterinsurgent governing. As Scheerer recommended, the United States sought to bring Ig-orots into manageable and visible labor regimes while disarming them in the process.[33] However, this work of "gradual civilization" required the labor of making visible a people and a terrain hitherto obscured to the United States.

If the colonial state could not account for all Igorot territory and popula-tions, it could instead govern through the images of racial stereotype. In other words, in the absence of arithmetic counting, the United States needed to account for its mountain subjects geometrically in an effort to one day coerce Igorots into visible and manageable spaces, pacified and productive for colo-nial industries.[34] In practice, the United States set out to declare and jus-tify certain features of abstract groups—manifestations of the "Igorot"—as metonymic to a whole. Ethnology, then, opened the practices of creating a colonial image world through which Igorots could be managed in groups and punished according to the terms of racial stereotype. It is important to note that the Scheerer report was not merely a recommendation document that the Philippine Commission valued greatly. It was an ethnological essay. Scheerer encouraged the United States to enact progressive governance via ethnological knowledge enforced, against an unruly people, both through discipline and requisite punishment. In other words, the ethnologies for colonial development were as penal as they were industrial.[35]

Ethnological governance drew upon new media technologies of the early twentieth century in order to justify projects of progressive rule. The most important feature of colonial rule in the mountains, where subjects could not simply be counted through censuses, was the camera.[36] Photographs of the empire's new subjects offered Americans a useful tool to account for the Cor-dilleras. However, as I showed previously, the visual economy of photogra-phy also served as a labor force through which Cordillerans could themselves express claims to self-representation or at the very least find economic and adventurous opportunities for themselves. Furthermore, not everyone in the Cordilleras necessarily agreed to be photographed for the state, much less so if (in the case of Ilongot territory) they were at war with Americans. In order to establish an industrial order in the mountains, American colonial officials such as Dean Worcester and his subprovincial governments prioritized the ethnological uses of the photograph. Despite colonial fears of warlike tribes in difficult terrain, that quality of belligerence meant that Cordillera bodies possessed an innate energy that might prove useful for work. Ethnologists consistently remarked on their subjects' musculature in their notes: "[The Ilongots and Ibilaos] are strong, robust, and tall."[37] But while Americans across the Pacific took to photography as the predominant way of consuming the Philippines, colonial officials took to other visual and literary media as well. Photographs, travelogues, performances, maps, and films together constellated around the production and circulation of capital in the Cordilleras. If, for Americans, the people of the Cordilleras could not easily be counted arithmetically, then the land itself—and the potential energy of the people who dwell on it—could be abstracted as aesthetic terrain.

In the mountains of Luzon under American imperialism, racialization and resource extraction contended with a colonial aesthetic: the pastoral. As historian Rebecca Tinio McKenna argues, Americans in Baguio deployed discourses of naturalism to obscure the architecture and infrastructural practices of development and the displacement of Ibaloi peoples in Benguet. While urban development, at the scale of Baguio, did not take place across the mountains, American mapping of the region reflected the US desire to infrastructuralize the landscape as a built environment. Furthermore, Americans put the pastoral to work on other Cordilleran groups, differentially along their terrain but always attuned to the prospect of developing capitalist order in those regions.[38] The Bureau of Insular Affairs took to the visual practices of City Beautiful to envision, perhaps, a "Cordillera Beautiful" through the cartographic practice of the blueprint. In 1909, Dean Worcester commissioned the Philippine Constabulary to draw out maps of extant roads and towns in order to ascertain their conditions and future avenues for development.[39] As with all blueprints, carrying out the plans required the mobilization of a workforce, and the marked roads and potential throughways necessitated that budgets be put in place for wage labor. Furthermore, these expeditions furthered the state's penetration into underexplored regions and establish a police presence in areas that continued to wage war against the United States.[40]

Across the Pacific, visual industries put the pastoral to work on Igorots as well to not only justify colonial rule but also obscure the actual work behind the Igorot village shows. Organizers of the Igorot village troupes advertised midway performances as "the head-hunting, dog-eating Igorottes" from the "mountain fastnesses" of Luzon. The show invited audiences into an immersive space that brought the Kodak Zone from Philippine Cordillera to midwestern amusement park.[41] Igorot workers built nipa huts in wooded areas in order to mimic the imagined mountain fastnesses of Luzon.[42] Furthermore, other than dog cooking and eating, performers made some extra income by selling wares that implied headhunting and raids: axes, machetes, shields, and bows and arrows.[43] Therefore, Igorot village shows were popular simulacra of imperialism, serving as metonymic built environments for the Cordilleras to the American public, themselves based on imagined notions of the mountains that Americans were only in the process of documenting.[44]

This pastoralism, in idyllic landscapes worked by Indigenous skill, was always under constant threat of losing itself to a natural and wild state of being "warlike." As Scheerer urged and the Philippine Constabulary attempted to carry out, Igorots must be disarmed of weapons to pacify the Cordilleras and establish order. However, the warlike headhunting Igorot proved to be a popular commodity for visual and material consumption across the Pacific. In between disarming Igorots through counterinsurgency and gun confiscation, the lance and the *bolo* (machete) knife took on new currency, arming the headhunter in the colonial imagination. Certainly, the lance and the bolo aided in raids and headhunting expeditions, but mountain peoples used these—as lowland peoples did—as tools for hunting and farming. Under the ethnologist's observations, from the photographs, and in the captions and lectures given about them, the bolo became a "head-knife."[45]

Worcester's caption for this image in the Newberry Library reads as follows: "Ilongote head-knife and scabbard. The knife is also used for clearing trails through the forest and for domestic work of various descriptions." The bolo is an all-purpose tool for cultivation and self-defense. In the mountains, Americans reduced the bolo into a primitive artifact of warfare through photography but with the potential to do industrial labor. By placing the white sheet behind the artifacts, the photographer divorces the weapons from any other context and renders it open to other imagined interpretations. In this case, whereas the bolo is a tool of industry in the lowlands, it poses violent threat when wielded by warlike non-Christians.[46]

When sold on midway attractions and displayed in American museums, the bolo also became metonymic for headhunting. These displays submerged the Indigenous production for which it is used, highlighting instead a material artifact for the "warlike" Igorot who resisted American civilization. Accusations against Igorots took place through the "head-knife," but the Philippine Constabulary did not confiscate these weapons, for they were easy to forge and were essential to Igorot economic life.[47]

While the warlike image tended to stand in for all Igorots in colonial government reports, it also obscured a gendered logic behind mountain

FIGURE 4.1
Photograph 2-c 37 1/2,
Dean Worcester
Photography Collection,
Newberry Library,
Chicago, Illinois.

governance. The observations of musculature made by the Bureau of Non-Christian Tribes fixated on men's bodies. In most Cordilleran tribes, head-hunting expeditions were affairs for men, and ethnological observations that Americans made about warlike tendencies fixated on masculine activities.[48] In practice, the Philippine Constabulary recruited men, and the workers who carried the cargo for American expeditions were also men. Furthermore, across the board, surveillance documents made by the constabulary in Ifu-gao compiled biographical profiles of valuable members in barrios, marking their valor or laziness, property values, warring history, and loyalty to government.[49]

Every entry in this document was identified as a man. The metonyms for governing Igorots co-opted masculine labor and warfare, but femininity be-came the impetus for invasion and establishing settlements. As historian Tessa Winkelmann and cultural critic Nerissa Balce show, European and American settlers capitalized on marriages with native women to establish their academic and entrepreneurial careers. In the visual archive, photo-graphs of nude women pepper Worcester's collections, from which he con-structed ideas of savagery and Philippine docility to US power. As Balce suggests, the Filipina's breast became a visual metonym for native hospitality toward American invasion in the islands.[50] Women's death and grief (as this chapter later explores), and not just bodies and sexual intimacies, could also be put to work to justify colonial benevolence, even if its practices were violent. In a 1911 massacre in Kalinga, Dean Worcester justified his American crony's brutality by fixating on the jawbone of a woman killed by a Cordilleran soldier in the Philippine Constabulary. Rather than blaming his institutions, he blamed instead the Igorot's natural propensity to be a headhunter. Worcester used the death of this woman—by "one of her own"—to continue disciplinary regimes in the Cordilleras.[51]

The United States put the imaginaries of pastoralism as well as threats to its idyllic nature (such as headhunting) to work in their uneven conquest of the mountains of Luzon. Dwelling on the different practices of this work across regions reveals how headhunting emerged syncretically between imperial and Indigenous economies in the mountains. While a homogenized headhunter circulated across the Pacific, its formations were nonetheless subject to native production and combat that fomented the stereotype's emergence.

Basi and Bolo

In major American colonial archives, there are far fewer documents—both visual and military—on Ilongots than there are on Cordilleran tribes, especially compared to the Ifugao and Bontoc tribes.[52] However, Ilongot insurgency against Spain and the United States gained currency in the colonial imagination, from which Americans would concoct the headhunting savage. While Ilongot histories and political cultures share characteristics with Cordillera tribes called "Igorot," Ilongots today do not, by and large, identify as Igorot. The Ilongot homeland is located south of the Cordillera Central into the Caraballo Mountains and intersects with the Sierra Madre chain across the eastern spine of Luzon. In the colonial imagination and in cultural productions about the Philippines, the Ilongot often bled into discussions with Cordilleran tribes, all of which Spain and the United States continued to call "Igorot," or "from the mountains."[53]

Ilongot territory was long desired for its proximity to the Cagayan Valley as a potential site for road building in order to facilitate commodity flows from the fertile tobacco lands to Manila. This territory was especially coveted because of its location at the intersection of two major mountain ranges, because a mountain throughway could produce the most parsimonious path for Philippine tobacco to be processed in Manila. During the late eighteenth

century, Gaddang and Ibanag natives of the valley and Ilokano settlers from
the Amianan's northwest coast were among the first peasants incorporated as
coerced labor for the Spanish tobacco monopoly and its private successors.
But because maritime and overland commodity transportation needed to
ford dangerous distances, the colonial state renewed its desire to conquer the
mountains of Luzon. Spanish military and missionaries offered their services
to subject Ilongot territory to militarized Christian rule. The reconquista
project made the southern Cordilleras a bloody war zone, with sustained
cases of headhunting throughout the region, the memories of which lived on
in Ilongot descendants in the mid-twentieth century.[54]

Initially, the Bureau of Non-Christian Tribes made little headway into
Ilongot territory. Instead, the Philippine Commission relied on interviews
and secondhand accounts from Spanish missionaries in the region who occupied the Sierra Madre with increased military presence in the hopes of coercing Ilongot displacement into Christian settlements. From these failed
missionary efforts, Dean Worcester wrote Ilongots as both cowardly peoples
and warlike headhunters, instilling these armchair ethnologies into official
government policy in the region.[55] The former stereotype of cowardly am-
bushers developed in response to Ilongot ambush combat styles. The latter
feature, as warlike headhunters, emerged as observations of landscapes of
violence specific to the Cordilleras. In reality, Ilongot fighters simply took advantage of their Indigenous knowledge of thick vegetation and undulating
terrain while maintaining raiding practices that continued into the second
half of the twentieth century.[56]

Throughout the course of the Philippine Commission's rule (1898–1914),
Ilongot territory continued to represent a dangerous frontier in the American
imagination. Nonetheless, this frontier was also a resource frontier for both
natural resource cultivation and human resource extraction. An undated publication, written by Worcester himself in the early days of Philippine Commission rule, speculated that the mountains could be cultivated with "sweet
potatoes, gabe, Indian corn, onions, and garlic," with harvests of rice "sown in
places in the forest which have been cleared up a little."[57] Rather than ascertain the soil quality of the region, Worcester's report suggested that the Ilongots were far too savage to express sophisticated agriculture but had the
potential to cultivate rudimentary crops when needed.[58]

Written accounts of expeditions into the Caraballo–Sierra Madre junction
echoed visions of Ilongot land as inchoate frontiers but essential to the infrastructural development of the colony. In a 1910 travelogue Cornelis de Witt
Willcox, a lieutenant colonel in the US Army, described a journey up through

the Mountain Province into the Caraballo Sur. The closer Willcox and his expedition approached the Caraballo Sur, he remarked, the "wild incoherent mountain masses [looked like they were] thrown together apparently without order or system. . . . And then, as [their] trail wound in and out, different aspects of the same elements would present themselves, until really the faculty of admiration became exhausted."[59] Wilcox said that upon approaching Ilongot villages in earnest, he found the Ilongot to be the "real wild man" in the Philippines: "[The Ilongots] have the reputation, and apparently deserve it, of being cruel and treacherous, as they certainly are shy and wild."[60] Most likely, the aforementioned Ilongot reputation came out of Worcester himself or other associates, priming the expedition goers to the expectations of the mountains and their peoples. Despite the difficulty of entering this region, Willcox emphasized that "the indispensable material condition of success was to make the mountain country accessible. Only those who have had the fortune to travel through this country can realize how difficult this endeavor has been. . . . In spite of the difficulties involved, however, a system of road-making has been set on foot, the labor needed being furnished by the high-landers themselves in lieu of a road tax."[61] Willcox lays bare the civilizing mission, which was to extract human resources through pacifying their supposedly violent tendencies.

Photography, as elsewhere in Luzon and the un-Christianized Philippines, remained the major means of rendering Ilongot territory visible for a larger public and for legitimizing the colonial project in the Caraballo Mountains and the Sierra Madre. Despite Worcester's success in the other subprovinces, he was only able to acquire comparatively few photographs of Ilongots due to precarious relationships in the region with local people. However, when his photographs were not of dance postures or head shots, the shots he took revealed a colonial interest in agricultural labor. In this first photograph (figure 4.2), taken in about 1903, a topless man grasps with his right hand a tall sugarcane, towering about fifteen feet including the fronds at the top. In the stark sunlight, his musculature is accentuated on his biceps and thighs as well as a well-built torso. His fit body amid endless fields of unharvested cane suggests the possibility of a bountiful harvest and plentiful native labor, if only exposed to the right technology. Worcester's caption in the Ayer collection is as follows: "An Ilongote clearing planted in part with sugarcane. Note the gigantic size of the cane, which grows luxuriantly in the rich forest earth."[62]

The second photograph (figure 4.3) captures a common method to make *basi* (sugarcane liquor). Again, a muscular man stands erect and flexed but this time in a clearing with a machine against a tree. The man's stance is rather

FIGURE 4.2 Photograph 2-a 21, Dean Worcester Photography Collection, Newberry
Library, Chicago, Illinois.

FIGURE 4.3   Photograph 2-b 46, Dean Worcester Photography Collection, Newberry Library, Chicago, Illinois.

awkward: his feet weigh down on the rope to immobilize the machine, and his hands do not quite grasp the horizontal rod but instead lean against his groin. His torso leans forward, as if ready to release the mechanism or work it when compelled to. Worcester, drawing from ethnographic observations of the process, described the industry as follows:

> Ilongote bassi mill. Bassi is a kind of weak rum made from the fermented and undistilled juice of the sugar cane. In this instance, the stem of a sapling is pivoted at a point near its larger end, where it passes between uprights. This end rests upon a thick block of wood. At a point considerably removed from the pivot is fastened a strand of bark extending to the foot of the uprights. This bark strand or rope forms a sort of treadle operated by the foot. In actual operation the foot is worked up and down rapidly in this treadle. The long free end of the sapling soon gets to vibrating violently, and the short end pinches down upon the wooden block with great force. A man feeds in sugar cane between the short end and the block, pushing the stalk in a little each time the short end is raised. Grooves on the sides of the block cause the juice to run down and drip into a receptacle

placed beneath to catch it. It is then fermented and imbibed during dances and fiestas.[63]

As in the first image, this second picture suggests a ready labor force, complete with Indigenous engineering that could be made efficient if sold toward a larger market instead of remaining within the ceremonial confines of the *kanyaw*. The musculature of the men in both paragraphs is emphasized, as is the fecundity of the landscape and the presence of a local industry. Worcester's fixation on the process of transforming the raw material (sugarcane) into a consumable commodity suggests his prospecting for a primitive industry, the energetics of which, through colonial knowledge and development, can be extracted for American—and personal—profit. This is commensurate with Worcester's first compilations of knowledge from Nueva Vizcaya's Indigenous peoples, based on interviews with ex-missionaries in the mountains: "They are strong, robust, and tall. . . . Although inclined to be indolent, nevertheless they take good care of their crops." Americans viewed land and labor as potential resources for extraction through prospecting corporal vigor and commodity agriculture.[64]

Ilongot land, while wild and undeveloped, therefore presented an opportunity for sugar cultivation, an industry long coveted by Americans through the nineteenth century. In the 1860s before the United States bought the Philippines from Spain, the Boston-based trading company Russell Sturgis & Co. looked to the Visayas as a supplier and planned for expansion across the islands well before 1898. Sugar refiner corporations such as Spreckels Sugar Company initially turned to the Philippines for its biggest supply of raw sugar and only turned to Hawai'i after the 1875 Reciprocity Treaty between the kingdom and the United States.[65] That the implicitly industrial photo captions appear in the acquisitions of one of the nineteenth-century's infamous robber barons, then, should not be overlooked. Worcester captioned these photographs simultaneously for a business magnate and the potential massive audience that Gilded Age money could buy. After fighting in the Southwest during the American Civil War, Edward Ayer made his fortune by supplying timber to railroad companies. The Ayer collection on Native American and Philippine ethnologies was acquired through conquest and genocide and the cultural fascination of the savage contemporary to nineteenth-century westward expansion. Paired with the two dollars he received for his prints, Worcester purchased cultural capital for his conquest and investment in the Philippines, cloaked in the language and technology of social science.[66]

However, the danger of an overgrown territory, coupled with "the warlike nature of the Ilongots," haunted Americans in this region.[67] Despite the potential for labor and colonial development, the Philippine Commission imagined the Ilongot as "tigers dedicate[d] to the shedding of human blood . . . on account of superstitious motives and a certain necessity relating to their savage life."[68] Worcester's initial ethnology was conducted from his armchair, compiled from Spanish and lowland Filipino secular missionaries who entered the Sierra Madre as part of reducción missions, and thus his descriptions of Ilongot headhunting derived from an especially bloody time of military invasion and imperial violence in the late nineteenth century. Prior to his own photographic expeditions into Ilongot territory, his eyewitness accounts fixated on the sword.[69] Worcester's interviewees described the *kampilan* (spelled "campilan" by Worcester), supposedly a variant of the bolo, that is achieved by sharpening down a bolo from an industrious machete into a purely warlike weapon for raids.[70]

Worcester did not capture images of Ilongots in the midst of a raid. However, he implied their warlike nature by fixating on their weapons, and imploring the photographic viewers at the Newberry Library to do the same. The ethnological profile preceding the photographs notes that Ilongots are "head-hunters, but seem to be a cowardly people, who almost invariably attack from ambush. In taking the heads of their victims, they do not use head-axes, but employ large knives (bolos)."[71] For example, figure 4.4 depicts a photograph taken in a settlement called Canadem. The photograph depicts young and teenage boys in a row, all wearing loincloths. The second boy from the left holds a bolo, gleaming in the sun. A topless older woman, less tanned from the outdoors, stands at the right, and an older man stands on the steps. Above a young caped man to the right of the older man a knee is visible, as is a fully clothed young boy at the window. While the photograph spreads out in front of a stilted nipa hut, the Newberry caption implores a particular locus of attention: "Note especially the dilapidated character of the house and the head knife in the hands of the man in the middle foreground."[72] This may indeed be a headhunting expedition, but neither this photograph nor any of the other ones in the Newberry series on "Ilongotes" suggest cowardice, as Worcester claimed. However, the caption addresses a lack of engineering prowess (the rudimentary house) and a natural propensity for violence (through the "head-knife"). The two features to which this caption ascribes meaning implores that the photograph's spectator view the scene as evidence for colonial development.[73]

While photography could serve to popularize the colonial mission, the logistics of military and industrial invasion into the mountains required maps.

FIGURE 4.4 Photograph 2-a 20, Dean Worcester Photography Collection, Newberry
Library, Chicago, Illinois.

As in other parts of the Cordilleras, the Philippine Commission mapped the
intersections of the Caraballo Sur and the Sierra Madre by means of blueprints. The blueprint of Nueva Vizcaya or, more specifically, terrains with
Ilongot settlements that rivaled Spanish and American roads, marked the
landscape as a site for future development.

The map in figure 4.5, compiled by the Philippine Constabulary deployed
in the region, depicts the undulating terrain that impeded efficient tobacco
circulation from the Cagayan Valley (to the northeast of this region) to Manila (to the southwest) since the late eighteenth century. The map marks
"Ibalao Rancherias" (Ilongot settlements) with dark circles and "Ibalao trail"
with thin dotted lines. "Christian towns" (presumably Ilokano, Gaddang,
and Ibanag barrios) are marked in rectangles, with "good trail" in thicker
dashed lines. The Ilongot trails do not appear comprehensive but instead are
mapped according to skirmishes between American forces and Ilongot
resistance. These are the roads that Worcester and his ex-missionary interviewees cite as strategic paths for headhunting raids. Good roads, on the
other hand, were those under the patrol of constabulary and local barrio law
enforcement and maintained by pacified native labor. The blueprint, then,

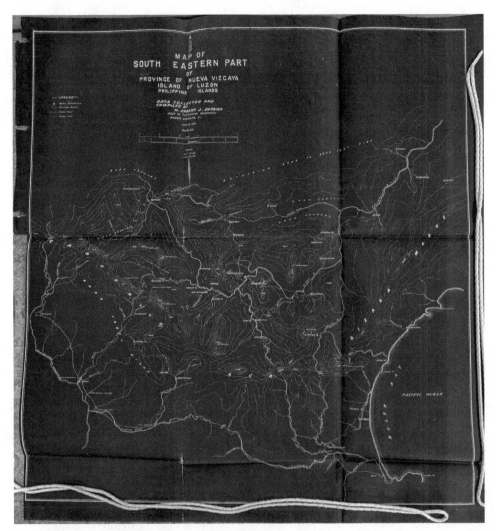

FIGURE 4.5 "Map of South Eastern Part of Nueva Vizcaya," box 3, volume 15, folder 4/4, Hatcher Graduate Library, University of Michigan.

visualizes attempted conquest in which colonial capitalism competes with Indigenous geographies through warfare over the land.[74]

Ilongot land remained inaccessible until well after World War II, and headhunting continued as well. Under the United States the colonial development project was a failure, but its racializations of Ilongots as headhunting savage remained potent. In 1965, President Ferdinand Marcos relaunched the infrastructural and legal conquest of the Caraballo Sur with financial support of the World Bank. He proposed a plan for a Pan-Philippine highway from

Laoag in the Ilocos to Zamboanga in Mindanao. In 1972 under martial law, the Philippine government sent firing squads to quell headhunting, with militarized enforcement made possible through the new highways.[75] Marcos's postwar reconquista, long after its Spanish and American forebears, incorporated modern construction technologies but with the same logic as American development: infiltrate the mountains with native labor, incarcerate lifeways considered deviant from state power, and build infrastructures to circulate trade from Manila to its hinterlands.[76]

"The Most Wonderful Rice Terraces"

In Ifugao, as in Ilongot territory, Americans put the pastoral to work for capitalist development while grappling with the specter of headhunting in the eyes of a progressive state. However, unlike the thick obscurity of the Caraballo Mountains, expeditions in Ifugao and neighboring Bontoc reveled in the vistas of the rice terraces. These terraces were later believed to be over 2,000 years old by American anthropologists, a narrative that has persisted until only recently through the efforts of archaeologists in Ifugao. According to Stephen Acabado, the principal investigator of the Ifugao archaeological expeditions, Ifugao people did not merely flee to the hills in response to Spanish colonialism but also cultivated the rice terraces as a strategy against conquest itself. Against Spanish conquistadores, the Ifugao people earned the moniker *tribus independientes* (independent tribes). This sustained success over three centuries of Spanish lowlands rule can be attributed to wet-rice agriculture that stretched across the valleys of the region and supplied the mountain populations independently.[77]

While rice paddy cultivation was an advantage against Spanish techniques of conquest, by the early twentieth century the sedentary nature of Ifugao cultivation proved to be its own undoing. Unlike Ilongot land, Ifugao was swiftly subjected to American colonialism and its military structures in the mountains. With Ifugao already under Spanish colonial military command, the United States merely continued the occupation, making use of native policing labor as its imperial forebears did. This practice was encouraged by Otto Scheerer as a means of quelling conflict and headhunting in the area, immediately subjecting the region to a carceral government by means of ethnological knowledge.[78]

From 1898 to 1909 in the name of counterinsurgency, occupation forces built a surveillance state in Ifugao and collected plentiful information on locals. Local leaders, who had become wealthy as lowland traders in the nineteenth century, were among the earliest to surrender to the United States and join the civil government as collaborators.[79] With the collaboration of local leaders, subsequently appointed as *cabecillas* of their local *barangay*, the Philippine Constabulary built its major barracks in both Banaue and Kiangan. The lieutenant governor's quarters were also built in Kiangan. Both complexes were built atop uncultivated land on the sides of both valleys, overlooking the Ifugao rice terraces.[80] Colonial photographers, both professional and amateur, found that the settlements afforded them an ideal—and idyllic—landscape of their nation's new imperial acquisition. Atop the ridge between Kiangan and Lagawe near the colonial settlements established for the Philippine Constabulary, photographers captured landscapes such as the one pictured in figure 4.6. The panorama most likely captures the Nagacadan rice terrace cluster, the vantage point of which straddles Kiangan and the flatter region of Lagawe. The image consists of two photographs taken askew from each other from the same vantage point. The middle seam suggests an effort to align the rice paddies as best as possible without the luxury of an ultrawide angle lens or digital panorama production. Cropping for the photograph on the right must have taken place in the darkroom, as the developer focused on aligning the western rice terrace slope in the foreground. Such panoramas frequently appear in the American Historical Collection (Rizal Library) and the Dean Worcester (in the Newberry Library) and Owen Tomlinson (Bentley Historical Library) photographic collections, the three major visual archives for pictures in the Cordilleras. The sharpness of detail and the clarity of each step suggests that the cameras used were tripod-mounted, plate-glass large cameras, requiring—as in ethnological photographs—workers to carry the set up to the location. Behind the camera, considerable labor went into capturing a sublime vista devoid of humans but with Indigenous economic activity carved into the landscape.[81]

Furthermore, that there were many such photographs suggests inordinate energies invested in capturing and commodifying the landscape, which Americans frequently expressed as sublime. Despite the difficulty of the trek, writers paused on the sublime inexpressibility of the landscape in travelogues of journeys through the mountains. In her letters to her mother written in 1909, Nanon Fay Worcester, the wife of Dean Worcester, described the experience of traversing through rice terrace country in length:

> The river channel [of the Agno Valley] was rather narrow with high banks, and above these banks and extending back to the mountains on both sides were rice terraces filling every available space. This necessitates

FIGURE 4.6 Oversize folder 1, Owen A. Tomlinson Papers, Bentley Historical Library, University of Michigan.

paddies of all sizes and shapes, making one of the old fashioned crazy quilts. Even the fancy stitches are represented by the stone walls that separate paddies and hold up terraces. The rice is in full head but still green and every blade stands up as straight as an arrow. Can you not imagine the beauty of it all? The bird scaring devices added to the picturesqueness of the scene and interested us not a little.[82]

In describing Ifugao cultivation and irrigation systems, Nanon wrote in the passive voice—"above banks . . . *were* rice terraces," "*this necessitates* paddies," and "the fancy stitches [of the crazy quilt] *are represented*"—giving action to the agricultural infrastructures, as if they are removed from the Ifugao engineering behind them and the ongoing maintenance conducted by local farmers. Nonetheless, no matter how submerged, Ifugao economies and ecological skill speak back. The "crazy quilt" of Nanon's description of the rice terraces hides, beneath its passive voice, Indigenous engineers who figured out how to harness and cultivate slopes in an esoteric—"every available space"—yet sublime and breathtaking way.[83]

For Nanon, the beauty of the rice terraces also made them desirable photographic subjects even if a physical photograph did not circulate. Nanon wrote to her mother, "Can you not imagine the beauty of it all?" In a later passage in the same diary, Nanon wished that "a photograph could give [her mother] some idea of [the mountains]."[84] The private economy of the photograph between mother and daughter is not the profitable visual economy of the World's Fairs. However, Nanon's desire to possess the landscape suggests the place of photography, as an idea and possibility, to extract value from empire. Nanon desired to convey to people back home a sense of needing to see the sights before her, preferably with a camera, and to convert the spectacular Cordilleras into a spectacle for colonialism.[85]

The rice terraces in Ifugao were a pivot for absorbing the Philippines into the Kodak Zone. Nanon Fay Worcester was not a professional ethnologist and was not part of the colonial government's civil service, nor was she an avid photographer like her husband and his colleagues. However, even in her private writings and photographic circulations to her mother, Nanon Worcester drew upon the language of photography and capitalism to articulate her adventures in the Cordilleras. Dean circulated photographs to explicitly further his political agenda against Philippine independence and maintain his investments in non-Christian regions. As shown in chapter 3, Dean Worcester's midway clients, Truman Hunt and Richard Schneidewind, advertised their "head-hunting, dog-eating Igorrotes" as "interesting visitors" to the

American towns in which performing troupes conducted their work. Through colonial visuality, the Worcesters' associates justified capitalist development and labor regimes in Ifugao. This cadre includes Nanon Fay Worcester herself.

Photographs and travelogues unconsciously captured and gave pastoral beauty to Ifugao economies. The panoramas, such as that of Nagacadan above, are not terrae *nullius* for America's taking. Instead, they offer visual evidence for Indigenous labor and engineering inscribed in the slopes. Recounting the Bureau of Non-Christian Tribes' early expeditions in 1902 and 1903, David Barrows remarked that they were "the most expert agriculturists in the Islands, with their marvellous terraces and irrigation works, their strong compact towns, et cetera."[86] In his 1905 index to the Newberry Library, Dean Worcester described the Ifugaos as builders of "the most wonderful rice terraces to be found in northern Luzon, and for that matter, anywhere in the world."[87] His photographs of Ifugao attempted to capture both the landscape's beauty and its people's potential, all for Americans' beholding and for colonial industry.

In practice, the verticality of the landscape remained a challenge for Americans in the region. Within the political unconscious of American photographs and travelogues lies a jealousy of Ifugao economies and engineering for having filled, as Nanon Worcester noted, "every available space" of cultivable slope with well-irrigated rice cultivation.[88] The rock walls that separate each terrace are crucial to the irrigation systems in the land, and the proliferation of terraces made it difficult to appropriate the slopes to build roads. As ethnic studies scholar Vernadette Vicuña Gonzalez remarks, transportation infrastructures did not supersede landscapes of Indigenous economies but rather built around them in order to monopolize the beautiful vistas for imperial eyes.[89] Indeed, to this day road building proves to be difficult in the Cordilleras not only because of the mountainous terrain but also because these rice terraces and their cultivation practices have been declared UNESCO heritage sites.[90]

For the colonial government in Ifugao, the solution was to target the people themselves in order to capitalize on extant Indigenous economies for American benefit. Writing about his 1903 expeditions in his Newberry photographic collection, Worcester remarked on Ifugao economic potential for future audiences. However, in writing about the rice terraces, he composed his statement in the passive voice, focusing his rhetorical attention on the landscape while disempowering ongoing Ifugao maintenance of their production: "Their almost perpendicular rice terrace walls sometimes attain a

height of thirty or even forty or more feet, and water is skillfully led in irrigat-
ing ditches or systems of troughs along the precipitous mountain sides for
great distances to [the] tops of these systems of terraces."[91] The benefit, for
Worcester, is not immediately a profitable economy for the American prospector (and indeed, rice cultivation was at the subsistence level within valleys) but rather the visual commodification of a beautiful landscape: "The
trip from Quiangan [Kiangan] to Banaue affords one continuous series of
wonderful views of terraced country which cannot be matched elsewhere in
the world." Implicit in this ethnological profile is that any future road through
Ifugao could afford both commodity circulation and the added value of aesthetic beauty, perhaps for the future tourist.

As a metric for industrial progress in the region, Worcester referred to the
success of the US military occupation of Ifugao according to the suppression
of headhunting. In two short years, he claimed, Banaue went from being
"very warlike" and "actively engaged in head-hunting" to being "very friendly
towards the Americans."[92] In this description, Worcester decontextualizes
headhunting from the ongoing warfare in the region, then called a counterinsurgency after the formal declaration of peace.[93] Earlier in the paragraph, the
Ifugaos were described as "a tribe of warlike head-hunting savages" but then
become suppressed from "very warlike" tendencies, implying a residual warlike nature that should justify American occupation. Worcester, via the Philippine Constabulary forces, figured the visual Ifugao as a savage to justify
industrial development.

Photographs were not practical means of accounting for what Americans
needed to establish power in the region. For the Philippine Commission, racial archiving necessitated continued military rule that, as Otto Scheerer had
recommended, should stem from the protoconstabulary system under the
Spanish.[94] In the place of Worcester's annual expeditions, the constabulary
carried out the work of amassing geographical and ethnological knowledge
while maintaining police presence.[95] However, Americans in the region consistently remarked on the problem of population dispersal as well as constant
warfare, hindering their desire for readily available colonial labor. In 1910,
Lieutenant Governor Jeff Gallman offered a solution that envisioned Ifugao
self-policing by means of a road labor tax. He declared that deploying a full
criminal justice system in Ifugao outweighed needs for efficient road building. In order to quell conflicts, Gallman oriented discipline from barrio-based
justices to a compulsory road tax.[96] In doing so, insurgency would not only
be a crime against the state (or an embryonic American state structure in the
mountains) but would also most effectively be a crime against industry. In

the absence of infrastructure, producing a glut of outlaws also generated non-working masses, which—as other Americans feared—would be unproductive to the project of pacifying "warlike" natures. Rather than creating an army of insurgents, the road tax would produce a reserve army of colonial labor. For Gallman, this road tax also had the benefit of instilling a culture of self-policing: "An Ifugao who would never think of reporting the existence or whereabouts of a neighbor who is evading the authorities on account of a murder committed, will very promptly come in and want to know why I do not require so and so to work on the same as he is doing."[97] Rather than criminalizing headhunting, the road tax penalized unproductivity.[98]

Road labor and maintenance was not the only way that Americans endeavored to extract value from their subjects in the mountains. Under the watch of the Philippine Constabulary, Gallman and Senior Inspector Owen Tomlinson (who later became lieutenant governor) compiled a robust archive of key players in Ifugao leadership and economy. Initially hired as senior inspector of the subprovince, Tomlinson amassed photographs and surveillance profiles from his kinships in the region. From his small town of Whitesville, Indiana, he joined the US military to fight in the Philippines in 1899, mostly participating in campaigns in the Luzon lowlands. By 1909 at the establishment of the Kiangan government settlement, he became well regarded for both his leadership and his language skills, and soon after his constabulary appointment to Banaue, he gained fluency in oral and written Ifugao.[99]

For the Philippine Commission, Tomlinson's most important skill set was his affinity for economic ethnologies. By developing kinships quickly among Ifugaos, Tomlinson paid attention to whomever controlled political and commercial power and compiled this knowledge to sustain the occupation. In 1911 Gallman commended Tomlinson's enthusiasm as a senior inspector, remarking that he "has a thorough knowledge of what the people have to sell and what they desire to buy, and in my opinion is in every way fitted for handling the exchange opposition."[100] Ifugao, through its rice terraces and its people's deep knowledge of highland-lowland trade, exhibited robust commercial activity to which Americans were attracted. It was on this basis that Gallman recommended Tomlinson's appointment as his successor for lieutenant governor: "In the case that he is appointed I would recommend that he first organize the Ifugao exchanges. They are going to prove a great success, when properly handled. At present it is impossible to keep a stock on hand of the demand for the goods."[101] With ethnological work, Worcester and his constabulary colleagues sought to control Ifugao markets by policing commodity flows. Just as in Baguio, where Americans sought to govern Ibaloi markets through physical marketplaces, Gallman and Tomlinson implemented formal sites for exchange, doubling as value extraction and colonial policing.[102]

Through sustained occupation and interviews with locals, Tomlinson composed a massive document titled "Biographical Sketches of the Subprovince of Ifugao."[103] This document charts out notable individuals, rich and poor, in the different barrios of Ifugao. A profile of each listed individual remarked on political position, approximate value of holdings, industriousness or laziness, measures of loyalty to the United States, and histories as war leaders. Headhunts and other killings are relegated to the past in order to ascertain that the "warlike" nature of Ifugaos was being phased out. Killings after 1909, on the other hand, were individualized as murders rather than as a part of ongoing conflict in the region. Tomlinson commodified his kinships with locals in order to ascertain what nodes of the Ifugao social fabric could be exploited for economic gain, with the implication that economic development was necessary to suppressing savagery.[104] Every single entry in the "Biographical Sketches" was about a man. The report posited that Ifugao men were the key to exploiting labor and trade, while women were implicitly part of households' domestic spheres. Men are tabulated as both economic and undisciplined entities, to be disciplined out of their "warlike" nature and harnessed as workers or as conduits for colonial trade.[105]

Women appear instead in the photographic record as bare-breasted commodities for both public spectacle and private consumption. The written records of Tomlinson and Worcester in Ifugao are devoid of women's activities, but their visual archives are replete with women's bodies. Tomlinson kept an extensive collection of photographs that he preserved in his private albums, which his grandson donated to the University of Michigan in 1979.[106] The subjects of Tomlinson's early photos (taken as a soldier) are mostly Manila scenes and photographs of his American comrades. His photographic collection during his time as senior inspector and lieutenant governor focuses on three subjects in roughly equal parts: landscapes, his constabulary and male colleagues, and the women of his communities. The women are not as nude as in Worcester's photographs but do tend to be topless. Whether or not they were naturally so before the photographs were taken I cannot ascertain. However, Tomlinson took to the camera to capture naked women in abundance for his personal pleasure.[107]

Most disturbingly, Tomlinson's personal pleasure over Ifugao women may have involved child trafficking. An October 1911 letter from a colleague named "Bell" thanks Tomlinson for his "kind attention to the matter of the little *mestiza* girl at Quiangan, also for sending me the stool, baskets, and plants.

They have all been received and I understand settled for, at least I hope so. I heard that the people in Baguio are delighted with the little girl. She certainly was a beauty and would be considered a beauty not only in the Philippines but anywhere on earth."[108] For an undisclosed price, Tomlinson seems to have sold a petty assortment of gifts to a friend in Luzon's urban centers. The nature of the mestiza girl's work is not disclosed, whether it be sexual work, pageantry, service labor, or all of the above. The mestiza girl—mixed race, perhaps a child of a local and an American soldier—made Tomlinson some immediate profit, but her future value as an exhibition through circulation (indeed, her photogenic nature) would profit the incorporation of the Philippines into the Kodak Zone of the world.[109]

More than most other Cordillera regions, Ifugao proved exemplary as a zone for economic development. In 1922, the anthropologist Roy Franklin Barton published a paper titled "Ifugao Economics" in *American Archaeology and Ethnology*. Barton remarked on Ifugao Indigenous economies and their propensity for labor, as they work for wages and should seek to supplement income between rice terrace harvests. Through colonial occupation and policing, ethnologists partitioned Ifugao lifeways into separate spheres of "war-like" culture and potential economic profit. By the 1920s, it appears, the combination of a road tax, colonial policing, and the circulation of small coin took effect in Ifugao, to the benefit of American profit. Through racialized and gendered aspects of colonial capitalism, the American occupation commodified landscapes and lifeways for various forms of value.[110]

However, not all aspects of headhunting and masculine vigor could be commodified in terms of colonial labor. Just as performances were labored spaces in the visual economy of colonial photography, the ethnological images of these noneconomic activities could also be extracted for value even in death and in grief.

"A Freshly Decapitated Body"

The photographs in figures 4.7 and 4.8 appear in an "Igorots of Benguet" series in the Newberry Library, the prints and indexes of which were acquired by the library's Edward Ayer in 1905 from Dean Worcester. At one dollar per print, thousands of photographs made Worcester rather wealthy, in addition to the other industries he invested in. The group of eight photographs—what I will call the "Ifugao funeral sequence"—are brought into motion through the Worcester photo index, as Worcester himself sought to guide the beholder onto particular features of his photograph for his own ends. Unlike

Tomlinson's private albums, Worcester's visual products were meant for public circulation to further his political agenda against Philippine independence.

The obscured left side of the photograph in figure 4.7 (marked 7-b 77) appears in the Newberry print itself and supposedly blocks out a scene of a
family in bereavement over the burial pit. When the photograph is grouped
with accompanying images, we might glean insights with the photograph
into the production and circulation of headhunting imaginaries for colonial
purposes. We shall also uncover the ways in which these images resisted complete commodification from photographic subjects and the spectators beyond the photographer's intent.[111] Out of respect to the deceased and the
grieving family, I will not show the rest of the photographs. However, below I
will walk the reader through each photograph, first on its own terms and then
in sequence, identifying the unshown photographs by their archival label. My
readings of the Ifugao funeral sequence will be juxtaposed with Worcester's
own ways of animating the photographs in order to hold them accountable to
the structures of power behind their composition but also to pose challenges
to the claims they make, to poke holes perhaps, as Ifugao mourners did at the
funeral, in the shroud of these colonial images of petrified grief.

The first photograph (7-b 72), which is not shown here, was most likely
produced in Worcester's 1903 annual expedition. David Barrows remarked on
this practice among the Ifugaos, or the "most expert agriculturists in the Islands," supposedly happening in the offseason of rice terrace agriculture, and
that Worcester snapped this photograph on such an occasion upon finding "a
freshly decapitated body."[112] Rice terraces are visible in the background of the
photograph, along with a young man with long hair peering at the camera. A
decapitated body, with combat wounds on the left buttock and the upper
thigh, is tied onto a rod to be carried home by two individuals. The body's
knees are lifted into a fetal position, and the arms are folded, with the hands
up where the head should be, and the back rests on a shield. The left lower leg
and buttock are open with gashes from battle wounds—possibly from bolos
or bayonets—long left open from the journey home. With the body brought
back to Banaue, the photographer stopped to request that the funeral carriers
pose for a photograph. The carrier on the right, with a loincloth and white
hat, is off-scene, while the visible one on the left covers his mouth with his
right hand. This is not a natural pose and is worth pausing on; his face looks
distressed, and he may have been covering expressions of his grief. The day is
bright (and many areas of the film are overexposed), and the photographer
rendered a shallow depth of field, blurring the background and bringing a
clear image of the corpse (with all its gashes) in the foreground.

FIGURE 4.7 Photograph 73-b 77, Dean Conant Worcester Photographs, Edward Ayer
Collection, Newberry Library, Chicago, Illinois.

Later in this expedition (it is not entirely clear if it would have been on the
same day), the subjects put together a funeral. Not captured in this sequence
are the rites that lead up to the funeral, such as processions and dances.
(Tomlinson's collection captures these rites.)[113] With the same thin-pole nar-
row shovels they use for rice cultivation, some of the group dug a hole in the
ground among thick overgrown vegetation to act as a grave for the body.
Most men of the band are topless except for one at the back, who is dressed in
the uniform of the Philippine Constabulary; this gives credence to the location of this photograph, in Banaue, where the constabulary's barracks are

FIGURE 4.8 73-b 78, Dean Conant Worcester Photographs, Edward Ayer Collection,
Newberry Library, Chicago, Illinois.

located. The headless body is laid down in the pit (center left of the photograph), and some subjects look into the camera. (7-b 73) In the next photograph (7-b 74), two band members work with the body to move it deeper
into the pit. The constabulary member is off-scene for this one, suggesting
that the photographer may have wanted to capture mostly naked subjects for
this ethnological sequence. One band member in the center of the photograph has his bolo sheathed in a clear scabbard, but it shines in the broad
daylight. In 7-b 75, more men enter the scene on the bottom right, while the
men in the pit prop the body upright. In 7-b 76, still more men enter but this
time with their shields. One man in the middle scowls at the photographer,
presumably squinting from the sunlight that shines more or less into his face.
Another man in the middle, crouched atop the pit, has a white cloth on top of
his head. In 73-b 77 (Figure 4.7), all the same subjects look into the pit, obscured by an incomplete or postprocessed development that whites out the
entire left third of the photograph. The social and emotional gravity points
toward the obscured portion of the image unlike the rest of the images, the
subjects of whom turn their faces in different directions, including toward the

camera. The following scene (7-b 78, Figure 4.8) shows various young men filling the hole, marked horizontally with the same rod with which he was carried home. At the bottom right, six young men, one middle-aged man, and an elderly woman scowl at the camera or at the people behind it. The displeasure is apparent in their faces, and the middle-aged man and elderly woman show evidence of puffy eyes, as if they have just been crying. This is most likely the family of the deceased; the looks of disapproval on their faces suggest that this photograph was an egregious violation of a moment of grief. The final photograph (7-b 79) shows a filled hole and one man in a loincloth and cape, with sheathed bolo on waist, standing vigil and peering at the camera with a curious look.

Worcester's captions attempt to objectify the funeral for the purposes of study. In 7-b 72, which is described apart from the rest of the funeral scenes, Worcester turns the spectator toward a particular object: "Note that the shield was split in the fight."[114] The impersonal description glosses over reasons for the fight and elements of collective bereavement among the community. Instead, the description essentializes the Ifugao as naturally warlike and that this scene was simply an effect of Ifugaos' nature during the early occupation. Worcester claims that these photographs were taken in 1903, before the establishment of full colonial rule. The subsequent photographs are described in motion with one another, and the caption narrates the burial almost completely in passive voice. For instance, in 7-b 73, the victim *"was buried in a grave* . . . across the upperside of which stands one of the wooden spades *with which it was dug."*[115] Worcester describes the burial position as follows: "The arms and legs *have been bound* against the front of the body. . . . The blanket *was first chopped full of holes."*[116] Similarly, the captions animate 7-b 78 and 7-b 79 in the same removed passive voice: "The grave *is being marked."*[117] In all the photographs, the index captions completely erase any indication of a subject looking at the camera or, in general, as agents of a funerary rite to honor a fallen comrade. Like the landscapes and Ifugao economies, the captions of the Ifugao funeral sequence fixate on the products in the land, or the essential actions of the people in the photograph, except in one picture.

The image in 7-b 77 (Figure 4.7) presents a crack in the ethnological voice, a moment of agency from which the historical subjects speak. This photograph and its caption capture a family in grief. I quote the caption in length: "In 7-b 77 the mother and immediate friends of the deceased, standing on painted war shields, are going through the final ceremony, in the course of which they asked the deceased why he had gone away and gotten himself killed, leaving his old mother without means of support, especially in view of the fact that he had a house full of tobacco. They, however, promised to take vengeance upon his enemies."[118] No matter how removed and ethnological the captions might be, challenges to scientific objectivity can be found in the visual record. The photograph in question obscures the grieving mother, and it is unclear why this was so. The lens seems to have partially been covered with a sheet or a card, or this photograph may have been only partially developed in postprocessing. However, all heads are turned toward the left. An Ifugao expedition companion will have been translating for the caption to be made possible. Unlike the rest of the captions, which merely describe motions of the funeral, this one takes into account grieving for the dead. The mother and immediate friends express anguish over the deceased victim, and the voice of the caption moves from passive to free indirect discourse. Free indirect discourse is a mode of narration in which the third-person omniscient narrator moves into the consciousness of a scene's subject, describing motivations and possible thought processes as well as speech while maintaining the third-person voice. By melding with a subject's consciousness, this mode of narration establishes complete empathy between an omniscient narrator, the subject, and the reader.[119] Used in an ethnological caption, it emerges as a rare ethical response to grief and a moment in which the writer is compelled to honor that, despite better interests. Worcester did not speak Ifugao, so the translator is also given voice and implicit presence here, democratizing the production of this scene. Perhaps too, not fully developing the photograph was a failed way to restore some ethnological objectivity or perhaps another implicit response to grief. Perhaps Worcester would have wanted to maintain some face with Edward Ayer, his wealthy client, and future spectators of the photograph. We bear witness to a moment in which the social gravity of death supersedes a temptation to objectify the subject if only for a brief and painful moment.

The funerary rites and continued presence of headhunting suggest the presence of what anthropologist Renato Rosaldo called the emotional and cultural force of death. In his introduction to *Culture and Truth*, in which he simultaneously works through understanding Ilongot grief and his wife's sudden death during field work, he posits that taking literally a subject's force unflattens anthropological practice. Instead of placing grief within a larger web of abstract relations, or—in Worcester's photographs—a set of photographable customs, force demands paying attention to "a particular intimate relation's permanent rupture," of "learning . . . that the child just run over by a car is one's own and not a stranger's."[120]

I suggest that the rupture caused by the force of death simultaneously ruptured the American ethnological gaze. In a previous scene, the friends stabbed holes into the shroud, which Worcester had reduced to passive voice, distilling it simply into custom.[121] But in the case of image 7-b 77 (Figure 4.7), we might see evidence of this force through the single locus of attention, common to all heads turned toward the obscured grave, and the caption that unexpectedly animated dialogue and subjectivities. The developer in the dark room may have felt this force, petrified into the emulsion, compel the friends' practice to give grief its due privacy. Captured in these photographs, the subjects in question are Ifugao bands in relation to other groups around the Cordilleras and the armed Philippine Constabulary occupying Banaue and surrounding areas. Since agriculture and infrastructural development in the Cordilleras required coerced cheap labor—precarious yet still in abundance and certainly living—abundant deaths could not be productive in an industrial labor regime. Nonetheless, the cultural force of death in this funeral became yet another source of value for the white Americans who claimed private sovereignty over Cordilleran homes. For eight dollars—at a dollar per print—Worcester and his troupe put the Ifugao mother's grief to work.

The corpse too became a visual commodity to justify American occupation. Of the eight pictures of the Ifugao funeral sequence, photograph 7-b 72 (the victim on the pole) entered into wide circulation. In *The Head Hunters of Northern Luzon*, the military officer Cornelis de Witt Willcox described his travels into the mountains among headhunters but does not given an account on any actual instance of headhunting. He wrote extensively about traveling into the Caraballo Sur, noting the material and visual evidence of headhunting: "The men were fully armed with spears, bows and arrows, shields, and head-knives; gee-strings apart, they were naked. Some of them wore on the head the scarlet beak of the hornbill; these had taken heads."[122] But the photograph paired with the Ilongot narrative was not an Ilongot one but rather an Ifugao image, specifically, the first picture from the Ifugao funeral sequence. The caption reads as follows: "Headless Body of Ifugao Warrior. Being carried to burial on his own shield, suspended under a pole. Such a sight would be impossible to-day."[123] Certainly, the caption specifies that the subjects are Ifugao, but the matter of dispersing Ifugao photographs—taken in the context of an ongoing military occupation—suggests that the publishing process allowed these racial images to circulate within the confines of a multiregional travelogue. The Cordilleras became a dangerous but commodifiable site for the conquest and literary description of soldierly white men.

In 1914 and 1915, the Philippine Assembly banned the photography and exhibition of non-Christians both in the islands and abroad.[124] In response, Worcester replaced village shows with films and lecture tours, taking on the work himself to do expositions. In his original film plans, he had wanted to include "a headhunting party taking the trail and a head-dance on their return" and to "have a young man being talked to and guyed in a typical auto, by the old man, having it represent that he is trying to pursuade [*sic*] him that he ought to take a head."[125] However, no implications of headhunting made the final cut of the resultant silent film. Instead, Worcester or other presenters in the film circuit would have had to lecture over the screening, performing the work of ethnological captions but without the visual evidence.[126] Through Worcester's lectures, the racial images of the warlike savage circulated around the United States but without the popular audiences of the World's Fairs and other extractions. Nonetheless, through his various economic investments in the region, Worcester continued to extract value from the Cordilleras at the expense of the native peoples he came to consider as a ready labor force.[127]

AS THE US POPULAR ATTENTION TURNED to the world war across the Atlantic, a savage Philippines became a visual afterthought to the American public. By 1915, Filipino elites successfully eradicated visual productions of headhunting and dog eating from the Cordilleras. However, visual respectability did not Indigenous justice make. Eradicating visual productions of headhunting did not eradicate circulation of the warlike headhunter image. Colonial and postcolonial governments continued to occupy the Cordilleras to profit off of the region. With death squads—the contemporary iteration of the Philippine Constabulary—the Philippine government quelled headhunting in the Cordilleras, referring to its efforts at counterinsurgency as "modernization" and "development."[128] Meanwhile, Indigenous arts such as tattooing have become a source of tourism in the region, while Indigenous activists have become branded as terrorists.[129] Urban development and mineral extraction, launched in its modern forms by the United States, continues today.

When and why did Igorots count as "Filipino," and when and why not? As this section showed, the archival productions of Spanish and American capitalist development reoriented the "non-Christian" toward Igorots' relationships with colonial production and infrastructures. Being more dispersed and resistant to colonial rule, Igorots were brought into an American consumers' imperium through their incorporation into the Kodak Zone.[130] To shape respectability politics among elite nationalists, the Igorot became someone to disavow in favor of a "modern" Filipino subject in the global arena.[131] While Cordillerans' lifeways became subject to military and capitalist rule, the Igorot proliferated as a stand-in for the twentieth-century Filipino, to be expropriated or disavowed. Across the Pacific and in modest numbers—and constrained to Hawai'i—at first, Americans began to fear new hordes of Filipino men, which amounted to a "third Asiatic invasion."[132] For Americans, these hordes did not take heads. Rather, these invading Filipinos threatened two other possessions over which white settler men in the United States claimed ownership: white women and jobs. Many hailing from Ilocos and its diasporas, these young men became known as *sakadas* and *manongs*, or, altogether, Filipino Americans.

Part III
Lowlands

CHAPTER FIVE

Sugarcane Sakadas

In December 1906 with ten of their fellow townsfolk from Candon in Ilocos Sur, Simplicio Gironella and his four sons arrived at the 'Ōla'a plantations on the *Claudine* interisland steamship of Hawai'i.[1] Royal D. Mead, chairman of the Bureau of Labor and Statistics for the Hawaiian Sugar Planters' Association (HSPA), assigned these first fifteen Ilokano field hands to the humid and mountainous rain forests of 'Ōla'a because of its similarities to Luzon's monsoon weather patterns. While the climate, at least in Mead's imagination, may have been similar, the labor remained backbreaking and demoralizing. Asthmatic and homesick, Manong Simplicio requested alternative arrangements to help the planters recruit more workers from his home region but not as a field hand.[2] After a month and a half on 'Ōla'a, Simplicio and his manager, John Watt, arranged for his return to the Philippines with his fourteen-year-old son. Watt and his associates hoped that Simplicio could build momentum on the HSPA's recruitment schemes in Northern Luzon. With his youngest son, Simplicio returned to Ilocos Sur, and his three older sons stayed behind, working the fields. Francisco Gironella, his son, stayed behind with two other brothers, working as the interpreter between planters and the migrant workers.[3] Through the Gironellas, the HSPA could recruit more workers from Candon and elsewhere in Northern Luzon. Over the next decade, these first Filipinos on HSPA fields served as the model for future Filipino labor recruitment by sugar and pineapple companies in Hawai'i. In community histories, these workers eventually became known as the *sakadas*: pioneers of the large diasporic community on the islands today.[4]

But did these migrants understand themselves as Filipino in the first place? The archival construction of the Filipino, according to plantation records, reflects the language of the corporate oligarchies that effected occupation over the Kingdom of Hawai'i since the late nineteenth century. A longer genealogy of the term traces the Filipino to the *criollo* of the Spanish colonial period, the anticolonial articulation of the Filipino by Manila *mestizo* nationalists, and the American-guided governmental nationalism of the early twentieth century. North of Manila Bay, however, other ethnic groups did not necessarily conceive of themselves as Filipino. Local intellectuals in the Ilocos region did not always subscribe to the Tagalog-dominated nationalism movements that surged elsewhere in the archipelago.[5] Under American rule, the Filipino ethnic identity subsumed different groups across the islands.[6] Likewise, while Ilokanos became Filipino in Hawai'i, this construction finds its genealogy in the colonial systems of mass agricultural production in Northern Luzon's lowlands, through which Ilokanos were displaced from subsistence cultivation to migrate around the island to find work on plantations. The HSPA coveted the Filipino in Hawai'i as cheap and subservient labor, easily acquired from an American colony and imagined to be an always already rural worker.

This chapter centers the disproportionate impact of single-crop plantation industry in the lives of Ilokanos from Northern Luzon to the labor diaspora in Hawai'i. I argue that the racial formations of the sakadas emerged not exclusively by anthropological and policy-making means but instead through the private practices of accumulation and resource management on plantations themselves. The Filipino in Hawai'i—alternatively as cheap peasant or vagrant dissident—crystallized out of the joint corporate techniques of sugar plantations, the HSPA, the Philippine Commission, and the financial institutions that executed the dealings of the sugar oligarchy. Recognizing that the first arrivals from Northern Luzon were recruited by the Olaa Sugar Company, this study focuses on that particular plantation and its surrounding regions as well as its primary financial executor, Bishop & Company (now First Hawaiian Bank). Until the inauguration of Filipinization policies under Woodrow Wilson's presidency, private profiteers and financial institutions controlled the management over a fledgling transpacific Ilokano diaspora. Through these industrial stakeholders' practices of recruitment and accounting, they first constructed a corporate form of the Filipino on Hawai'i. In turn, these American financial institutions capitalized on Philippine racial structures put in place through the forced ruralization of Northern Luzon through nineteenth century Spanish agriculture, which generated an inland Ilokano peasantry through dispossession, coercion, and hunger.

Transplantations

While other visions of the Filipino proliferated throughout the turn of the twentieth century, such as the Igorot savage in the 1904 St. Louis World's Fair, the Filipino mobilized for commodity production was crafted as a third world agrarian imaginary.[7] Through plantation labor, environmental destruction, and knowledge production in the nineteenth century, the Ilokanos in Luzon became potential human resources for extraction and use in Hawai'i's plantations.

Altogether, the sugar elites, financial executors, and the Philippine Commission called these human resources Filipino.

The early twentieth century Filipino in Hawai'i, as migrant peasant, was the cultural product of nearly a century and a half of industrial agriculture in Luzon and the reorientation of the colonial Philippines toward commodity production. The Ilokano, like the Kapampangan, the rural Tagalog, and the Pangasinense in Northern and Central Luzon, lost subsistence land and livelihoods through a systematic colonial process of converting arable land in the Philippines into profitable commodities. Ilokanos moved around the island in search of plantation lands to lease, often becoming precarious and migratory in the process. In turn, photographers and social scientists from Europe and the United States recorded their observations of the various "tribes" of the Philippines. In the process, the Europeans and Americans decontextualized the endemic migrations of farmworkers in Luzon, rendering these histories of displacement into ideas of race and peasantry. Born of industrial agriculture across the island of Luzon, the Ilokano as a Filipino migrant peasant became essentialized as transplantable work, from plantation to plantation.[8]

As Candonians, the Gironella boys and men and the ten others who joined them came from a locale deeply intimate with the effects of land disposses-sion and plantation agriculture. In 1898, likely in coordination with Emilio Aguinaldo and Manila-based revolutionaries, local Candonian leaders de-posed Spanish priests and economic elites in the city who had been large landholders throughout the nineteenth century. During this period, agrarian revolutions spread across Ilocos and its inland diaspora. Bursts of unrest and emigration corresponded with various phases of Spanish colonial reforms as the empire sought to incorporate the rural Philippines into a global commod-ity market.[9]

Early Spanish colonialism in the Philippines did not exhibit the same in-frastructural investiture of rule as that which marked colonial rule in the Americas.[10] Across the Pacific, the ease of transatlantic maritime transporta-tion facilitated the development of widespread plantation labor systems and tenacious rule by conquistadores. The Philippines, by contrast, served pri-marily as a port to facilitate the galleon trades between the Spanish Empire and China. Spanish colonial officials and merchants concentrated around Manila, leaving lowland provinces elsewhere in the islands under the control of clergy. Catholic priests and friars centered rural life in Luzon and the Vi-sayas around the church and the *barrio* (village), converting the majority of lowland populations to Catholicism and collecting tithes to maintain local rule. Until the American colonial occupation, most native peoples encountered the Spanish colonial state not through public bureaucracies or despotic criollo-led pockets of power but rather through representatives of the Catholic Church.[11] The lack of infrastructural power through the Spanish colonial state and the absence of large-scale extractive economies until the late eighteenth century allowed for subsistence livelihoods in Northern Luzon's lowlands to flourish. These Indigenous economies consisted of coastal fishing, multiple-crop agriculture, and commodity trade. Of the latter, Ilokanos primarily traded with Spanish and Chinese merchants, especially in the coastal port cities of Laoag and Vigan, as well as with Cordilleran traders along mountain slopes.[12]

With the exception of the port cities, most of the Ilocos remained rural through Spanish rule. However, Ilocos's conversion into an envisioned natural resource frontier, as opposed to merely being religious and colonial borderlands, emerged as Spain launched initiatives to orient the Philippines toward a global commodity market. The British invasion of Manila and the destruction of two Spanish galleons revealed two core weaknesses of the Spanish East Indies: the vulnerability of *las islas Filipinas* amid rival empires in Southeast Asia and the economic precarity of Spain's island colonies under maritime war capitalism.[13] Under the government of José Basco y Vargas, the Philippines severed its former status as a province of New Spain (and Mexican political dependency) and shifted the islands' economic dependency from the galleon trade to the mass production of profitable commodity crops. Through the cultivation of choice products across the archipelago and aided by investments from British and American profiteers, Basco's regime partitioned the colony into geographic commodity specialties. Negros and other islands in the Visayas became sugar plantations for global production; Luzon, especially the Ilocos, produced tobacco, which were rolled into cigars in Manila.[14] Spanish colonial leaders enforced the tobacco monopoly in Luzon for a century. From 1781 to 1882, Spanish friars, under the initial orders of Basco, established the first *haciendas* of Spain's Southeast Asian colony. Unlike haciendas in the Americas, however, these landholdings of mass agricultural production were not passed down through familial means (as in the criollo class of the Americas) but instead were held as institutional property of the Church and the empire. Through the tobacco monopoly, the Church became both the religious and commercial sovereign among farmworkers and intellectuals in the Philippines. When Spain abolished the monopoly in 1882, tobacco remained the Philippines' major export.[15]

Over a century of the hacienda system pushed Ilokano farmers from small-plot subsistence cultivation into plantation labor. Municipalities such as Candon, which had been ruled by the local Catholic Church as a Christian township and from which the first fifteen sakadas came, quickly shifted into tobacco colonies. Church rule gave way to a growing wealthy Spaniard (and Spanish-sympathizing mestizo) elite to manage labor on tobacco plantations and accumulate capital across the Philippines. Furthermore, in the nineteenth century, colonial changes in irrigation that favored large-scale agricultural projects siphoned off the watersheds of Ilokano lands toward industrial tobacco production. Throughout the nineteenth century, Ilokanos moved up and around the mountain slopes of the Cordilleras toward Northeast and Central Luzon to find work on plantations as wage laborers or sharecroppers. Furthermore, a plague of rinderpest and the famines brought about by El Niño–Southern Oscillation episodes devastated agricultural production in the late nineteenth century. This phenomenon rendered Ilokanos, already dispossessed of their subsistence crops, into destitute workers, depending more on wage work on plantations. Due in part to the decimation of labor animals such as *carabao* (water buffalo), hit particularly hard by rinderpest, hacienda bosses demanded more labor power of Ilokano migrant farmers while maintaining crop production levels.[16]

Industrial capitalism and environmental destruction birthed the modern Ilokano diaspora. Dispossessed of their subsistence economies and displaced from their livelihoods, Ilokano families tilled plantation soils across Luzon as migrant workers in the nineteenth century. The local textile industries of Laoag and Vigan, which had increasingly become vibrant through the mass cultivation of *abacá* (Manila hemp), also suffered because craftspeople found their income unsustainable.[17]

In the midst of widespread ecological degradation and equipped with notebooks and cameras, ethnologists mapped out what they envisioned to be the racial landscapes of the Philippines. For anthropologists such as Ferdinand Blumentritt in Central Europe and Dean Worcester from the University of Michigan (who later served as the first secretary of the interior of the Philippines), the islands contained immense developmental potential if subject to a government that promoted a capitalist work ethic among its people and harvested its tropical landscapes.[18] Treatises in Spanish and English on the late nineteenth century Philippines recorded Christian agricultural workers in Central and Northern Luzon working the fields, subject to uneven power relations between landlords and workers. Ferdinand Blumentritt, one of the most prolific Philippinists of the nineteenth century (but who had never been to the Philippines), wrote on the "Ilocoans [sic]" as migratory due to the injustices done to them through incapable rule of Spanish colonial land-holders and friars.[19] In *The Philippine Islands and Their People* (1898), Dean Worcester also noted the migratory tendencies of Ilokanos, observing state plans to harness this mobility for the purposes of developing "public lands," that is, uncultivated borderlands on other islands such as Palawan.[20] These writers noted the role of the Spanish Catholic state in the subjugation of rural people but took for granted that Christian natives had long farmed for com-modity crops, such as sugarcane. For ethnologists of the Philippines in the nineteenth century, while the tobacco monopoly connected the islands to a global market, the relationship that land commodification played in produc-ing a migrant rural race was not immediately obvious. These writers did not capture the environmental and subsistence economy destruction under nineteenth-century land development, and only in 1911, when crops failed fol-lowing the eruption of Taal Volcano, did American scientists acknowledge systemic famine.[21] However, the labor potential of migrant workers to culti-vate land was considered paramount as a method to develop the people into modern economic subjects.[22]

At first, these publications did not find audiences beyond small intellec-tual circles in Manila, North America, and Europe. However, the 1887 Madrid and 1889 Paris Expositions deployed ethnological images of race, paired with artifacts and performers from non-Christian regions of the Philippines, and reached increasingly popular audiences. Furthermore, the Spanish-American War of 1898 and the US purchase of the archipelago from Spain produced an outpouring of visual culture on America's "new possessions" for the enthusi-astic consumption of an American public. The visual and ethnological seeds planted by late nineteenth century social scientists suddenly found an eager market to satisfy. Through travelogues, novels, and photographs, Americans consumed the Philippines as sources of tropical commodities and exhibi-tions of tropical races. The vast amount of popular literature on the US colo-nies and America's own industrial expositions (such as the 1904 St. Louis World's Fair) brought ethnological racial formations, already decontextual-ized from the contexts of commodity production and environmental de-struction in the nineteenth century, to a middle-class American audience.[23]

On the ground, the supposedly peaceful peasants of the Philippine low-lands waged agrarian wars as guerrillas under Aguinaldo's command and on behalf of their own towns. Through the declared "victory" of the United States over Aguinaldo's forces, lowland farming communities garnered suspicions from American colonial officials and army infantrymen as potential enemies, more commonly called *ladrones*. When the Philippine-American War was declared "over" by American victory, the ongoing warfare became criminalized as petty rebellions against the modernizing regime of the United States.[24]

Just like counterinsurgency campaigns, the ideological warfare of Philippine pacification remained an ongoing process throughout colonial occupation.[25] William Howard Taft, who believed in landownership as a means to discipline agrarians into loyal subjects, argued that the staunch traditional peasantry of the Filipino was to blame for failure to adopt private ownership.[26] Other officials such as Dean Worcester fought Philippine independence through various media: selling photographic prints of his renditions of the Philippines' "tribes," publishing prints and op-eds against Philippine independence in *National Geographic*, financing "Igorrote village" savage shows and documentary films, and presenting slideshows to academies and politicians on his anti-independence visions of Philippine politics.[27]

White Europeans and Americans, as they observed lowland Philippine peoples, envisioned a migrant peasant ready for agricultural work. These visions were not particularly unique to the Philippines in the age of industry. Elsewhere in the colonial Global South, imperial plantation managers also sought agricultural workers whose racial characteristics exhibited migrant peasantry. In her study of migrant workers and Darjeeling's tea plantations in northeastern India, anthropologist Sarah Besky traced the development of a third world agrarian imaginary among planters and tea advertisers in the cultural constellations that constructed the tea worker.[28] Likewise, in the sugar plantations of Louisiana and the Caribbean, planters and policy makers imagined the third world agrarian worker as the "coolie."[29]

The Corporate Construction of the Filipino Peasant

The sakada, subsumed into the immigration history of Filipino America, was cultivated out of the systemic ruralization of Northern Luzon in the nineteenth century. The term is likely derived from the Ilokano phrase *sakasakada amin*, meaning "those who work barefoot."[30] The term "sakada" (meaning "their feet") stands in, then, as a synecdoche for a racialized imagined rural workforce, generated out of the political economy of the tobacco monopoly in the Philippines. The sakadas, like the Fujianese, Cantonese, and Nepalese workers in South Asia and the Americas, proliferated within the discourses of the third world agrarian imaginary that plantation recruitment sought.[31]

However, for the HSPA, the pacified agrarian vision of the Filipino was not only a cheap labor force. The Filipino as migrant worker was imagined to be a buffer zone between unruly and clandestine "Oriental" labor from Northeast Asia and white settlers working on and managing the plantations.

On plantations such as the Olaa Sugar Company, spanning the majority of the Puna district of Big Island, Hawai'i, the Filipino proved to be a valuable resource for the racial and industrial issues that managers faced. Ironically, the managers' problems were not merely exacerbated within plantations; the plantation structure itself was a central node through which capitalists produced race relations among workers. The Koloa Plantation, one of the earliest plantations, was established in 1835 by the Bostonian capitalist William Hooper. He built the plantation with both profit and a racial mission in mind. While the venture was ultimately unsuccessful, Hooper's mission to transform Kanaka Maolis into subjects of an American market civilization laid the grounds for the racial economies of American plantations in Hawai'i. In the pursuit of efficient sugarcane harvesting and cane juice extraction, Hooper contended that native workers he had recruited from the area could not be civilized through American labor regimes. Meanwhile, as Hooper complained of insufficient (and inefficient) native workers, Kanaka Maolis suffered rapid depopulation throughout the first forty-five years of European contact. Political efforts, such as "return to the land" movements in 1832 and the promotion of native agricultural labor to rehabilitate population decline, attempted to remedy such labor shortages. Later industrial plantations in Hawai'i, as in plantations across the nineteenth-century world in Louisiana and the Caribbean, instead opted to import forced and indentured nonwhite labor. This took the form of slaves in the Atlantic and the Pacific, coolies from East and South Asia, and migrant workers from the Philippines.[32]

The establishment of the Olaa Sugar Company in 1899 sought to take advantage of business oligarchs' new exclusive access to colonial governance through the United States. After the overthrow of Queen Lili'uokalani and the territorial annexation of Hawai'i, American business oligarchs invested in building a sugar plantation in the geologically volatile 'Ōla'a region of Big Island. The company was founded as a "progressive plantation." Initially, the Olaa Sugar Company nominally favored independent farming and promoted the Americanization of Hawai'i through European immigration and eschewing Kanaka Maoli homesteading. Similar to the imperial conquest of the American West, investors envisioned the Olaa Sugar Company as a gateway plantation for white settler colonialism in Hawai'i through the small yeoman farmers' enterprise while maximizing profits. However, the numbers of haole settlers did not catch up to the company's desired bottom line, and the Olaa Sugar Company quickly turned to Japanese labor to grow sugar.[33]

The plantation in Hawai'i generated forms of race concomitant with each group's capacity to work. Along various sliding scales of industry and civilization, plantation elites produced and classified racial knowledge according to their evaluated performance across all modes of commodity production. However, when workers on plantations struck, these strikes exacerbated the precarity of the racial project on the fields. Not only did strikes destroy swaths of crops, planted in coordination over several years, but in addition the techniques of evaluating racial fitness and coercing racialized workers into paternalistic dependency gave way to antiworkers' incarceration and violence.[34]

The Filipino, as constructed by the HSPA, appealed to planters because Filipinos could be used to break strikes. In 1905 and 1906 Japanese workers struck, leading to severe labor shortages on HSPA plantations.[35] In search of cheap labor, HSPA recruiters targeted the Ilokano regions of Luzon at the recommendation of the Philippine Commission. However, the importation of Filipino labor was not met with the fanfare of "immigrants" from Spain and Portugal. Cheap Filipino labor was the most prudent approach for Olaa in order to recover costs from the Japanese strikes, although bringing in European workers was thought to promote the US government's tolerance for labor from the "Orient."[36] John Watt, the manager at Olaa, set out a course to house the new workers in the old and dilapidated Japanese quarters while distancing them from striking Japanese workers.[37]

Anticipating a shipment of 200 Filipino families for distribution across HSPA plantations, Watt warned Bishop & Company (henceforth Bishop & Co.), the executors of Philippine labor recruitment schemes to Hawai'i, that "none of this [Filipino] labor should see or come to Honolulu or know anything of what city life is or they will be as surely spoiled for plantation labor."[38] On the Olaa plantation, Filipinos were not the only ethno-racial group to be classified as corruptible by the city; Puerto Ricans too were subject to the same types of comments.[39] This warning gestures to early twentieth-century racial ideas of migrant labor in urban contexts. Peasants may have been kept off the city in order to maximize their affective ties to the land and agricultural labor and minimize their desires for opportunity and other skilled industries. Some white Americans believed that the city could corrupt the quality of agricultural workers and rendered their desired Filipinos unfit for plantation labor.[40]

The Olaa Sugar Company and the HSPA had initially desired approximately 200 families to settle Hawai'i from the Philippines. These families were not to be afforded the same benefits of the homesteading contracts of white workers, but family-based labor settlement was central on the Americanization efforts of the Olaa Sugar Company.[41] However, recruiting entire families to move to Hawai'i was not a simple matter, even as the HSPA offered to loan recruits money to pay off outstanding debts in the Philippines. Only 15 families arrived, mostly men. Simplicio Gironella and his 4 sons were the among these 15 who arrived from Candon City in Ilocos Sur. Simplicio's wife opted to stay behind, and he would return to her within a year. As soon as two months after the first 15 sakadas arrived, migrant workers declared that they wanted to bring their spouses to Hawai'i. The provision in the emigration deals between the Philippine Commission and the HSPA stated that no women could move to Hawai'i alone unless already married to a worker. Family reunification required a "marriage certificate, babies and *all other evidences of married life that they possess.*"[42]

This provision—to provide all "evidences of married life"—is worth pausing on. By 1906, the Philippine Commission had just launched its first colony-wide census. Establishing civil government in the Philippines was swift but haphazard. Cultural geographers and historians of the American occupation have demonstrated the integral role of ethnology in establishing civil government differentially across terrains and islands. For instance, the so-called lowland Christianized tribes could be easily governed and surveyed, because Spanish hacienda rule had consolidated control over an agricultural farming population. In practice, because of the nascency of the civil government in the Philippines, recruits often eluded this provision by pairing women in their families with uncles and cousins in order to distribute potential emigration to Hawai'i.[43] Furthermore, while the terms of contract guaranteed free transportation and board for families, it was also advantageous in the early twentieth century for one partner to remain in the Philippines while the other worked for the HSPA so as to send remittances back home and purchase mortgages for landownership while also paying back the debts that the HSPA had bought out.[44]

Nonetheless, early recruitment efforts by the HSPA clearly coveted some semblances of Filipino family settlement in Hawai'i, even if the legal technics prevented it from putting family-based working into practice. George J. Wagner of the Matson, Lord & Belser Company, the Manila-based partners for the Filipino labor recruitment schemes, suggested to the company an initiative to attract more workers to Hawai'i by disseminating photographs of pleasant working conditions in the islands. Wagner requested photographs of gangs of women in the fields, and specific requests were made for Ilokano women to show future recruits in the Northern Luzon region. The Olaa Sugar Company was requested to provide these photographs as well as shots of various aspects of modern plantation edifices but could not furnish any requested pictures of women. The company simply did not have any.[45]

Why, then, did the HSPA covet family migration from the Philippines to Hawai'i? The desired use of photographs as well as requests made for Olaa workers to send home letters to their families suggests a family moral economy that the HSPA sought to capitalize on. From the lessons of previous Puerto Rican workers, the HSPA did not restrict correspondences but instead encouraged them in order to attract future families to Hawai'i.[46] It seems that like plantation managers in the nineteenth-century Caribbean, the HSPA wanted to erect a racial barrier between white Anglo-American profiteering elites and unruly Oriental labor, literally through Filipinos' reproduction. But unlike Caribbean managers, by requesting photographic subjects familiar to homeland families, the HSPA also wanted to capitalize on the larger kinship structures of Ilokanos in Northern Luzon in the hopes that families—reproduced back home—could continue to promote a better life abroad. Nonetheless, these racial fictions did not manifest in Hawai'i; however, families in later years developed cultures from the return migrations of Hawayeños, family members who had gone to Hawai'i and returned with *pasarabo* (gifts from journeys) and stories to tell. Despite the early failures of these family programs, the HSPA was actually remarkably successful in its reproductive engineering across generations.[47]

Once Ilokano recruits settled into the plantation, human resource management practices consolidated their Filipino ethnic identity. Unlike the Chinese and the Japanese, migrant workers from the Philippines were exempt from the anti-Asian immigration laws. These workers occupied a legal gray zone that declared their status as US nationals but without the full protection of American citizenship. As US colonials, Ilokano recruits could move about the United States and its colonies without the surveillance regimes imposed on other Asian workers after the Chinese Exclusion Acts and the Gentlemen's Agreement between the United States and Japan. However, this legal status also meant that plantation management could not impose the same systemic disciplinary measures on the sakadas that they could on Japanese workers who escaped their cane fields. While lunas in the fields attempted to maintain the rank and file, Filipinos who left tended to do so most often in response to harsh treatment. On one hand, no centralized migration regulation and grievance system existed for Filipino workers until 1913. On the other hand, sakadas could simply leave the plantation altogether if dissatisfied with their working conditions.[48]

High worker turnover made annual crop harvests precarious. While Olaa hailed itself as a newer experimental plantation, the company cane was prone to parasites, variable rainfall, and lava flows from nearby Mauna Kea. Thus, the sugarcane enterprise was precarious from the onset.[49] The Olaa Sugar Company measured productivity by output, which meant that the labor on ʻŌlaʻa's terrains required more effort than flatter and less volatile ground. However, sakadas in the first decade of Filipino labor in Hawaiʻi often left anyway for neighboring plantations, schools in Hilo, and lumber mills, where they could be paid higher wages. Furthermore, leaving the company provided opportunities for sakadas to pursue diverse career options and education in Hilo.[50]

For the planter oligarchy, the Filipino was both a legal entity and a set of bank accounts. Until 1909, Bishop & Co., as the "official representatives" of the Philippine Commission to the HSPA's Filipino labor recruitment schemes, skimmed two dollars per head from their early Filipino recruits. Like other migrant workers to ʻŌlaʻa and other plantations, sakadas were assigned bangos (derived from the Japanese word *bangō*, meaning number) that corresponded to their name and payroll. Planters used the bango identification system to track and punish dissenting Japanese workers during strikes.[51] For sakadas, each name and bango also corresponded with a series of bank accounts with Bishop & Co. that accounted for their debts, payrolls, and store credits. A "Filipino laborer" leaving the plantation could be followed but not brought back. Furthermore, the resources necessary to bring such workers back to their plantations outweighed the opportunity costs of simply requesting more recruits from the Philippines. However, if a worker were to depart without having fulfilled the minimum contract term of three years, the Olaa Sugar Company pursued the work as a debtor to the company and to Bishop & Co. until such time that the worker's accounts were paid off. The outstanding debts of these migrant workers on financial records became vagrant accounts. If planters could not govern and exercise control over sakadas in the same way as their other Asian workers, they could do so through financial means.

Failure to pay off outstanding balances rendered a sakada into a debt fugitive. On January 24, 1908, reporting on monthly "Filipino accounts" (a separate line item in Olaa correspondences to Bishop & Co. during the first two years of sakada labor on the plantation), Bishop & Co. reported three outstanding balances with Olaa stores from Silvestre Clarin, his wife Perpetua Lazo, and "Dusca." Two weeks later Dusca was found to have died—and thus a sunk cost—but Clarin and Lazo had still not paid off their store balance.

Clarin had owed \$11.20 to Olaa, and when debtors came to collect, they found that he had left the plantation altogether to work with the Hawaii Mill Company. It took almost one and a half years to track Silvestre Clarin to a different company on the island of Hawai'i, not simply because he escaped effectively, aided by his legal status as a "national." Known primarily as "Laborer #3119" and his wife as "Laborer #2415," Clarin and Lazo were traced to the Hawaii Mill Company, and their employers interviewed them regarding the \$11.20 they owed to Olaa. Clarin and Lazo were not bothered by Olaa since.[52]

The Filipino, then, was regulated first and foremost along relationships between employers, mediators, and employees, in other words, along the spaces of commerce. Already understood as cheap labor, Filipinos received less pay from Olaa administrators than other workers from Asia, justifying their lower pay by means of their industrial output compared to Japanese workers.[53] They also entered the plantation in debt to begin with, having had their outstanding debts to Luzon planters bought out by the HSPA. Their arrival as migrant workers subjected them to financial systems of indenture that held themselves, their transnational families, and their landholdings under the auspices of the plantation. Furthermore, workers' relationships with plantation stores—the ebb and flow of their accounts—also generated data that planters ascribed to racial capacities. For example, a 1910 circular by the HSPA observed that across the plantations "the Filipino is very incapable of caring for himself. Placed entirely upon his own resources he is likely to spend his money for fancy groceries and consequently be insufficiently nourished." The HSPA then suggested having other Asian cooks tend to the Filipinos so that they can develop to be "stocky and robust" and suitable for plantation labor.[54] Therefore, the plantation stores acted as a means of governing sakadas' bodies and deducing racial fitness.

Because of their status as US colonials, the Filipinos on Hawai'i were afforded mobility that other migrant workers subject to exclusion acts did not possess. Through that mobility and through the financial means of assembling racial knowledge, sugar companies and banks played an intimate role in constructing the Filipino during the early years of migration to Hawai'i.

"Weeding Out Your Inefficients"

As colonial workers, sakadas were not beholden to the international regulations of the anti-Chinese immigration laws and the Gentleman's Agreement between the United States and Japan. Thus, they were accumulated en masse by the HSPA with the assistance of the Philippine Commission and transnational financial institutions. Furthermore, as a migrant (and vagrant) peasantry, recruits from the Philippine agricultural lowlands were not merely cheap workers; they were fresh sources of labor tied directly—*sakasaka*, barefoot—to the crops and soil on which they historically worked. Banks and planters too adopted ecological discourses cognate with the accumulation of migrant peasants. Known contemporarily as "waves of migration" of Filipinos to Hawai'i, labor recruitment schemes instead referred to them as "fresh labor supply."[55] In the schema of crop production, organized in terms of future harvests, Bishop & Co. and Olaa demanded "fresh labor" for the cultivation of new sugar in the wake of constant departures and labor unrest.

Like crop turnovers, labor turnovers were predictable and manageable aspects of tending to the Olaa plantation. However, by 1914 the accelerated dispossession of rural farmers in Luzon, combined with the rapid success of labor recruitment after the first fifteen sakadas, led to a glut of Filipino emigrants eager to find work in Hawai'i. The labor surplus generated a minor crisis among plantations, who did not want to take on the numbers that the HSPA demanded. In response, Olaa charted out a course of action to deal with the supposed surplus. These strategies not only replicated the ecological discourses of "fresh labor" but also constructed its opposites: "We [at Olaa] are gradually letting out the *poorer lot of the field hands, especially the Filipinos,* and under the circumstances it would be unwise to take on new men unless they are considerably above the *average in usefulness.*"[56] Concurring with Olaa's plan, Bishop & Co. encouraged its methods further:

> At a recent meeting of the HSPA the situation was discussed and a resolution passed that the Filipinos now on hand be absorbed by the Plantations on their sugar tonnage basis. Our allotment is 37 people whom the HSPA want to ship Saturday. We know of course that you will be loath to take this party on at present but we must do our share in the matter of providing employment for these people who come here under a contract to work. However, *by gradually weeding out your inefficients*, no doubt you will be able in time to reduce your labor force to the point required by the conditions. (Emphasis added.)[57]

From their first encounter with HSPA recruitment agents in the Philippines to their regular activities on plantations, Filipino field hands at the Olaa plantation were subject to various forms of assessment that determined their efficiency. In the fields, timekeepers and lunas watched workers' output, while managers compared their industriousness with extant data on Japanese labor efficiency.[58] Some fields contracted to Filipinos, as with Japanese fields, were measured in terms of tonnage produced, with contracts based on commission based on harvest.[59] Workers were also subject to frequent medical examinations, as demonstrated earlier with the HSPA reports on Filipino diets. Through various measures of time, health, and harvest productivity, Olaa enacted systems of evaluation that quantitatively imagined a Filipino worker's body. Before the 1914 labor overflow, if a Filipino field worker did not meet prescribed standards of crop output, the worker could be moved into a different role indoors, such as kitchen work.[60]

As a part of the Filipinization reforms under the Woodrow Wilson administration, the Philippine Bureau of Labor was founded in 1916.[61] Extant HSPA recruitment systems, which began to centralize in 1914, partnered with the new bureau.[62] Now a government-regulated industry, the discourses of Filipino labor migration to Hawai'i were caught in an impasse between two vocabularies: fresh labor supply and "Filipino immigration." Until 1914, the Filipino on Bishop & Co. correspondences had been referred to variously as "accounts" and "laborers." However, the growing number of emigrants produced a glut of labor headed to HSPA plantations. As "immigrants," they were understood to be potential settlers on Hawai'i, but because the plantations were their points of entry, companies such as Olaa needed to take on the burden as their civic duty to the United States. Under the revised labor practices of this period, especially through the centralized collection of names and laborer numbers, sakadas became subject to a new regime of surveillance and evaluation, cultivated on plantations in earlier years. No longer dealing with a perceived dearth of labor and citing the supposed migratory tendencies of Filipinos on the islands, Olaa could opt to deploy its productivity metrics in order to simply let workers go. Through a centralized migration bureaucracy that managed an abundant labor force, the vagrant worker would no longer be a problem.[63] "Fresh labor supplies" could be replenished to produce sugarcane, and Filipino workers were no longer chiefly the wards of the plantation. They were, instead, wards to a corporate sovereignty, acting as a state within the US empire.[64]

From 1906 to 1914 as the sakadas migrated to plantations to cultivate cane and pineapple, the "Filipino" between the Philippines and Hawai'i emerged out of labor management practices across several institutions. Through the built environments of stores and dwellings, the infrastructures of recruitment sheds and steamships, and the management methods of financial surveillance and bureaucratic paperwork, "Filipino" families and lives were commodified for the purposes of agricultural production. However, manufacturing the "Filipino" in Hawai'i did not end with the "weeding out" of "inefficient" working lives. On occasion, the "Filipino" worker, after death, haunts the archives through outstanding balances on plantation accounts. As a vagrant account, even after passing away, the worker could exist and persist as a specter of debit and credit, waiting to be exhumed or laid to rest:

> FILIPINO LABORER NO. 1129, GRACIAS PROCTUOSO: This Laborer died in the latter part of May leaving a balance to his credit of $9.10. A Brother-in-law of this man by the name of Louis S. Kasipit, made a demand for this balance of $9.10 on behalf of the Sister of the Deceased. This party gave the Sister's name as Mrs Feliza S. Casipit, address, Aminos, Pangasinam [sic], Philippine Islands. We refused to pay this man this balance, and think the proper method of handling the same should be through the Planters' Association. If we are right in this matter, you may pay the $9.10 to the proper authorities in Honolulu, after the advice of which we will credit same up to your account on our Cash Book.[65]

Planters and the HSPA accounted for workers' deaths from the moment workers set foot on a transpacific steamship and throughout their tenure on a plantation.[66] However, these deaths were registered as sunk costs in financial statements whenever payrolls and outstanding store debts came up for review. The Gracias Proctuoso case was impeded by inconsistencies in the spelling and account numbers between Olaa and Bishop & Co. Unable to verify the case on their own, they sent the $9.10 credit to the Bureau of Labor and Statistics.[67] Beyond this, I have not yet been able to find Gracias Proctuoso in subsequent Olaa records. It might be that his credit had been claimed by the brother-in-law or reabsorbed back into plantation revenue. Gracias, even after death, remained a vagrant to be accounted for. Minute matters of spelling and managing bangos across financial statements, within and outside of the corporate infrastructures that comprised the Olaa Sugar Company, were not mere inconveniences that required rectification. As nine dollars and ten cents, Gracias challenged the self-proclaimed efficacy and success of American capitalism. His corporate death, then, could haunt empire through ledgers and annual audits.

Cultivating Life between Cane

The chief racial marker of the Ilokanos was their supposed propensity for migration. The vagrant state of the Ilokanos made them ideal cheap laborers for plantations in Hawai'i, and the machinery of the HSPA mobilized across the Pacific to channel workers to its fields in large numbers. However, movement

did not so neatly conform to the HSPA's infrastructures of labor management, and even when it did, movement was not as smooth as the HSPA
would have liked. Ilokanos, like their Tagalog and Bisaya coworkers, moved
along the dispossessed and industrialized landscapes of Big Island, Hawai'i,
in clandestine but relatively free ways. They were regularly incarcerated for
vice (e.g., gambling) and violence (e.g., strikes) but, as shown previously, enjoyed much mobility in ways that challenged the prescribed movements of
the transpacific infrastructures of commodity production. Along the way, Ilokanos found ways to elude the legal and financial binds of the HSPA through
their microlevel interface with its technologies. Recruiters, labor executors,
and plantation villages registered what seem like inconveniences to them but,
upon closer inspection, actually reveal small ways in which sakadas made do
in the early periods of their community's nascence.

These multilingual and mobile expressions of slippage in between the
corporate machinery of the HSPA constitute what historians have called
infrapolitics. Historians such as Robin D. G. Kelley, Glenda Gilmore, and
Stephanie Camp have studied actions of enslaved and oppressed Black people
that escaped the obvious radar of overt political action. These small acts include ecological countergeographies outside of plantations, loud conversations on a segregated bus, and aggressions against white women on a North
Carolina street. Infrapolitics, Kelley argues, are not necessarily orchestrated
acts of "political resistance" against a larger consciously acknowledged power.
More often than not, these small acts constituted everyday political acts of
making do under duress for some measure of social wiggle room.[68]

Consequently, sakadas had a lot of literal wiggle room. While their rooms
on Mountain View and other Olaa camps were quite cramped, their status as
US colonials provided them access to movement across islands and to the
continent. Their propensity for movement frustrated plantation managers
endlessly. While the HSPA sought to coerce young men into serving out
company-exclusive three-year contracts with boat tickets home, sakadas had
other agendas around the cane field and far away from the plantation altogether. These divergent acts were myriad ways in which sakadas could preserve their own notions of time and value, in other words, the terms of their
labor. These acts of preservation frustrated plantation managers and other
profiteers precisely because their idealized cheap labor forces refused to conform to the discipline of capitalist ecologies on the plantation.

In a massive act of anticapitalist iconoclasm, the Japanese, just years earlier
in 1905, set fire to cane fields across Hawai'i.[69] For late nineteenth-century
plantations such as that of the Olaa Sugar Company, cane fields conjured up

pastoral images of agrarian labor and American ecological prowess.[70] But while King Sugar produced the groundwork for race relations and financial oligarchies in Hawaiʻi that persist to the present day, the landscapes and images that the industry produced were, in reality, always at risk of ruination. The monoculture of sugar demanded favorable soils and precise timing from planting to harvest over a three-year period. Sugarcane production demanded large volumes of irrigation, of which the rainy ʻŌlaʻa had plenty, but also predictable and pleasant tropical weather, which ʻŌlaʻa lacked, being right next to the seismic activity of a volcano.

Contracts and languages, urban migration, and recreation constituted measures of action not simply, then, against an exploitative plantation elite. These disobediences, incongruences, and incommensurabilities constituted a challenge to the efficiency of the industrial plantation, manifesting as inconveniences in paperwork and labor management. However, at stake behind these inefficiencies was less time and energy put into working the soil for profit. These myriad modes of infrapolitics revealed sakadas' refusal to be alienated wholesale as cheap workers, and their active detracting from field work constantly posed a threat to the precise life cycles of each sugar crop.

Preserving measures of free choice began at the contract, the point of transaction through which the Ilokanos alienated their labor power from themselves as exchange value for recruiters. For American recruiters, contract was the primary *Weltanschauung* through which social and economic relations were viewed since the postbellum period. By the late nineteenth century, contract workers, with consent "freely given" through the signing of the contract document, were understood to sell their labor time in exchange for wages.[71]

Less understood is the actual implementation of contract for colonial subjects. While Ilokanos who migrated inland found wage labor in various industries, including plantations, many others preferred sharecropping, purchasing mortgages for plots of land from former haciendas. Contract work was also found in American colonial public works projects such as road building in Benguet, and recruiters recognized the use of Ilokanos in these projects as well. Based on the inconsistencies of its implementation, the form of contract implemented by the HSPA in Northern Luzon seems to be an American innovation. Recruitment, as discussed earlier, worked through local networks of Ilokanos across the region and deployed advertising materials such as photographs and letters from family abroad. The moral and visual economies of recruitment, in theory, gave way to its legal mechanisms once the worker agreed to out-migration from the Philippines to Hawaiʻi. In practice, this does not seem to be the case; rural Ilokanos recruited by Philippine-based agents expressed various levels of literacy (if at all), and staff claimed that they read the contract terms every day as Ilokanos and their agents awaited the steamer.[72]

In Luzon, since small numbers of HSPA labor recruiters were at the mercy of local collaborators and the various languages of the region, the language politics at hand deserve some pause. Consent to contract terms for the HSPA and their partners seems to have amounted to the mere fact of having heard (if they did) the terms as they awaited the steamship. Who did the reading, in what languages, and how effective were the translations from English to (presumably) Ilokano? It seems that the labor card itself was poorly translated—this is presented in the Ilokano language below—and many workers refused to sign it.[73]

However, negotiating and avoiding contract terms on Hawai'i proved more difficult than in Ilocos and Manila. Without a foreign power to address their labor concerns, sakadas turned to racial leadership from their own communities. As JoAnna Poblete has shown, Filipino religious leaders between 1912 and 1946 served as mediators on plantations between white elites and workers. Pastors such as Simon Ygloria in O'ahu tended to worker congregations in English, Spanish, Tagalog, Ilokano, and Bisaya. However, before the rise of Filipino pastors, Filipino camps and plantations favored multilingual individuals drawn from the workers' ranks. At the Olaa Sugar Company, Francisco Gironella—one of the first fifteen pastors and educated in Candon City—served that role. Since he was a fellow Candonian and the son of the elderly Simplicio, other workers quickly came to trust him. As early as 1907, Francisco was tapped as a translator and a contract negotiator, working between English and Ilokano. So favorable too was Francisco to the plantation managers that by February 1907, they endearingly began to call him "Frank" in everyday correspondences as well as in Filipino account statements.[74]

Francisco's translations—and the sway that the HSPA thought he would have—were far from perfect. The Olaa Sugar Company asked Francisco to translate a statement from the civil government in the Philippines pertaining to migrant workers in Hawai'i, to be signed by workers acknowledging their recognition of Bishop & Co. as their corporate sovereigns. The labor blank that he translated and edited is as follows:

YTI AGTURAY TI CO

Daguiti ramramit iti Gobierno idiay Islas Filipinos, a' iso nga agay can cadaguiti Filipinos a' trabajadores. Amin a' cayat a' saludsuden daguiti

trabajadores sipapalubus, qet sicaycayadanto nga agaramid iti sobre escrito no ania iti cayatda nga ammuen tapno siayat dantumet a' mangibaga.

BISHOP [Agturay] &. CO

The decrees [*ramramit*] of the Governor of the Philippine Islands
pertain to the Filipino workers [*a' iso nga agay can cadaguiti Filipinos a'
trabajadores*]. All that the migrant workers [*daguiti trabajadores sipapalubus*] want to ask, and you will be the one to make the letter [*sobre escrito*]
of all necessary information [*no ania iti cayatda nga ammuen*] so that they
will be able to address your issue well [*tapno siayat (nasayaat) dantumet
a' mangibaga*].[75]

The original (which the author has not found) is summarized by Bishop &
Co. as stating that "Bishop & Co of Honolulu are the Agents of the Philippine
Government in this territory, and that the laborers can refer to them in case of
need."[76] The translation is clunky in composition, as Francisco most likely had
to find alternative ways to express corporate language in more literal terms.
For instance, "all necessary information" directly translates, from Ilokano, to
"all that they would want to know." Furthermore, the direct translation of
"Bishop"—as *agturay*, meaning "authorities"—can, on one hand, be read as a
frivolous approximate translation of a proper noun. On the other hand, it also
suggests a possible slipped translation of the Ilokanos' understanding of the
company itself. Ilokanos in Hawai'i, through Francisco's translation, came to
understand Bishop & Co. as the corporate sovereigns over their affairs.

Over 200 labor blanks in Ilokano translation were approved by Francisco
and printed between September and December 1907, to be distributed to
new workers. However, these cards were rarely signed. When Filipinos struck
against the HSPA and Bishop & Co., they cited contract violations as their
primary grievance. Workers noted that they had not heard of any provision
that two dollars per month were to be removed from each person's salary to
set aside for the steamship journey back home. While this statement may not
have truthful—it may have been mentioned in those auditory contracts read
while waiting for the steamship in Manila—the labor blanks, which are the
documents that themselves required signature as a contract, merely serve to
defer all labor issues to Bishop & Co., not to the plantation.[77]

A plantation system's linguistic proficiency over contracts and worker coercion was necessary to maintain discipline over a non-Anglophone labor
force. The Olaa Sugar Company sought to maintain workers for three-year
periods, at first through the promise of a return journey to the Philippines.

These three-year periods, like waves of migration commissioned by particular plantations, corresponded to three-year periods of sugarcane planting and harvesting.[78] Local multilingual leaders such as Francisco were paramount to the HSPA's labor management practices, but trivial matters such as clunky translations would hinder plantations' desired levels of workers' discipline. The workers resorted to reading these incongruences as denigrating sources of racial knowledge of the "Filipino," calling them vagrants who are "practically worthless" and should not be treated with "excessive kindness," lest they make unreasonable demands.[79]

At the end of this labor dispute, the Olaa Sugar Company simply opted to let sakadas go should they choose to leave but without the guarantee of a paid return passage. The "Filipino," at times of labor grievance, was weeded out as an economic inefficient. Observing that workers opted to leave in large numbers anyway, we might surmise that they simply made the choice to move on to other plantations or to the continent or chose to seek new lives in cities. Certainly in 'Ōla'a, some Filipino workers had plans beyond remaining on plantations to work. Many, including fresh recruits, used the plantation recruitment schemes to launch searches for economic opportunities in Hawai'i. Hilo, the closest major city to 'Ōla'a, became a popular destination, as plantation managers urged that interisland steamships land directly on 'Ōla'a's shores out of fear that the city would contaminate their workers with disobedience. Hilo, like Honolulu on O'ahu and Manila in the Philippines, was believed to have housed labor agitators who fueled the fires of the Japanese strikes in the mid-1900s or otherwise produced degenerate states of vagrancy and labor agitation.[80]

Many of the Ilokano labor agitators who landed in 'Ōla'a opted to pursue lives in Hilo in order to attend school.[81] Hilo also served as a popular destination for temporary travel and recreation, among other forms of rest and relaxation. However, despite the HSPA's approval for weekend baseball excursions, this form of relaxation drew the suspicion of Olaa's managers, as many did not return in a timely manner. A group of twenty sakadas left to play baseball on January 17, 1908, but did not return until the 20th and the 21st. Upon their return, they supposedly began to cause trouble among earlier recruits and continued to refuse to sign any contracts. However, it seems that these Ilokanos had used the Hilo baseball trip as a covert excursion for labor organizing, as just weeks later more workers refused to make their two-dollar deposits, to the ire of Bishop & Co.[82]

The benefits of refusing contract terms, incongruences between languages, and the mundane ways in which workers simply left or took extra days to rest attest to the precarity of plantation management on Hawai'i and reveal the ways in which workers navigated their place in commodity production. Contract negotiation across languages joined recreation as discursive and physical spaces of political action that, while not immediately coordinated as a wide-scale attack on industry, eluded the capitalist plantation's exacting demands for time and energy.

THE "FILIPINO" IN HAWAI'I, rooted in the long nineteenth-century process of land dispossession and industrial production, was consolidated through American capitalists' infrastructural participation in the globalized Philippine agricultural market. Cane fields, bank books, plantation stores, management schemes, and workers' politics gave shape to a transpacific infrastructure through which race emerged out of Ilokanos' (and other Filipino groups') circulation. Non-Tagalog workers from Northern and Central Luzon, who had not been implicated directly in the intellectual production of the "Filipino" by Manila's mestizo nationalists, became "Filipino" through their movement toward Hawai'i as a labor commodity of the Philippine Commission and the HSPA. Imposed with the moniker "Filipino" through "Filipino accounts," "Filipino contracts," "Filipino camps," and other plantation racial management schemes, their interface with the corporate infrastructure of companies such as Olaa generated the groundwork for what would become the sakada community in Hawai'i.

The generation of the "Filipino" did not end with the forced concatenation of Hawai'i and the Philippines in a plantation infrastructure that produced food commodities and migrant workers. Further removed from their Northern Luzon homeland yet remaining inextricably haunted by it, Ilokanos in the American West also became "Filipino" according to the particular regional infrastructure they reckoned within their specific geography of the American commodity empire. Just as with the sakada in Hawai'i, the circulation of young Filipino men around the commodity-producing infrastructures of the American West crystallized into another racial identity that, while standing in for all Filipino migrant workers, remained inextricably Ilokano. But unlike the barefoot and destitute sakada, the "Filipino" who emerged in Alaska, Seattle, and California became the vagrant and masculine *manong*.

CHAPTER SIX

Manongs on the Move

In *America Is in the Heart* (1946), the Ilokano Pangasinense novelist Carlos Bulosan tells a "personal history" of migration from the Ilokano *barangay* (village) of Binalonan to a fantastical vagrant life all over the American West. At the height of his writing career, he affiliated himself with Hollywood writers as a part of the 1930s and 1940s Cultural Front, a radical leftist movement that stretched across Hollywood writers to novelists and cartoonists. At his most influential and at the moment when he crafted the vagabond migrant worker into his mythological Filipino America, Bulosan sought to be the literary mouthpiece for a vagrant community whose energy fueled the US commodity empire. However, he did not actually perform much of the labor that his protagonist, Allos, does. Because Bulosan was sick with tuberculosis, he was restricted to some brief stints on the fields and domestic work in cities.[1]

But as one Seattle community activist puts it, Bulosan was a good listener. With Allos, Bulosan took on the many stories of his peers in order to tell a coherent story of Filipino America. These young men were known by younger Filipino Americans after 1965 as the *manongs* (Ilokano for "older brother") and became memorialized in community histories. The manongs traveled by steamship, train, and jalopy to different places of work all over the West. They stopped for rest and recreation in cities, sporting their best suits to gamble and dance with white women in taxi dance halls. When working conditions were bad, the manongs bummed around in cities in search of scarce jobs and later joined the labor unions that proliferated during New Deal America. Allos, whose travels and travails stood in for both Bulosan and his contemporaries, might be considered as the colonial beatnik. However, unlike the beatnik, most of the manongs' movement around the continent did not take place on highways. While the Beat Generation's extravagant postwar road trips reflected the rise of car culture in the United States, the prewar manong circulated through coal capitalism. Steamships and railroads provided the arteries of industrial agriculture in the American West, and in the process manongs experienced cultural geographies only made possible by the infrastructures of capitalism in the continent. Map 6.1 shows where Allos traveled in parts one and two of *America Is in the Heart* before he begins his involvement with union politics:

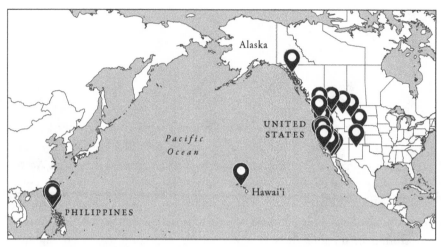

MAP 6.1 Allos's travels in Carlos Bulosan, *America Is in the Heart*.

The icons in the bottom left cluster around a very small region in Luzon between various *barrios* in Pangasinan, the American city of Baguio in the Cordilleras, and Manila. In part one, Allos either walks, takes a bus, or travels by train between these three locations. His feet are callused, and the searing heat and torrential downpours make his agricultural life difficult. Noting the deterioration of his home region, Allos became impatient and footloose, entering into a diasporic life that led him to travel by transportation modes beyond barefoot walking: buses, cars, and trains. In part two, Allos encounters more formidable edifices of migration: transpacific and Alaska coastal steamships, the great American railroads of the West, and the economic temptations of West Coast Chinatowns. He experienced the Pacific and the continental West at a faster pace, made possible by the transportation technologies fueled by coal and gasoline.[2]

I blueprint this geography with a work of fiction for two reasons. First, while in no way does a fictional novel serve as a source of historical fact, it attests to the potency of narrative in understanding Ilokano migrant cultural geographies. Some of the Ilokano oral histories I studied at the Filipino American National Historical Society (FANHS) emphasized that their lives were shaped by rural spaces and the railroads that took them from field to field. Second, narration suggests that commodity infrastructures did not only circulate products and capital; they also produced affective landscapes for the workers who circulated within them. Ilokanos not only found work through these infrastructures of movement but also made lives out of how capitalists captured seasons and accelerated the flow of commodities. As human media on fields and in freight cars, Ilokano migrants shaped kinships and notions of being "Filipino" out of the affective experiences on the infrastructures that sought to mobilize their corporal energies as abstract labor.[3]

This chapter traces a geography of Ilokano masculine migration cultures in the American West. Centering Ilokano oral histories and diasporic literature, it considers the production of the "Filipino" on the continental United States in a settler colonial and industrial capitalist context. Like the plantations on 'Ōla'a and across Hawai'i, the diasporic "Filipino" emerged out of capitalist infrastructures that displaced Indigenous peoples from their land and restructured the environment in favor of commodity production. However, whereas the *sakadas* in Hawai'i were constantly subject to the documentation of financial institutions and plantation stores, the manongs (as the young men became known later in the twentieth century) led highly mobile lives. While recognizing that minimal archives are available for understanding the personal and affective experiences of migrant workers outside of cities, historians have investigated the manongs in terms of urban recreation and livelihood or by their experiences as labor organizers in farmworkers' unions. While working-class ethnic histories of urban space continue to flourish, my attention instead turns to the structures that linked cities and workplaces together: infrastructure.[4]

Focusing on ethnic narrative as the subject of analysis allows us to read— and listen to—what anthropologist Brian Larkin calls a poetics of infrastructure. Defining infrastructures as "matter that enable the movement of other matter" but also as technologies of mobility "come[s] to represent the possibility of being modern, of having a future, or the possibility of that possibility and a resulting experience of abjection."[5] For Carlos Bulosan and for interviewees at FANHS, infrastructures of American imperial mobility allowed the ethnic worker to envision a constellation of possibilities at being modern, whether that be "picking gold from the street" as one migrant noted (whom we shall meet later), working enough to buy a tailored suit to take to dance halls, or being able to write a great American Anglophone novel as a peasant boy from Pangasinan. Ethnic narratives reveal migrant workers' affective landscapes as they encountered the different temporalities of the US empire: swift and thrilling yet disciplinarian and exhausting. Despite their vast geographical distances from each other, Ilokano migrant workers collectively felt these possibilities of industrial time, experienced on infrastructures that harness the ecology of the American West.[6]

I argue that Ilokano young men experienced Filipino America as a collective experience of rhythm in an industrial and settler colonial landscape.

Rhythm, or an orderly set of movements at prescribed intervals of time, marked the experience of migrant travel, disciplined industrial labor, and urban recreation. Ilokano young men related to being diasporic Filipinos in terms of their insatiable need for adventure, experiences of tiredness as temporary seasonal workers, stories of tramping on railroads, and relaxing in cities. All these reported experiences attest to their understandings of ethnicity as an affective landscape wherein they carved ways of living in a racial logic that wanted them only as temporary wage labor.[7]

Throughout the myriad stories and anecdotes I have curated in this chapter, an underlying question about these subjects emerges: Are these Ilokano continental workers settler colonizers? Some, such as Juan Mendoza, strategically exploited legal loopholes to purchase land and accumulate wealth through property ownership and became entrepreneurs. Many others, however, long envisioned their sojourns into the continent as a temporary one, and for most of their travels they remained precarious workers who were exploitable as "US nationals." But nonetheless, particularly with Ilokano men who brought with them a sense of adventure, such affective landscapes of adventure are made possible through settler colonialism in the continent and the infrastructures of mobility that accompanied imperial expansion. Their mobilities as well as the imaginaries they brought with them (i.e., tabula rasa images) are built upon the technologies of extraction that followed settler colonial expansion into what is now known as the American West. In these stories, with the few exceptions of those Filipinos who settled on land with the intent of exploiting it for profit, there is no concrete moment in which hypermobile colonized labor becomes a settler per se. Nonetheless, the structures upon which they experience this unsettled labor movement (with some possibility of settling altogether) might be understood as settler colonial capitalism.[8]

This chapter begins by excavating the sense of adventure that Ilokano young men reported feeling as they considered leaving Luzon and entered into labor circulation. Moving toward Montana, an understudied region of Filipino migration in the United States, I show how Ilokanos built ethnic kinships by maintaining railroads and harvesting fields at certain times of the year. Next, this study moves into cities wherein young men became diasporic dandies: wandering spectacles who sought pleasure and recreation in the undisciplined rhythms of urban life. This chapter concludes by exploring the feeling of loneliness and homesickness and how interethnic (Philippine) social groups and cultural education served to centralize that homesickness into a synchronous diasporic nationalism. I show that narrating Filipino

America as migrant workers meant narrating a battlefield of alienating capitalist time in hinterlands and resource frontiers and organic rhythms among young men who cultivated a sense of adventure and recreation.[9]

Rhythms of Empire

Filipino migrant workers understood their ways of life through Alaskan salmon canneries, Yakima Valley hops fields, Stockton-area asparagus, Central Valley grapes, and Chinatown recreational spaces. Ilokanos knew these geographies by word of mouth, and they circulated through kinships born out of this vast geography. By the 1920s and 1930s, the expediency of travel—for commodities, cultures, and workers alike—was facilitated by the massacres of the Indian Wars just decades prior and the scramble for land by big agricultural and railroad businesses. The industrial ecology in this region gives a sense of the infrastructures upon which Ilokano migrants made their lives and told their stories in later years.

Capitalism captures ecology and time in order to profit off of its products. As historians have shown, American westward expansion and genocide was not merely a matter of clearing land for white settler colonialism. Whites sought to harness the ecology and resources of the continental interior and the coasts for themselves. Projects of capitalism and colonialism in the continental West industrialized seasonality and ecological time, built through the cheap labor of nonwhite workers such as Filipinos, whose livelihoods became intimately entangled with these infrastructures.[10]

Seasonality, ecology, and economies marked what I continue to call the rhythms of life in the region: movements and courses of action over regular intervals of time at various speeds. Indigenous economies in these regions had harnessed these rhythms in order to expand regional power, but many groups moved to follow the resources rather than remain sedentary. For instance, the Comanches in the Southwest—Comanchería—established what Pekka Hämäläinen calls a "kinetic empire," predicated not on building classical civilizations but instead by imposing a hegemony on resources of ecology (grass) and mobility (horses) and a dialectic of trade and raiding.[11] In the Pacific Northwest, Kwakwaka'wakw, Duwamish, and other Coast Salish people followed the salmon up and down the coast. By the late nineteenth and early twentieth centuries as with many other Indigenous nations, several performed in the World's Fairs and expositions and worked in hops fields to earn supplementary income yet still anchored themselves—to the ire of white agricultural industrialists—according to the movements of salmon.[12]

As American empire expanded across the continental West, it did so through the deployment of genocidal violence and state expansion.[13] While Indigenous dispossession was carried out materially through legal and material violence, it was justified and reinforced through the processes of cultural and epistemic imperialism. Whites conceptualized Indigenous people in the plains into a diminishing fixity in order to make the "transit of empire"—the intellectual, cultural, and material mobilities of settler colonialism and industry—as smooth as possible. As cultural theorist Jodi Byrd argues, Indianness under American imperialism was constructed to render Indigenous peoples as minorities under a liberal framework while relegating them into an exceptional past, excluding Indianness from the forward-moving progress of civilization.[14]

The transit of empire facilitated the circulation of capital. With every nineteenth-century technological construction on setter colonial landscapes, mythologies abounded around how they marked the rise of American civilization. The robber barons embodied capitalist greed but also the economic potential of building on the continental tabula rasa. American arts and culture, from literature and Wild West shows to film and photography, facilitated the imaginary of the smoothness of imperial power. What resulted was a smooth American landscape of land and sea upon which travel could be imagined and mythologized as a condition of modernity.[15]

Large-scale monocrop agriculture in the nineteenth century, especially immediately before and after the American Civil War, was facilitated by massive ecological destruction. Since a crop's cultivation is fixed on climate, sunlight patterns, and nutritive soil, irrigation became a means to maximize input for swiftly growing agribusiness in California. Unable to control planetary seasonality, irrigation and environmental change maximized economic output through monocropping over large swaths of land.[16]

Railroads accelerate the flow of commodities across larger expanses of space while reconfiguring their markets away from local geographies. In the United States, railroads funnel livestock to slaughterhouses and meatpacking factories in midwestern cities such as Chicago and Cincinnati. Not every modern state was able to successfully implement such an infrastructure, and the United States could only truly do so in large part through a genocidal expansion campaign in the West.[17] Railroads also channeled crops to centralized markets and diverted market power away from the immediate spaces of rural townships to big cities, pumping capital and provisions into metropolitan spaces, especially in the Midwest.[18]

Transportation infrastructures are always in danger of deterioration. Railroads, like farms, need constant maintenance, especially in meteorologically variant regions such as the Big Sky states. In the 1920s and 1930s places such as Montana grew sugar beets, which needed to be moved around through the railroads that connected them to processing in the East and West Coast. Ilokanos staffed railroads' maintenance, and this circulated by word of mouth around the manong communities of the American West.[19]

The temporality of capitalist production in the imperial United States was predicated on acceleration to accommodate for commodity flows and the disciplined repetitive rhythm for production. Besides fossil fuels such as coal and gasoline, the US commodity empire is fueled by a massive labor force mobilized from the Global South to tend to its productions and infrastructures. On the continent, chattel slavery fueled the bloody rhythms of cotton and tobacco plantations. US economic power and industrial agriculture was built on the bodies and souls of Black folk. The steamship and the railroad accelerated commodity flows across the continent, including enslaved labor commodities.[20]

Abolition of chattel slavery in the hemisphere did not abolish labor exploitation. Because of the development of northern-led industry after the American Civil War, industrialization in the United States grew through northern capital and westward expansion. Migrant workers from Asia and Latin America were brought en masse to replace formerly enslaved African Americans, and an increasingly racialized labor force expropriated from the Global South facilitated Indigenous dispossession in the American West and the consolidation of American industry on the continent.[21]

Workers generated the energetics of industry in the American West, built for the optimization of profit through the volume of production and the velocity of circulation. In order to extract as much labor as possible, various technologies emerged to maximize labor and minimize costs. For instance, high-calorie foods and nutritional sciences sought to maximize energy outputs of workers for an increasingly productive US economy. Since the eighteenth-century Industrial Revolution, sugar, tea, coffee, and bread carbohydrates served as primary fuels of industrial empires; these crops were also some of the largest produced in colonial spaces. Through nutrition and advertising, empires sought to reform working-class and racialized bodies, while workplaces extracted as much as possible through long working days. Labor unrest and unions demanded higher pay per hour (the unit of industrial work), limits on daily labor, and social programs to tend to deteriorating health exhausted by physical work. Modern life was marked by increased tempo, and the pace of labor needed to satisfy companies' demands for production and profit.[22]

By 1919, the success of environmental and infrastructural reconfiguration in the American West produced high-commodity outputs, which to be sustained required cheap labor. Due to the 1882 Chinese Exclusion Act and the 1907 Gentleman's Agreement with Japan, commodity producers were without the ability to recruit more Northeast Asian labor. Because of their status as US "nationals" with free movement across American colonial and metropolitan spaces, Filipino peasants were favored to power the human engines of commodity production in Hawai'i and the American West.[23] As shown in previous chapters, the political and environmental conditions of Northern Luzon, combined with kinship recruitment efforts on the ground, made Ilokano young men favorable recruits for plantations in Hawai'i. By the 1920s a more liberal culture of emigration proliferated, perpetuated both by readily available transportation modes and affective energies at home that promoted emigration. Like the working-class young white boy in Mark Twain's *Huckleberry Finn* (1884), working Ilokano men felt a need to "light out" to the West. (They, of course, traveled east to the West.) The archive of oral histories at the FANHS might give us some sense of the affective landscape as Ilokano men tramped and worked in the American West.

Adventure Time

Many Ilokano young men and a few women left for the United States for education and adventure. Many studied at the University of Washington or the University of Southern California. When education became difficult to afford, many workers indulged in seasonal labor and urban recreation, and one individual I have found relocated briefly to Missoula, Montana, to continue his education there. Education, of course, was a primary driver for emigration, especially with the promise of better jobs and more options to support oneself as a student. Since the *ilustrado* and *pensionado* generations, educational emigration became a popular choice for leaving home. However, as some interviewees attest, American education was more desirable because of the opportunity for adventure and seeing beyond the small geographies of Luzon.[24]

Migrants' desires for adventure are much less understood than educational opportunity. While it is unwise to homogenize what adventure could mean, its predominance among interviews is noteworthy. Most interviewees do not elaborate on the notion of adventure, and interviewers do not press further, so it is necessary to reconstruct what it might mean with the few clues we have. Drawing from consistent contextual source materials since the 1300s, the Oxford English Dictionary defines the term "adventure" variously as the following: "chance, fortune, luck"; "chance of danger or loss"; "a course of action which involves risk"; and "a novel or exciting experience."[25] Adventure is not simply travel but is a form of travel that increases the variance of risk and reward by undertaking such a course of action. Despite modest economic means, an adventurer cannot be pragmatic, or *kuripot*,[26] in order to maximize the breadth of experience and thrill. From these definitions, then, a worthy cognate of "adventure" is "gamble."

How did Ilokano men cultivate a sense, or an itch, for adventure? Not simply a fact of traveling to a new place, adventure also suggests an affective landscape cultivated from an individual and collective imaginary. Faced with a dearth of sources, I conjecture with narratives that express homeland conditions before departure. Since the Gironella family and other Candonians departed for the 'Ōla'a plantation in 1906, Northern and Central Luzon became a hotbed for out-migration to plantations. Letters, photographs, and return migrants (Hawayeños) flaunting their earnings encouraged cultures of emigration.[27]

One such adventurer was Juan Mendoza. A young boy from Ilocos Sur at the cusp of his eighteenth birthday, Juan disembarked a ferry from southwestern British Columbia into the port of Seattle. It was the first Thursday of May 1927, and Puget Sound began its slow ascent into its brief summer. At the port, the smell of saltwater and smoke mingled as freely as the city's transients. For Juan, his arrival in Seattle was simply an accident of his ambitious travels to the United States, "just a chance." He remained steadfast in leaving home to go to school, and as he stepped onto Seattle's industrial shores, he recalled his old Ohioan baseball manager's fervent encouragement to go to America. As Juan imagined it, America was to be the land of his manhood and the terra nullius of his prosperity. From his agrarian province to the transpacific steamships, he imagined in his mind's eye the prospect of scouring the streets for his chief harvest: "picking gold."

JUAN MENDOZA: Oh, the old guys just came from high school, you know, we thought we came in here pick golds from the [street]. Well, that was economics, you know, but I always have the ambition to go to school, you know, I came over here, so I went to school.

DOROTHY CORDOVA: What make you land here in Seattle?

JM: Huh?

DC: Why did you come to Seattle as opposed to another place?

JM: It was just a chance that I came over here, I didn't select Seattle, it was just a chance that I came in here, just a chance. I don't know anything about this country.

DC: Were you encourage[d] to come here by some of your teachers?

JM: Well, yeah. As the matter of fact, I use to play baseball, high school, you know, I was the member of our team and our, sort of a manager was an American, well, they encourage us to come to the United States at that time, believe it or not. And so—

DC: He was an American teacher?

JM: Mhh, hhh, yeah, he was a white fellow, yeah. He use to be from Ohio and so that's the way it was. Well, I came in here for the main purpose of picking gold from the street but I always have [in] my mind that I was going to school, that was the ideal because I thought, well I have known lots of people they all, they all went to school. So I went to go.[28]

Juan admitted that he did not know anything about America except from the cultural imports that came to him at school. Baseball, brought by American educators as a way to discipline physical activity among colonial wards, was immensely popular among Filipino children and teenagers.[29] Unsurprisingly, in an American recreational space, Juan's midwestern team manager used the sport to perpetuate an imaginary of the United States as a land of opportunity. Prior to the Great Depression, the Midwest was a regional node for American industry and became the center of railroad traffic and a booming meatpacking industry. Due to urbanization and industrial expositions in the region, an ideology of progress and modernity had circulated around the Midwest, which midwesterners brought to their classrooms in the rural Philippines.[30]

Mariano Angeles, from the province of Abra, wanted to go to America "for education and adventure," also encouraged by teachers from the Midwest. His Demonstration Project for Asian Americans interviewer, Cynthia Mejia, asked him who inspired him to move to America:

MARIANO ANGELES: Well, it is always my ambition to go abroad and well, I had a friend over there, a townmate who was in Iowa during that time, Des Moines, Iowa, who used to write to us over there about America. And that was the time also that I was in high school, in first year when [missionaries] came over here. I was still a young man when they visited and also the missionaries were boarding in our home and they told me about—told us what America is, what kind of people they have and what government they have. And then in my high school years ... mostly [all] of our high school teachers are American. They came from Michigan, [come] from Wisconsin, came from Nebraska, from Utah ... from Cleveland, from Ohio, Cleveland, Cincinnati.[31]

Not coincidentally, the teachers who imparted the vision of America as a land of opportunity came from west of the Appalachians, and many others came from west of the Mississippi River. These American teachers were embodied products of the subjectivities of settler colonialism, themselves articulating visions of imperial modernity through westward expansion. By articulating visions of their settled homes in the West, they imparted an imagined geography of beauty and opportunity upon their students in order to transmit that desire to them. As evidenced by the feelings of adventure and seeking opportunity, these stories certainly had some considerable effect.[32]

Teodoro Aguinaldo Ranjo, an orphan from Pasuquin in Ilocos Norte, first learned about America from the Thomasites and the soldiers who stayed behind after the Philippine-American War to become teachers. Ranjo recalled that his teachers were from the Midwest and introduced the United States by way of teaching the students Great Lakes geographies:

CYNTHIA MEJIA: What did you want to do in America?
TEODORO RANJO: Pursue my studies and adventure....
CM: What [did] you hear about America, better standard of living...?
TR: It was "land of opportunity" of course ... you must remember that when I left home, I was already aspiring to be an educator, a teacher, you know, right. I [was] smart enough to get something like that in the United States. But it was very hard at the time.[33]

Ranjo, like other migrants, declared his intent to go to school and seek adventure. Since Ranjo was already an aspiring teacher with training to teach, the United States was imagined as a place to engage in that profession. America was an opportunity to not just make money but also be a productive subject. He would get that wish not in his chosen field but rather in the fields and railroads of the US commodity empire.

Circulating media and remittances between families at home and emigrants also generated a feeling for adventure. Since 1906, many Ilokanos left for Hawai'i to work on sugar plantations. Called Hawayeños at home, many left for the continent after their three-year terms were complete but during their sojourns sent back letters and photographs of their prosperous life as an emigrant, which attracted further migration. Rudolfo Andres, from Pangasinan and a 1930s arrival, recalled seeing the suited photographs from friends in the United States and seeing dollar signs from emigrants, and this inspired him to get in on the adventure for himself:

> HELEN HATCHER: So what made you decide to come to America?
> RUDOLFO ANDRES: Well, I see these guys over here when they are in America, they lefted [sic] the Philippines and they send picture and they are, you know, they got the suit. They are, they look nice. And not, not only like that, they send money too. When I find out how they send money, they are six in a group, this man Juan will send their paycheck and next month the other guy, that's his turn you know. "So how come, you are only just arrive in there and they send lots of money?" You know already the value of Pesos over there is two to one. That make you interested to come there.[34]

As Andres describes, the desire for adventure was a transpacific feedback loop of capital. Since Filipinos could not own any property and worked vagabond lives, they wore the capital they earned on their bodies and flaunted it through circulating photography and money. Andres's fixation on both suits and money produced an affective desire to work in the United States not just because of some vague idea of opportunity but also because of the visual and material cultures that made their way back to the Philippines. For Andres and other migrant workers, money and capital that could be seen and felt contributed to their desire for a footloose working life.

Ilokanos' desire for adventure was also felt as a collective affect in the Amianan.[35] Trinidad Rojo from Ilocos Sur, who moved to the United States to go to school and earn a doctorate in literature at Columbia University, observed that insatiable itch to travel among his fellow young Ilokanos. Even though he paid his way through school, Rojo noted that the opportunities for self-supporting were greater in the United States by virtue of the work options available in the American West. However, he had the option to work in the Philippine government under the Ilokano senator (and later president) Elpido Quirino. While that would have been the more pragmatic choice for schooling, Rojo admitted that he got swept up in a feverish culture of emigration: "There was movement around me."[36]

That movement could be attributed in part to the increasingly tiny holdings that peasants held in the early twentieth century and the impossibility of cultivating without periodic misery. In order to afford the steerage ticket for steamship voyages, some families supported their sons' emigration by selling off plots of land or otherwise through loans, which they could expect to be repaid once their son was employed.[37] After a childhood of displacement and precarity, Allos, the protagonist of *America Is in the Heart*, describes the underbelly of feeling restless and adventurous in Ilokano settlements of Luzon: "I was getting restless and fearful of the uncertainty that pervaded our household. I felt like running away—anywhere. I wanted to cast off the sudden gloom that shadowed our family, and I thought the only way to do that was to escape from it. I would also be escaping from my family, and from the bitter memories of childhood. 'I am leaving now, Father,' I said one day."[38] Prior to wanting to depart, Allos's economic world spanned the farms and wetlands of Pangasinan, from Binalonan to the shores of the Lingayen Gulf. His father was a farmer on small family plots, while his mother sold beans in various neighboring barangay on foot. His family's farmland, prior to his emigration, had been bought out by men from Manila, and what was left over was the poor-quality land from which his father could hardly cultivate enough for subsistence. It was not productive for Allos precisely because uncertainty and loss were accompanied by a lack of action or by a lack of options for courses of action. Instead of spiraling into destitution altogether, the affective experience of escaping would allow uncertainty to become risk, paired at least with some course of action. Finding work in an American library in Baguio, Allos learned about Abraham Lincoln's life. Allos fixated not on Lincoln's Emancipation Proclamation or the American Civil War but instead on his trajectory from poor peasant farmer to president of the United States.[39] For Allos, Lincoln and the America he learned in the library meant possibility; he would find a course of action to board a ship across the Pacific.

Through the promise of mobilities—in the plural—adventure created an affective landscape that reconfigured the relationship between Ilokanos and American economic opportunity. Migrants did not leave for the same reasons, but the general affective landscape in the region was shared. They felt, intuitively and in their community, a need to move and to enter into a transpacific and continental structure of mobility. While education provided a safe option for social mobility, well known in the Philippines through the Spanish and American introduction of public schools and the civil service, adventure draws a broader continuity between its affect in the homeland and how America was constructed as a land of "opportunity" of many forms. The evidence of adventure was not simply the experience of thrill and opportunity but also a material relationship with American wealth. Juan Mendoza encapsulates this relationship with his first payday: "I still have it [my first pay]. My first pay I have it, you know. Because I went to Alaska in Quadra Bay, that's where he sent me and when we came home, they paid us in gold piece, The Bank of California, gold pieces."[40] This was before the Great Depression.

Adventure's affective landscape was cultivated out of these imaginations of America as a land of economic opportunity. However, the outcomes of this affective landscape was only produced for men. Ilokano women such as Rosalia Villanueva Mendoza, the wife of Juan in Missoula, also felt that itch for social mobility and travel within Luzon. She expressed frustration that despite there being movement around her—as Trinidad Rojo had felt—she was halted by her family and her schools. Her cousins and her sisters denied her the opportunity to go to school, despite the fact that she could have gone if she paid the matriculation fee. She was encouraged to graduate from nursing school at the San Juan de Dios Hospital in Vigan. Rosalia could only move to the United States by reuniting with her lover Juan, whom she met in school. Juan, of course, had already been able to indulge in adventure, facilitated by transportation infrastructures that favored masculine mobility and foreclosed women from its transits.[41]

Gendered migrant labor was not just enforced through national and imperial laws. Social reproduction took place most effectively at home and in everyday life. As earlier chapters show, what scholars have identified as a "culture of migration" arose out of the decontextualization of Ilokano dispossession from Northern Luzon in the nineteenth century. Rosalia's story reveals the micropolitics of everyday life through which the gendering of migrant labor was dictated through family and educational pressures. These cultures of gender exclusion reached into the intimate spaces of family and childhood life, replicated by the perceived and actual danger for women to be in places such as steamships and rail cars. While a sense of adventure was felt across genders, the ability, encouragement, and resources to take on such courses of action segregated Ilokano men and women.[42]

How did Ilokano migrants make lives and survey the United States, their fabled land of opportunity? While cities are where many Filipinos eventually settled with property, a vagabond lifestyle took them to the far reaches of the US commodity empire on the continent. Alaska, California's Central Valley, and the Yakima River Valley in southeastern Washington state are just some places where Ilokano, Bisaya, and some Tagalog workers circulated. Between field and mining work, the promise of eventual recreation, and lives on railroads (through which many labor camps traveled), one understudied region of Filipino labor migration provides a microcosm of the varied spaces of Ilokano lives in an industrial West.

Missoula, Montana, 1934

The Big Sky city of Missoula, Montana, fell under a blazing sun in the summer months of the mid-1930s. The Wilma Building, then the tallest edifice in Missoula, bustled with its modest mix of guests. Many came by way of railroad, touring the vistas of the Rocky Mountains or on their way to the Pacific Northwest. Fewer of these wayfarers arrived than perhaps half a decade prior; it was the middle of the Great Depression. More patrons, also arriving by way of railroad though not always legally, looked to settle in after months of tramping for work. Locals knew them as Filipinos, fresh from a Montana mine, a Yakima Valley farm, or a Hawaiʻi sugar plantation.

One of their *kababayan*[43] was a favorite of Mr. and Mrs. William Simons, the owners of the Wilma Building. Juan Mendoza, this man in his early thirties, worked the elevator and the door greeting guests from desk to room. A former tenant himself, Juan became intimately familiar with the Wilma's halls and the local high society that gathered downstairs. By 1934, unlike many of his fellow Filipinos, he led a home life that looked more like what the white folks led: after work, he drove his small car to a residential area just outside of the downtown core and into the driveway of a modest house. His wife, Rosalia, would greet him with their newborn daughter in her arms. In their yard, a small garden boasted two tropical treasures: hanging leafy vines with long green gourds and low bean plants that nestled the grassy ground.

Passers-by may have been forgiven for overlooking the unassuming house except for two features. First, the owners were Filipino at a time when Filipinos could not own a house. With some laughter, Juan later recalled their legal sleight of hand, which allowed them to purchase this property: they registered it under their American-born daughter. Second, the garden might have drawn some attention to a resident or a pedestrian looking in. Neither plant that grew in abundance was familiar to the Western Hemisphere. The gourds were *paria*, or bitter melon, quite foreign to the average Montanan palate. The beans were *balatong*, or mung beans, cooked whole with seafood or meat. Neither could have grown, Juan recalled, in Western Washington, where the air was chilly and the rains were cool. In Missoula, the summer climate was favorable for a small harvest of these hardy plants. One might have heard the thuds of a knife cutting paria or the fishy and savory aromas of the stews that followed a potful of whole balatong. At work, Juan might have been the Filipino lift operator, but at home and in the garden, the Mendozas were unmistakably Ilokano.[44]

Big Sky Balatong

Adventure came about through transportation infrastructures that encouraged movement and the seasonal workplaces that kept Ilokanos working and moving. Filipinos' status as "US nationals" allowed them relatively unfettered movement across metropolitan and colonial spaces in the US empire. Coal-powered steamships, railroads, and factories were the edifices of imperial incomes. The new industrial order harnessed steam to accelerate the circulation of commodities and, in the process, expanded the geographies of workers who sustained its production and its infrastructures.[45]

Crossing by steamship to Puget Sound, many Ilokanos arrived in Seattle first. The affective experience of arriving in Seattle was itself described as quite an adventure. Juan Mendoza from Vigan described the Seattle landing as "just a chance." Teodoro Ranjo did not choose Seattle and only arrived there because that was where the boat was to take them to America. That chance feeling was a product of the transpacific steamship routes that rendered Seattle and the Pacific Northwest into a gateway for commodities, workers, and military-imperial power.[46]

Young men worked in western Washington state lumber mills and Alaska salmon canneries during summer months to pay for their studies in institutions such as the University of Washington.[47] Unable to afford tuition fees at the University of Washington during the Great Depression, some young men hopped trains to Montana, where they found easy employment on railroads and in sugar beet fields. The Big Sky state was a far cry from the ports of Seattle and the Chinatowns of the California West Coast but provided ample work opportunities for anyone who wanted to venture away from coastal economies. Three primary industries abounded in Montana where Filipinos worked: railroads, sugar beets, and mines. Anecdotes from interviewees suggest that Bisaya labor fueled the region's mines, while Ilokanos worked on railroads and sugar beet farms.[48]

In the mid-twentieth century, American sugar was king: Hawaiian cane and Big Sky beets. Sugar beets were most successfully cultivated in California, Utah, and Nebraska, with growing cultivation in Montana. The production shifted in earnest after World War II, when Japanese American sugar beet workers were interned from California. As the industry gained a foothold in the Big Sky states, Filipino and Mexican migrant workers provided the labor time for sugar beet's rise. Migrant work also maintained railroads that connected crops and other commodities, important work because Big Sky tracks were especially susceptible to the volatile weather patterns immediately east of the Rockies.[49]

Filipino American history in Montana and the Big Sky is vastly understudied. This history lacks the metropolis and the major Chinatown economies of West Coast cities, but as evidenced by interviewees and its appearance in Bulosan, the Big Sky states were as integral to the migrant worker's life as the Central Valley and the Yakima Valley. Well before becoming flyover states at the advent of commercial flight, the Big Sky was well integrated into the fabric of migrant work. Using Montana and the flyover states as an optic, we can understand how Ilokano and other Filipino workers most immediately experienced the affective landscapes as they encountered the industrial edifices of Big Sky industry.

A few Filipino families managed to buy property in Missoula, Montana. Juan and Rosalia Mendoza were one of two such families in the city, and they purchased a small house under their American-born daughter's name. Summer sun and heat provided the necessary climate to carve out a comfortable Ilokano life, and indeed, they grew a little garden of tropical vegetables despite their home's remoteness from other Filipino communities.[50] But for everyone else, Montana was a place of work or at least an immediate alternative to the sudden unaffordability of Washington state student life in the wake of the Depression. Prudencio Mori, an Ilokano who moved back to the Philippines later in his life, noted how food insecure he was until a relative suggested he move to Montana:

> PM: I managed to live on apples. Mostly on apples because apples at that
> time were pretty cheap, so after finishing my sophomore year, I quit
> the University [of Washington] and I wired to Montana what I made
> in bonds of Filipino Tramperos. You know what that means?
>
> DC: No.
>
> PM: It's the Filipinos who follow the craps [*sic*]. Tramperos. I worked in a
> sugarbeet [farm] because when during that summer, Summer I think
> 1933, a cousin of mine came from Montana and he found out that I was
> not in school and he said, oh you better come to Montana and I'll help
> you go to school there. I said why? Well, you'll work at the sugarbeet
> field with me and then I'll help you go to school. There is a university
> at Missoula, the University of Montana.[51]

Montana was not a first choice for Ilokanos, who chose Alaska or Washington state in order to support their Seattle education. During the Depression, Montana was a new option for affordable education and employment. If they did not work in sugar beet farms, they worked to maintain the extensive railroads that connected the Big Sky with coastal markets. Rudolfo Andres was one such Ilokano railroad worker who was employed by Japanese contractors to repair the tracks around Livingstone, Montana.[52] The Mendoza family knew the Ilokano railroad cultures well enough that Juan invested in a used car so he could find potential clients for his weekend business as a suit sales-man.[53] However, as Prudencio Mori highlights, many migrant workers hopped on freight trains as tramps.

Tramping was well known among Ilokano men and other Filipino migrant workers as the risky (adventurous) but cost-affordable way to move around the continent. For Ilokano and other Filipino migrant workers, trains repre-sented the freedom of movement—however risky—but also a measure of being masculine. Prudencio Mori, growing weary of working on a Montana sugar beet farm, looked to the freight train as a means of liberation from agricultural labor:

> PM: You know, by this field where we were working, a freight train goes
> by everyday and every time that freight train pass by the field where
> we were working, it was loaded with men and women alike. Those
> were the hobos. And even the Filipinos, the Filipinos who were
> working with me said that's the way they travel. They would jump
> into the freight train while it is moving, but you have to go outside
> the station, far from the station to board the train to get into the freight
> train because they would not allow you to board it while the train is
> still at the station. Those boys riding in the freight train, they can do
> that, so can I, I said.[54]

The train, as risk but also as promise of freedom and mobility, embodies an infrastructure of adventure. Prudencio Mori watched the train and familiar-ized himself with its schedule as it moved past the sugar beet field, the rhythms of transportation infrastructures. Because he wanted to tramp on the railroads, life on the trains was only meant to be temporary, between work stints. Hobos, as he saw them, were entire families of all genders who lived vagabond lives, working or not. But Filipino tramps such as Prudencio, mostly men, looked at tramping as a means of proving their masculinity: "[if the boys] can do that, so can I." For Prudencio, adventuring as a tramp was a masculine venture.[55]

Teodoro Ranjo, who was a stowaway on a transpacific steamship, remarked that many tramps were ambitious people without money, so tramping on freight cars was a "smart way of travelling."[56] Tramping itself as an option became known through word of mouth, and its own shadow organizing logics emerged. Rudolfo Andres noted that a head tramp is always the "last to ride" so as to ensure that his less experienced companions are safely aboard and free of patrol harassment. Montana, with its predominance of Ilokano railroad maintenance workers, must have been a safe haven for tramping workers who sought a familiar face. Bisaya workers must have also found refuge with fellow Filipinos and disembarked the train in order to work in Montana gold mines.[57]

In Montana, as in the agricultural fields of California and Washington state, laborers lived in makeshift camps between work shifts. The shape of the labor camps around sugar beet farms suggests how improvisational migrant work cropped up around seasonal commodities. Allos, Bulosan's protagonist, joined as an attempt to work away from his unproductive stints in cities. To maintain a transient lifestyle, few major luxuries could be afforded in settlements, and camps consisted of tents and dilapidated vehicles to take people around. Jalopies afforded more control in mobility than the average Filipino worker and were often deployed by Pinoy labor contractors.[58]

Because of the time and energy investment that tramping for work extracted, Ilokanos quickly learned how to quantify the landscape according to their desired earnings. They learned how to not only look at the landscape in terms of aesthetic beauty but also identify it according to how profitable commodity cultivation could be. As Prudencio Mori, "I said [to my cousin from Montana], 'By the way, how much can you make working in a sugarbeet field?' Oh sometimes you can make $500.00 after the whole season, after the season is over. So I went. I was not there one week and then we started to work at the sugarbeet field."[59] Through word of mouth, workers partitioned the landscape by their crops and industries and the possibility of extracting value should they sell their labor time during the ecological season. In short, Ilokanos perpetuated a settler colonial and industrial capitalist way of seeing the American West.

Seeing landscapes as commodities did not only mean valuating their products for personal gain. These commodified ways of seeing were reinforced by perceiving the landscape in pastoral and beautiful terms, ripe and bountiful for picking.[60] In his descriptions of migrant worker life, Bulosan also partitioned the landscape into its commodities. "As Long as the Grass Shall Grow," a short story published in 1949, depicts the halted relationship between an Ilokano migrant farmworker and a white woman teacher working with the farming community:

> [My] eyes were familiar with the bright colors on the hillside, the yellowing leaves of the peas, the sprouting green blades of the summer grass, the royal white crowns of the edelweiss, the tall gray mountains in the distance, and the silent blue sea below the clear sky.

I had arrived in America, the new land, three months before and had come to this farming town to join friends who had years ago left the Philippines. I had come in time to pick the summer peas.[61]

The protagonist's arrival onto the pea fields is marked with a colorful pastoral imagery upon which he establishes his knowledge of land and labor. For the narrator, America is a "new land," a tabula rasa for migrant worker economic opportunity made viable through established kinship ties from the Philippines. Because they were not able to settle or own land, America is figured as an abstract beautiful landscape, domesticated in the protagonist's eyes through the colors of the season. Because the colors are vibrant and not gray or white (as in winter), this is a fecund and productive landscape. Through his description of color and flora, Bulosan portrays seasonality, both pastoral and industrial, from which the mobile peasant might extract value and find oneself in the "new land."

Industrial rhythms and the spatial partitioning of a dispossessed landscape provided the rubrics of Ilokano men's migratory lives. As recent historians of Filipino America have emphasized, the lack of an urban foothold is not a sign of a failure to develop a viable ethnic community, as earlier Asian American historians once did.[62] While most Ilokano men interviewed expressed their initial intent to travel to the United States for education, the Great Depression foreclosed those options, and many were left to find other means of making and spending income. Perhaps, then, one of the most egregious literary injustices of Carlos Bulosan was to emphasize the aimlessness of migrant men. In the same story as above, the narrator observes that the older workers "seemed a bunch of contented workers, but they were actually restless and had no plans for the future."[63] In part 2 of *America Is in the Heart*, the protagonist undergoes a period of that aimlessness as well, working in the countryside and gambling in cities, wandering in a repetitive manner as he lets himself get carried into the flows of labor and capital around the American West. Nonetheless, while I have shown how the countryside and its connective tissues were integral to the lifeways of Ilokano migrants, cities and the vices they offered served as nodes of ethnic community building despite the vagabond nature of Ilokano and other Filipino young men in the prewar years.

Diasporic Dandies

For young Ilokano men, cities were double-edged swords. For one, Ilokano men could not own property and were made to work most readily in fields or canneries. For living abodes, Ilokano men settled for hotels in Chinatowns, whose economies were oriented to serve transient workers.[64] However, despite the accommodating commercial cultures of West Coast Chinatowns, cities were not friendly as long-term options for Ilokanos before World War II.[65] Chris Mensalvas recalled how rural spaces were places of survival, and while cities were places of recreation, they afforded few options for *dagiti kabsatna* (his brothers):

> We were mostly on farms where we can confine ourselves or canneries, hotels. That's how our people existed, survived you could say. That's one of our problems right now, because of all of those hotels right now, especially those that are gone now, were . . . mostly Filipinos. Now a lot of those hotels are gone. . . . There were very few hotels that the Filipinos could live even in Chinatown. . . . We are so crowded just like bums. That's one of the problems of the system. They're doing alright, they're staying in the city. They know there's no escape.[66]

Mensalvas noted that urban work was steadier but, without options for settlement for migrants from the Philippines, proved to be less viable than the work habits that many Ilokano men knew. Furthermore, unionization and strong mutual aid systems were organized in Alaska and other well-known labor sites.[67]

However fleeting, cities gave benefits that were indispensable to a viable migrant working life. In Los Angeles, young men could create masculinity in taxi dance halls, boxing tournaments, and gambling houses. Other Filipinos, such as Frank Mancao, who reached an ethnic middle-class status, remarked on the ostentatious cultures of worker gangs who arrived in cities. Seen otherwise as stoop labor in the fields, weekend recreation in urban spaces provided a way to stretch their legs, walk in their best clothing, and accompany white women, to the dismay of onlooking white men. In short, cities are where workers could see sights on their own terms and be seen in their absolute best. Urban centers, as small as Chinatowns in Reedley and as big as the metropolis of Los Angeles, served as these recreational ports. However, these spaces had the caveat of being the areas wherein Filipinos were most watched and most understood by local law enforcement and white vigilantes.[68]

When Ilokano men stepped into cities, they made sure to dress in their absolute best. The political economy of fashion among the manong generation was as mobile as the workers themselves. A voracious market for suits and formalwear became well known to companies as far away from the West Coast as Cincinnati. Ilokano men along the railroads were among the most sought-after customers for tailors, and salesmen such as Juan Mendoza made a living out of making manongs look sharp. He was hired by a suit company in Nashville as its representative in Montana in order to tap into a voracious Filipino migrant worker market. The job at the Wilma Building paid $60 per month, and each suit sold on weekends could garner a 25% commission, or roughly $20 per three-piece suit. Rosalia and Juan purchased a car in order to conduct business, and they followed the railroad tracks to different labor camps. From driving around the area, they noted that the people who worked the railroads and farms in Montana were mostly Ilokano, while Bisaya men worked in mines. Speaking the same dialect, Juan was a perfect salesman and tailor for this market of sporty bachelors who would not have been able to buy off-the-rack suits, which were far too big.[69]

After a picking or canning season, dashing young men in their best attire wandered in between working stints and bummed around in cities, and they were known for spending their cash in taxi dance halls and gambling sessions. However, when they stepped into cities as racialized transgressive figures, they made sure to be seen in their flashiest suits. These garments, including three-piece sets, rakish sportswear, and zoot suits, were not only made for community social events or the taxi dance halls in urban areas. They also served as signifiers of wearable capital in a time when the men could not own property. In suits and rakish sportswear, they commissioned that a portrait be taken so they could send a photograph to their home province, which encouraged further emigration among family and friends at home. The young man wearing a suit might gesture to some expression of respectability politics, outside the denigrated image of the Filipino farmworker. By contrast, much like zoot suits, the rakish sportswear signaled, along the lines of fashion, a rebellion against bourgeois white respectability. In donning their attire and wandering the town, the manongs could be thought of as diasporic dandies.[70]

Dandies, or in French, *flâneurs*, were young men in the nineteenth and early twentieth centuries who wandered the streets of European cities. They donned sharp, bright suits, sensuously experiencing urban life. Regardless of the city or the context, flâneurs fascinated writers such as Charles Baudelaire, William Makepeace Thackeray, Oscar Wilde, and Walter Benjamin because of their visual relationship with their wanderings: dandies watched and were watched. The flâneur was a walking visual signifier for nonproductive life in modern cities, spaces of capitalist modernity and wandering mobility. But simultaneously, *flânerie* provided a means of creatively setting the terms for how one was seen and materialized the mutual watching at the core of urban

FIGURE 6.1 Migrant workers in suits. Photographer: Frank Mancao.
Courtesy of Filipino American National Historical Society.

social life. As anthropologist Jamie Coates notes, the flâneur exemplified transgressive urban walking that maximized a creative and nonteleological means of experiencing the city's lifeways, as urban life itself was coconstituted by the flâneur. Carving out a visual identity in a city, "the *flâneur* used a wide range of ambulatory strategies and performances to establish his place in the world."[71]

Flânerie, then, can be understood as a visual interlocution among people in the city. Novelists, poets, and philosophers understood the social relations of urban modernity in intimate, visual terms. For instance, in "Crossing Brooklyn Ferry" (1856), the American poet Walt Whitman gave shape to this interlocution in free verse:

> Flood-tide below me! I see you face to face!
> Clouds of the west—sun there half an hour high—I see you also
>   face to face.
> Crowds of men and women attired in the usual costumes, how curious
>   you are to me!
> On the ferry-boats the hundreds and hundreds that cross, returning
>   home, are more curious to me than you suppose,
> And you that shall cross from shore to shore years hence are more to me,
>   and more in my meditations, than you might suppose. (1–5)

Every dandy was encountered in the city, but not every urban dweller was a dandy. Not donning the "usual costumes," the dandy was not simply curiosity but also deliberate visual transgression. The dandy seized that mutual act of seeing "face to face." By deliberately accentuating visual and performative modes of interlocution, dandies sought to control their right to look and their right to be looked at.[72]

However, not all flâneurs in Europe were white, and not all flânerie was regarded with equally wistful regard across racial and ethnic lines. For instance, the ilustrados in Europe, middle-class educated young men from the Philippines, led scholarly lives while also indulging in the modern sensuousness of urban culture. These ilustrados, young migrant men themselves, established a vibrant community of students in Madrid but from mostly mixed-race and middle-class households in Luzon. They organized as *propagandistas* (propagandists) to promote Philippine assimilation as a Spanish province. Since they were mostly in their twenties, they often spent time wandering cities in their best clothes or taking part in European recreation. José Rizal, nationalist intellectual and martyr of the Katipunan movement, saw Filipinos' ostentatious gallivanting in Madrid as anathema to a moral order necessary for enlightened nationalism. He complained of their unproductive decadence while he himself participated in many of their activities in his young adulthood. The Filipino Enlightenment of the nineteenth century was not merely an intellectual movement; it was also a homosocial kinship between young men who sought, at every political and public turn, to appear respectable despite their youth and racial identity.[73]

The similarity between the ambulant ilustrado and the manong is not merely coincidental or vaguely genealogical. The influence of the ilustrados in Philippine culture reached diasporic communities, and migrant communities deliberately drew upon the images of Filipino dandies in carving out their respectability politics.[74] While previous chapters warned against a nationalist historiography in determining the "Filipino" in the diaspora, this case is different. I suggest that for diasporic dandies, a nationalist genealogy is relevant at least in the case of men's portraits in early Filipino America. A visual economy of dandyism, from the middle-class Filipino diaspora in Spain to the working-class Filipino diaspora in the United States, constituted a transnational respectability politics for racialized men denigrated in their respective contexts.

Almost certainly, workers would have seen the ilustrados with fine suits in photographs. Many Filipinos were active in various mutual aid societies based out of Seattle and California towns. For instance, the Caballeros de Dimas-Alang (Gentlemen of Dimas-Alang), a pseudo-Masonic fraternity, sought to cultivate diasporic nationalism through the reverence of José Rizal. Other active mutual aid societies modeled their organizations after La Liga Filipina, Rizal's pseudo-Masonic nationalist group, and distributed nationalist literature to its membership. The members of the Dimas-Alang produced images of themselves in uniform and sent them to comrades and friends to depict their dignified dress.[75]

The manongs' diasporic dandyism is a collision between, on one hand, a Philippine masculine culture of migration and the respectable uses of Western fashion and, on the other hand, a material manifestation of migrant workers' economic destitution in the United States. Many migrant workers visited cities as pit stops in between contracts and during the Great Depression often found themselves with less employment and even less opportunity to spend their money on prohibitively expensive tuition.[76] Without education and abundant skilled jobs that the imagined United States promised to offer, workers' earnings needed to circulate by other means. Some were kuripot and cultivated good savings and investment skills.[77] However, for most, the experience of receiving money was an affective experience that required a

FIGURE 6.2 Pedro Alesna, a Dimas-Alang member, sending a portrait postcard
to Frank Mancao. Photograph taken in Moriyama Studio in San Francisco,
California. The back of the postcard reads "Remembrance for our meeting here."
Courtesy of the Filipino American National Historical Society.

repeated sense of thrill. Without the stability of the promise of education and economic mobility, cities provided other options for the manongs.

The cognate of adventure is "gamble." Speaking to the twentieth-century context, the philosopher Mario Wenning notes that gamblers "[engage] risk and [seek] fortune in situations marked by uncertainty." However, unlike other sports and games, "coping with contingency does not require the same degree of risk aversion." Rather than retreat from risk, the gambler instead attempts to increase the speed of transformation in hopes of profit. Without the disciplined diversion of finances toward education for the affective experience of learning, for Ilokano men gambling served as a secondary terrain of labor—after income has been made in the fields and in canneries—through which adventure might be experienced.[78]

Gambling was not looked upon favorably among fellow Filipinos. Bulosan, in *America Is in the Heart*, presented gambling as a moral dilemma toward the larger cause of a radical Filipino politics. However, while gambling presented a risk that moralists looked down upon, it also presented other modes of self-representation and ethnic agency. Unlike activities such as stock market investing, gambling in Chinatowns was predicated on performance and conspicuous display of capital. Like wearing expensive tailored suits, gambling was a dialectic of seeing. It put Filipinos in visual contact with other workers in Chinatowns and integrated them within a highly visible extralegal economy.[79]

While the Great Depression produced conditions of destitution and exhaustion, Ilokano and other Filipino young men took to cities to display conspicuous consumption and spirited public dancing. To the ire of white men who watched them in cities, young Filipino men frequented taxi dance halls. For ten cents a dance, they could woo one woman they desired or move between women and show off their dance skills. Filipino American cultural scholar and dramaturg Lucy Burns notes that observers called the manongs' taxi dance hall performances "splendid dancing." The dancing manong challenged the emasculation of the "Oriental" but also served as an embodied terrain. As sociologist Rick Baldoz argues, the sight of the rhythmic movements of interracial couples produced such vitriol that it mobilized white men's advocacy to ban Filipino migrant labor from the continent, hence the Tydings-McDuffie Act of 1934.[80]

The taxi dance halls commodified heteronormative choreography across racial lines, but their surplus value was the possibility of claiming one's own terms of rhythm and the chance at transgressive intimacy. For young men, despite the dangers of militant white men, interracial dancing provided an opportunity for the possibility of *panliligaw* (Tagalog for "courtship"). Their "splendid dancing" operated along axes of courtship in which they would compete among each other by means of their charisma. Among more middle-class Filipinos, these young flirtatious men exhibited an ethic of *panggulo* (Tagalog for "troublesome behavior"). Panggulo Filipinos are those not working in fields, or as Julian Ebat from Binalonan (a townmate of Carlos Bulosan) recalls, those who were not simply "helpers in the fields.... If you wanted to see a Filipino, the consensus of opinions is that he is here for the sugar beet, or he's a lemon picker."[81] The urban manong was troublesome for this respectable agricultural image. Teodolo Ranjo, from Ilocos Norte, recalled that what was being read as panggulo was a performance of masculinity and courtship, especially for young men:

> After we arrived, we thought we got our independence only, all of the sudden that why a lot, that why a lot of us got astray, got into some bad company and things, but not really.... Troublesome—but anyways we didn't, we did not do anything bad only when you know how it is when you were young and you are after one girl this and that, you have to show off a little bit that you are somebody that's the trouble here, so that the girl you are after will like you, right?[82]

Frank Mancao, a Bisaya (Central Philippine) photographer and business owner in Reedley, California, also noted how conspicuous consumption got Filipino gangs in trouble with law enforcement, who did not incarcerate them but rather chased them out of town.[83] Ranjo may have been alluding to being involved with these gangs that flaunted suits and nice cars and frequented taxi dance halls. For middle-class Filipinos and white law enforcement in urban sites, the movements of working men in places of recreation were anathema for each of their interests. Anti-Filipino racism during the 1930s cited panggulo behavior in cities, threats to both Filipino respectability and white men's masculinity. But panggulo, I posit, comprises urban micropolitics of dandyism, wherein migrant workers sought to see and be seen on their own terms and wander and dance according to their own rhythms.

From the discipline of stoop labor in fields, cities were places where farmworkers could stretch out and indulge in activities by claiming their own time. Gambling, dancing, boxing, and other recreational activities afforded opportunities for young men to immerse their bodies and minds into rhythms not subject to the disciplining temporality of the workplace. In order to reclaim dignity, they sought to see and be seen at the expense of their respectability but, at the very least, also at their own rhythms.[84]

From *Nakem* to *Kamalayan*

Life for the manongs was not all fun and games in urban recreation sites.[85] In order to get to the point of recreation, Ilokano migrant men needed to quickly find a way to establish themselves in a land not their own, often at a port not of their own choosing. Ilokanos first searched *para dagiti kailianda ken kailokuanda*[86] when they arrived on the continent. Some, such as the lumber worker Sinforoso Ordoña, found it in Valer Laigo, *ti kasinsinna taga-Bauang, idiay La Union*,[87] who found him work in Alaska.[88] Barangay transnational kinship structures were indeed important for establishing labor migration patterns in the West. *Tagnawa*, or the Ilokano ethic of mutual aid and social support for less fortunate kin (broadly conceived), perpetuated in a transpacific context. But these affective kinships were not afforded to everyone, nor were they always sustained no matter where Ilokano young men went for work.

It is important to note that the experience of alienation and loneliness that Ilokanos faced occurred in a multilingual context. Tagalog had not yet been implemented as a national language, so migrants from Northern Luzon knew some English, the occasional Spanish, and, of course, Ilokano. To conclude, I chart out, in three languages, the feelings of homesickness expressed by one migrant worker and how he made do with becoming Filipino in tongues not his own.[89] As you read the passage below, you may need to flip between the words on the page and the endnotes or otherwise between different modes of linguistic consciousness if you understand some of the text.

TAGA-PASUQUIN, IDIAY ILOCOS NORTE, ni Manong Teodolo Ranjo. Awan naganakna, nagnaed ni Manong Teodolo kenni ikit na. Nagiggian ni Manong Teodolo idiay Seattle ken barangay. Idiay Cosmopolis ti umuna a trabahona, idiay factoria ti kahon, ta nabaga ni gayyemna maipapan iti trabaho idiay Laud a Washington. Sumabat ti dua a gayyem idiay Batac, idiay Ilocos Norte met. Ngem inton-ano nagawatna ti surat ni kasinsinna, kunana ti narigat ken malidliday nga biag a trabaho idiay America:[90]

"The first time when I received a letter from home," *kunana ken Cynthia Mejia, ti babai taga-DPAA* [Demonstration Project for Asian Americans],[91] "it happened. It came from my first cousin, that letter hit me. I must have been homesick, lonesome, homesick. I don't know what happened, I went right between these pile of lumber, I read that letter and I cried in there . . . the first day that I worked over here, boy I thought that was some needles around here." *Nasangit ni Manong Teodolo, iti baro a lalaki, awan pamilya wenno kailokuan kaniana.*[92]

Nakasarita ni Manong Teodolo ti English ken Ilokano inton-ano baro isu idiay United States, ngem saan a nakasaritana ti Tagalog. Nagadalna ti Tagalog ken dagiti grupo a sabali a Pilipino, ngata saan a kailokuanda.[93]

"It is only here when I learn Tagalog. . . . So, you get, you don't get out of place if somebody talks in Tagalog."

Kailan nagaral na si Manong Teodolo ang Tagalog, nakapagsalita siya sa kanyang mga kababayan. At saka, nakapagkilala siya ang bagong uri ng pagkakamag-anak, sa labas ng bayan nila: Pilipino. O siguro, Pinoy. Sa Dimas-Alang, yung isang na mga grupo ng kapisanan, sa komunidad ng mga Pilipino sa mga lungsod, ay naging Pilipino siya. Yung "nakem" niya, nagbago yun sa "kamalayan":[94]

"We dream about the Philippines. These are the closest, especially Dimas Alang, we, they preach about serving the Philippines, and all that. We tried to help gain independence, you know. That's why we, we were really lonesome, homesick for the Philippines, to see the Philippines again. But it was impossible for us to go because we couldn't earn enough money for our passage at that time."[95]

MANONG TEODOLO, like many diasporic migrants, became "Filipino" away from the Philippines. It was an uneven, uneasy, and incomplete process of flitting between different tongues and registers, or what language historian Vicente Rafael might call a war of translation.[96] However, the "national language" was not only enforced in the homeland but was also a necessary tactic of ethnic survival in the diaspora. Just like how Ilokanos learned of America through an imagined geography, they learned the Philippines—and became Filipino—by imagining the archipelago in a language and history that was not theirs. The everyday experience of language alienation and diasporic code switching of folks such as Manong Teodolo attest to a multilingual—even creolized—linguistic landscape experienced by Ilokano, Bisaya, and other Philippine migrant workers. Without a shared vocabulary, they instead shared experience through the ways they saw the land, wished themselves to be seen, danced and rolled dice on their own time, felt thrilled by the pace of transportation infrastructures, and undertook the burden of the rhythm of labor discipline. Eventually some common grammar of Filipino diasporic life would arise but through an enforced language of Tagalog and a Manila-centric nationalist historiography.

The affective landscape shared by Ilokano and other Filipino migrants in the United States was one of unprecedented mobility at an astonishing pace but also of exhausting discipline and lonely displacement. Knowing a homeland synchronized diasporic Filipinos by nationalizing and centralizing their feelings of homesickness. Transnational groups such as Dimas-Alang, initiated by Filipino nationalist Andres Bonifacio and founded in San Francisco in 1921, served as diasporic mutual aid societies, with precedent in a rich mutual aid culture in the nineteenth- and twentieth-century Philippines. Mutual aid cultures called tagnawa (Ilokano), *bayanihan* (Tagalog), and *tinabangay* (Cebuano) tethered diasporic groups together through social and economic activities.[97] Masonic groups such as Dimas-Alang, Legionarios del Trabajo, and the Gran Oriente Filipino carried the extra feature of mimicking the lodge cultures of the Filipino ilustrados and drew from the symbolism of Rizal in order to commemorate Philippine political history away from home. Manong Teodolo joined Dimas-Alang in 1941, right before the war, when the organization was in full strength. Migrant workers who received aid from these groups also immersed themselves in the symbolism of Philippine nationalism and felt the need to give aid to their newly imagined homeland.[98]

In the process, Ilokanos translated their *nakem* into *kamalayan* and their native *utang a naimbag a nakem* (Ilokano for "debt from a good conscience") to their hometown families into a nationalist *utang na loob* (Tagalog for "debt from within") to a newly imagined *bayan* (Tagalog for "homeland").[99] Perhaps it was a good alternative to the feeling of alienation as migrant workers, which while thrilling was certainly exhausting and unbearably lonely. Nevertheless, an underlying ambivalence about Tagalog in Manong Teodolo's story suggests that another process of alienation, one of diasporic nationalism, tugged at the affective landscape of Ilokano men circulating around the United States. Without a place to call home and without a means to buy a house to call home, a homeland would have to be imagined, even if that homeland was not theirs.

WHAT DID IT FEEL LIKE to become Filipino in America? As this chapter has shown, those feelings of diasporic movement began with the American occupation in Northern and Central Luzon and how quotidian politics in school and at home generated a sense of adventure. The collective sense of "movement" stirred within young men and women a desire to undertake courses of action—in this case, educational travel—to maximize reward out of risk. However, out of the gendered character of capitalist infrastructures across the Pacific and the micropolitics of everyday life, fulfilling that mobility was only afforded to men. In the United States, they experienced a life of labor between two affective landscapes of time: the thrilling speed of circulation and the burdensome discipline of stoop labor. Cities provided spaces wherein Ilokano men could engage in rhythms of recreation on their own terms, including gambling, dancing, and wandering the city to be seen. However, the experience of alienation and loneliness was too overbearing compared to senses of thrill, especially during the Great Depression; mutual aid societies, ethnic community, and the Tagalog language provided a limited means of creating a vocabulary of home and synchronizing the diasporic experience of being racialized in the US empire.

Part IV

Filipino/America

CHAPTER SEVEN

Two Insurgent Ethnologies

Es ist niemals ein Dokument der Kultur, ohne zugleich ein solches der Barbarei zu sein. (There is no document of civilization [*Kultur*] which is not at the same time a document of barbarism.)
—Walter Benjamin, "Theses on the Philosophy of History," 1940

Our journey from the slopes of Northern Luzon to the railroads of the American West traced the racial cartographies of Filipino America. The ethnological division between lowland and highland peoples obfuscated the historical kinships across elevations, reducing Northern Luzon's native populations into an assortment of racial types. Lowland types were considered to be not only closer to civilization but also better workers. Highland types, the populations of which actually resisted colonization through trade and countercolonial warfare, became regarded as indolent and insurgent. The division of race, then, also served as divisions of labor.[1]

But what of the two thinkers in the introduction, the *dos hermanos de los selváticos*? In the heyday of modern ethnicity and Filipino ethno-nationalism, Isabelo de los Reyes and Carlos Bulosan opted instead to center their grounded visions of a global Ilocos, diving deep into regionalisms and hinterland lifeways. They did not shed the cultural partitions of imperialism but instead drew upon them in creative and subversive ways. Americans in the Philippine Cordilleras partitioned populations according to their capacities to work by producing ethnological ideas of culture, then criminalized those deemed deviant to industrial productivity. However, as these two Ilokano writers show, ethnology could also be a colonial genre of writing whose tropes and poetics could be appropriated for critiques of empire. As dissident thinkers of social movements across the Pacific, de los Reyes and Bulosan imagined an Amianan-centered Filipinas that did not divide the *indio* and the Igorot. Instead, they envisioned solidarities outside the purview of the state, built upon shared economic and political histories and made possible by the valleys and rivers of the Amianan slopes beyond state geographies.

This conclusion explores the politics and poetics of Northern Luzon in the writings of Isabelo de los Reyes and Carlos Bulosan. Despite writing decades apart, they together imagined an Amianan proletariat that recognized ethnic difference but constructed solidarities between the lowlands and the highlands. I suggest that their rhetorical modes of challenging the tribalism of imperial ethnologies amounted to a veritable insurgent ethnology through which they both appropriated the tribal rhetorics of empire but redeployed them in subversive ways. The insurgent ethnology draws upon the foundational work of political scientist Megan C. Thomas, whose work examines how Philippine scholarship deployed European Orientalism and racial sciences to anticolonial ends.[2] Examining the *ilustrado* transnational milieu, Thomas argues that the specific practices of disciplines such as ethnology and folklore brought about horizontal relations among peoples, connected by the mundane practices of everyday life. Certainly, they also brought about hierarchies, commensurate with the practices of colonization, but within these disciplines also contained their own subversion.

From their insurgent ethnologies, Isabelo de los Reyes and Carlos Bulosan produced a counterarchive of the global Philippines from Ilokano *Weltanschauungen* against the proliferation of Euro-American and Manila-centric knowledge formations about the archipelago. They accounted for an alternative vision of ethnicity attuned to the geographies of the northern Philippines and imagined a Filipino subjectivity beyond the Tagalog world but spanning Indigenous and diasporic experience.

Hermano de los Selváticos

Among his ilustrado contemporaries, Isabelo de los Reyes was considered a political maverick and remained at the margins of the Manila intellectual class. Born in Vigan and being an Ilokano migrant to Manila's bourgeois circles, de los Reyes became a prolific writer and printer by 1882. However, unlike his contemporaries, he did not leave the archipelago until his arrest during the Philippine Revolution, when he was exiled to Spain. As a young man, as Benedict Anderson has shown, de los Reyes was exceptional in that he found an international academic audience that regarded his work as cutting-edge scholarship. As a journalist and printer during the late nineteenth century, de los Reyes took advantage of the media ecology of his moment, eagerly distributing literature within the archipelago and across the Suez Canal to Europe. In European circles his work was met with great enthusiasm, particularly through the German translations of his works conducted by the ethnologist Ferdinand Blumentritt. De los Reyes's *El Folk-lore Filipino* (1887) won a silver medal at the 1887 Madrid Exposition for scholarly excellence.[3]

As Resil Mojares and Megan C. Thomas argue, de los Reyes's ethnological practice sought to unite people across divisions in the archipelago through precolonial ties. Folklore, as a specific practice of ethnology, initially served to recover the stories and practices of rural peoples in danger of becoming lost to industrialization. Inspired by Spanish intellectual circles, which demarcated field sites along regional lines as opposed to the English nationalist ones, de los Reyes drew upon a deep study of Luzon to infer on the nature of the Philippine *Volk*. Like Franz Boas, his global contemporary, de los Reyes deployed his scholarship to challenge the predominance of scientific racism in the late nineteenth century. By centering traditions and narratives, he put forward a native version of cultural relativism by looking at the shared stories among different groups. He challenged racial essentialism—that different races innately had different levels of civilization—by conceptualizing race itself in terms of culture. Instead, he posited that within racial groups themselves, different subgroups could change according to their contact with civilized spaces such as cities.[4]

After a systematic literature review of global folklore studies and positioning Philippine ethnology within the late nineteenth-century milieu, *El Folklore Filipino* begins with a touch of irony: "I am a brother to the forest peoples, Aetas, Igorots, and Tinguians, and born in this remote Spanish colony, where civilization shines albeit very dimly, I sincerely confess very little or rather said, I know nothing of the new occupation of human thought named Folk-Lore."[5] De los Reyes positions himself as not only a colonial subject but also an anthropological one. He names the peoples known to the Spanish as *infieles* and declares brotherly ties with them as a Christianized and literate subject. If we reference the two Ilokano words for such a type of kinship, we can see that the nature of this declaration is Janus-faced. On one hand, the adaptation of *hermano* in Ilokano is *manong*, or an older brother. As manong, he might claim a more elevated status than the *selvático* (forest people) siblings. On the other hand, the sibling (without Spanish loanwords, Ilokano is gender-neutral) is *kabsat*, or "cut from the same cord," which is a declaration of flesh-and-blood ties. Writing as a native ethnologist, de los Reyes straddled between the racism of the practice and its subversive potential.[6] The hermano figure, written as an Ilokano scholar, exemplifies this duality. Nonetheless, de los Reyes as the hermano—both as manong and as kabsat—claims an intimacy to which other ethnologists do not have access.

The specific practice of folklore studies, in which Isabelo de los Reyes may have found radical potential, came with the politics of what the discipline could collect and preserve. In particular, de los Reyes's folklore also turned to stories and oral traditions as a means of archiving race. On this front, de los Reyes cites Emilia Pardo Basan, a Galician folklorist, to determine the purpose of the discipline: "[The purpose of folklore is] to recover these fading traditions, these customs that are being forgotten, and these vestiges of long-gone times that are in danger of disappearing forever, to archive them, to avoid their total disappearance, to conserve their memory and form with them . . . a universal museum, where scholars can study the complete history of the past."[7] Folklore, for Basan—and by extension de los Reyes—is the practice of archiving race in the age of industry. However, de los Reyes markedly differs from Basan and other scholars in that he does not wholly subscribe to the fear of disappearance that European intellectuals expressed. De los Reyes gives his own "rigorous definition" of folklore as "the occupation of human thought, whose objective is to recover all the facts that unenlightened people know and have, that had not been studied."[8] This reveals an ambivalence toward what Resil Mojares calls the ilustrados' Philippine Enlightenment. Despite the nationalist potential of European radical texts on Philippine civil society, the knowledge not kept in libraries—that is, native ecologies and lifeways—might disappear. Losing Indigenous knowledge would be the price of progress.[9]

Regionalizing the ethnological study of the Philippines could be a way to counteract the homogenization of industrial progress. Ferdinand Blumentritt, the Bohemian ethnologist and de los Reyes's frequent collaborator, lamented to him sometime in the 1880s that progress "level[s] out all the races with its steamships, railroads, commercial activity and the telegraph."[10] As shown above, de los Reyes positions himself within the intellectual mission of archiving preindustrial cultures but does not wholly subscribe to the cultural obliteration that other ethnologists feared modern infrastructures would bring about. While discussing beings and venerated objects in Ilokano life, he recounts an animist moment on an 1880 trip aboard a ferry from the Ilocos coast to Manila Bay. At the behest of his *kailokuan* (Ilokano for "countrymen"),[11] they knelt in front of an oven-shaped rock formation (*peñasco en forma de horno*) in order to ensure good health once they disembarked in Manila. By depicting Ilokano devotion along the western coast of Luzon, de los Reyes gestures toward an Indigenous cultural matrix that adapts rather than disappears in the face of capitalist circulation.[12]

What became the published version of *El Folk-lore Filipino* focused almost exclusively on Ilokano folklore, with very brief sojourns into Zambales and Malabon, all along the western coast of Luzon.[13] In other words, the foundations for Isabelo de los Reyes's work encompassed his journeys across his

Amianan homeland as well as his observations from frequent trips aboard the Ilocos-Manila ferry.[14] Despite the geographical limitation of his work, he managed to become a celebrated native ethnologist in the European intellectual scene, particularly through the ways in which he problematized biological notions of race through folk culture. *El Folk-lore Filipino* gained international fame through its accolades at the Madrid Exposition in 1887, the same exposition wherein Igorot performers staged a village for Spanish audiences. On one hand, this exposition was an affront to the ilustrados' propaganda campaign to forge a respectable Philippines in the Spanish public. On the other hand, thanks to the insurgent ethnologies of Isabelo de los Reyes, Philippine social sciences became widely respected around the world.[15]

From his nineteenth-century social scientific works, de los Reyes's influence led to a deeper ethnological engagement with Luzon's far north. On one hand, ethnology served to extract human resources from the Cordilleras during the American occupation. On the other hand, the Amianan's visibility could also challenge the Tagalization of Philippine nation building. In a letter to Ferdinand Blumentritt, José Rizal grumbled that the rise of Ilokano folklore, among both native folklorists and the popular European readership, began to skew the racial formation of the Filipino northward. Rizal, like early twentieth-century opponents of Igorot shows, feared the preponderance of Northern Luzon in the making of a modern Filipino.[16]

Upon his return to Manila under American rule, Isabelo de los Reyes turned from recording folklore to producing it. He founded the Iglesia Filipina Independiente with the dissident secular priest Gregorio Aglipay and wrote prolifically on Ilokano moral philosophy and Indigenous Christian Protestantism. Furthermore, de los Reyes organized some of the first labor movements in the Philippines among fellow printers. Having been radicalized during his exile in Spain, he brought back to the Philippines rich source material for fledgling labor movements, such as those of Karl Marx and Mikhail Bakunin as well as the Italian anarchist organizer Errico Malatesta.[17]

The Amianan intellectual diaspora did not end with de los Reyes's nineteenth-century sojourns to Manila and Spain. Carlos Bulosan, an Ilokano from Pangasinan, saw power in the insurgent potential of ethnology, working it into his prolific career as a poet and fiction writer in the American West.

"Maybe One Day You Will See My Igorot Friends"

In chapter 6, a study of narrative and informal knowledge among manongs in the American West, we considered Carlos Bulosan's position as an oral historian—or, as Dorothy Cordova loved to emphasize, a "good listener"—of the early migrants. But those accumulated stories had to be rearticulated, and indeed Bulosan produced a large corpus of multigenre texts from which we remember him as a foundational Filipino American writer-activist. In 1972, E. San Juan, one of the earliest literary scholars of Bulosan, declared, "It is my conviction that Bulosan in the years to come will be justly recognized as the first Filipino writer in English who, in the period of transition from feudal-bourgeois to proletarian ideology, spearheaded the vanguard of the revolutionary working-class in its struggle against colonialism and exploitation."[18] Noting Bulosan's autobiographical statements throughout his life, San Juan traced the corpus to its roots in "the radical peasantry by indicting those obsolete, repressive institutions which blighted his childhood."[19] Rightfully identifying the entangled imperialisms of a Manila elite and the United States on the masses of the archipelago, San Juan nonetheless glides over the particular conditions pertinent to Bulosan's Ilokano family in the province of Pangasinan.

To understand Bulosan the writer-activist, I suggest that we must understand Bulosan the diasporic Ilokano. Bulosan's Ilokano Weltanschauung accounts for the literary archives he produced throughout his lifetime. San Juan centered the author's peasant heritage in his poetics, tracing the cultivation of a rural class struggle from the Philippines to the United States.[20] Intellectual historian Augusto Espiritu expands our understandings of the Bulosan corpus by arguing that Bulosan's modes of adaptation and narrative collection stem from his attempts to translate lowland Philippine oral traditions into English literature. However, both scholars begin from Bulosan's arrival in the United States or having already presupposed a sort of Filipino rural consciousness, despite the author's nonmetropolitan status.[21]

Most recently, scholars have noted the centrality of colonial industrial regimes in Bulosan's writing. Bulosan's diasporic storytelling, as theorist Sarita Echavez See argues, "return[s] to and transform[s] anticapitalist traditions of reciprocity, mutuality, and obligation." From his writing, we might glean the possibility of "an alternative economy of anti-accumulation."[22] See's subjects, read through Bulosan's short stories, account for the financially and linguistically illiterate as the central figures of anticolonial education. Like Isabelo de los Reyes, Bulosan imagined a sort of folk encapsulated through the seemingly aimless wandering of migrant workers. Allos, the protagonist of *America Is in the Heart*, valorizes the organic knowledge of his *tatang* (Ilokano for "father"): "Illiterate as he was, my father had an instinct for the truth. It was in this in-born quality, *common among peasants*, that had kept him going in a country rapidly changing to new conditions and ideals."[23] In this way, just as Isabelo de los Reyes constructed an Amianan-centered scholarly Philippine folklore in the late nineteenth century, Carlos Bulosan did so through folk narrative and poetics.

This reading of Bulosan's *America Is in the Heart* (1946) demonstrates the presence of the Amianan in his writing. Building from Espiritu's and See's readings, I suggest that Bulosan adapted Philippine racializations through insurgent ethnologies, taking on various aspects of American colonial and metropolitan visions of Igorots and subverting them. To demonstrate this, I follow depictions of Cordilleran peoples in some of his works.

The novel's first mention of the Igorots comes in part one, at a moment between Allos and his tatang, the latter teaching the former about foraging and natural abundance. The tatang and *anak* (Ilokano for "child") swim in a stony-bottomed river in the Pangasinan village of Mangusmana. On the way to making camp, the tatang picks some wild bamboo to stuff with shrimp and wrap with banana leaves over a fire:

> "This is called *doayen*, son," said my father, pushing the burning coals over the [bamboo] tubes. "It is more delicious than the wild boar."
>
> "How did you learn to make it, Father?" I asked.
>
> "From the Igorots in the mountains of Baguio," he said. "I lived with them when the revolution was broken in southern Luzon. I fought with them, and we were called guerillas. Someday you will understand, and maybe when you grow up you will see my Igorot friends."[24]

The revolution places this story in the nationalist periodization of the Philippines but traces the continuity of life at the margins under American rule and Southern Luzon political might. After the revolution, the tatang retreated into the mountains with the Igorots for refuge, invited to join in a long-standing Cordilleran practice of wartime safety. Doayen, then, comes out of the highlands knowledge passed onto a lowland comrade. Passing the culinary knowledge onto his anak, the tatang also transmits inter-Indigenous kinship against a dominant Manila-centered imperial rule.

Manila becomes a distant abstraction as life continues in the impoverished woodlands of Pangasinan. Once back in the family property, tenderly caressing the plants of his upbringing, Allos's tatang tells his anak that they lost the land to a man in Manila whose emissary—"a strange man [who] appeared from nowhere"—arrived to claim the property.[25] In these passages, Northern Luzon highlights an intimate relationship with the landscape as well as an intertribal camaraderie between the Ilokano and the Igorot, facilitated through highland and lowland solidarity. Manila, on the other hand, is the space of capitalist abstraction and of faceless proprietors who claim parcels of flat land without the native ethic for appreciating natural life.

Indeed, Allos does not meet his father's Igorot friends but learns firsthand of the historical ties between the lowlands and the highlands in an intimate economic space: the village market. Allos remarks that Igorots "come down from the mountains to trade with the lowlanders . . . [walking] among the people in their G-strings with their poisoned arrows and dogs."[26] Noting that Igorots "come down" implies that they did so on a regular basis—once a year—and this lowland-highland exchange forms the fabric of everyday life by the Amianan slopes. Like ethnological remarks on Igorot racial types, Allos fixates on their warlike "poisoned arrows" and implicit dog-eating temptations. However, unlike the American fixation on Igorot exotic dress, Allos continues that lowland people "did not even bother to look at [the Igorots] or at their dogs," suggesting the regularity of this visit. In Allos's profile of the market's visitors, he quickly moves past their appearance to emphasize their role in the fabric of lowlands Amianan life: "They were a peaceful people, bent only on hard work, and religious in their own way. They came to the lowlands villages once a year to trade their products, sometimes staying over for one season to help the farmers with their plowing and harvesting."[27] This passage emphasizes two counterclaims against prevailing stereotypes of the Igorot: peaceful rather than warlike and hardworking rather than indolent. Furthermore, while lowland peasants live predominantly as farmers, Allos's remarks suggest an awareness for Igorot agricultural prowess in the Cordilleran valleys as well. The practice of *tagnawa* (Ilokano for "mutual work ethic"), by helping Ilokano lowlanders out with the farming season, also suggests both a highlands-lowlands moral economy and a possible counterclaim against the penal ethnologies deployed against the Igorot. In those off-seasons in the valleys, rather than "reverting" to indolence or savagery, an Igorot continuity of agricultural labor in the lowlands reveals a countereconomy predicated on mutual aid (tagnawa) for food and financial security.[28] While this depiction is a work of literary fiction rather than anthropology, it nonetheless represents a discursive mode of counterconduct against early twentieth-century racial stereotypes, especially in this Anglophone American novel for distribution in the United States.

In chapter 9, Bulosan subverts the ethnological gaze through its most prevalent technology: the camera. In Baguio, when an American tourist offers him ten centavos to strip naked for a camera, Allos remarks that he had "found a simple way to make a living. Whenever I saw a white person in the market with a camera, I made myself conspicuously ugly, hoping to earn ten centavos."[29] Indeed, Allos found a means to make income while subverting the ethnological gaze by working the Kodak Zone. But in the same passage, Allos recognizes the exploitative operations of white Americans' ethnological appetites. He notes that naked Igorot women and children and sometimes "the old men with G-strings" are the preferred subjects for the Kodak Zone's emissaries: "They were not interested in Christian Filipinos like me. They seemed to take a particular delight in photographing young Igorot girls with large breasts and robust mountain men whose genitals were nearly exposed, their G-strings bulging large and alive." Through the Kodak Zone, the narrative flattens and excises the intimacies between lowlands and highlands, reducing native peoples into visual stereotypes. Only in the company of a camera's gaze does Allos remark upon the Igorot in the ethnological mode. The Dean Worcester photographs haunt this passage, unsurprisingly so. Popular publications such as *National Geographic* reproduced these photographs for mass consumption. Through this passage, Bulosan highlights photography's role in colonial ethnology as well as the voracious American tourist market that fueled the visual production of savage images. He distinguishes himself as a "Christian Filipino," both words rarely deployed in part one's Amianan context. Veering away from the Christian Filipino, the American camera produces a colonial pornography, highlighted by the passage's emphasis on sexual girth: "young Igorot girls with large breasts" and men "whose genitals were nearly exposed, their G-strings bulging large and alive." In the Kodak Zone, Allos notes that the Christian Filipino was "not interesting" and could be made abstract and invisible; the non-Christian, on the other hand, was formed through their sexualized hypervisibility for popular American consumption.[30]

However, this ethnological excising does not last in Bulosan's narrative, as the Igorot of *America Is in the Heart* also appears at the moment of Allos's education. Allos had already been literate but learned of the power of language and reading through the labors of Dalmacio, an Igorot houseboy in Baguio who became his friend:

> "I will soon go to America," he said one day. "I am trying to learn English so that I will not get lost over there."
>
> "I am planning to go to America in two years," I said. "If I save enough passage money to take me there."
>
> "You don't need money," Dalmacio said. "You could work on the boat. But English is the best weapon. I will teach you if you will do some work for me now and then."

He put a book in my hand and stated reading aloud to me.

"Repeat after me," he said. "Don't swallow your words. Blow them out like the Americans."

I repeated after him, uttering strange words and thinking of America.

We were reading the story of a homely man named Abraham Lincoln.[31]

English as a weapon suggests the insurgency of language amid domestic spaces such as the American Baguio home as well as the American metropole. Insurgency, as opposed to revolution, seeks not to overthrow a power but rather subvert its hegemony through modes of counterconduct.[32] In this case, Dalmacio's insurgent language teaching cultivates sufficient language skills to draw enough of a road map in America ("so that I will not get lost") and navigate daily life in the colonial metropole. Dalmacio does this by reducing language to a set of imitable exercises. "Repeat after me," he commands. Reducing American English phonetics to their bare physical forms ("blow them out"), he becomes the conduit for a didactic mimicry of American English speaking but also a mockery of linguistic prestige.[33] As a result, I conjecture that Allos cultivates the American aspiration after consonants such as "p" and "k" as opposed to neutralizing them (swallowing them) through Philippine phonemes. As a colonial native from the Philippines, Allos learns from his Igorot friend the insurgent act of code switching.

Rather than the Thomasite (white American teachers in the early twentieth century Philippines), the Igorot becomes the figure of insurgent education. For a simple barter of labor time ("if you will do some work for me now and then"), Dalmacio begins to teach Allos the art of American elocution while providing clues as to the more subversive aspects of American historical narrative:

"Who *is* this Abraham Lincoln?" I asked Dalmacio.

"He was a poor boy who became a president of the United States," he said. "He was born in a log cabin and walked miles and miles to borrow a book so that he would know more about his country."

A poor boy who became a president of the United States! Deep down in me something was touched, was springing out, demanding to be born, to be given a name. I was fascinated by the story of this boy who was born in a log cabin and became a president of the United States.[34]

The (heavily reduced) story of Lincoln serves as a touchstone for Allos as a means of imagining the United States in terms of possibility. Allos approaches his employer, Mary Strandon, who tells him briefly about American slavery and emancipation. Upon learning of Allos's interest, Mary Strandon gives Allos access to several history books in her study, then connects him to a job opportunity in the local library. The white woman becomes the first librarian in the labor of Allos's education. Behind Allos's historical curiosity—particularly a class-conscious one focusing on the poverty of Lincoln—is the catalyst of Dalmacio's pedagogy: to see within the tools of the colonial master the possibilities of subversion. As an English-speaking migrant worker, Allos takes this ethic across the Pacific.

Once abroad, Allos does not excise the Amianan from how he reckons with the continent. He makes sense of the landscapes of the American West precisely through the mountains and, in particular, from his relationship to the American colonial hill city in the Cordilleras. The first mention of the Trans-Mississippi West, "Spencer, Iowa," comes from Mary Strandon herself, who claims "that the trees there were as luxuriant as in Baguio."[35] Years later, escaping from being a witness to a murder in San Luis Obispo, Allos as a young adult arrives in New Mexico from Los Angeles. Renting a hotel room, he stares outside of the window: "The primitive beauty of Santa Fe reminded me of the calm and isolation of Baguio, the mountain city in Luzon where I had worked for Miss Mary Strandon. Morning was like a rose cupping its trembling dews, shattering and delicate, small but potent with miracles. But the nights were tranquil with millions of stars."[36] The Amianan appears as palimpsests in Allos's encounters with the American continental landscape. This passage suggests the centrality of the "mountains of Baguio" (as Allos's tatang called it in part one) to the making of a Filipino American transpacific consciousness. As historian Rebecca Tinio McKenna elucidates, Baguio was central to the "architecture" of American imperialism, through which built environment and capitalist market subjectivities dialectically shaped the nature of colonial rule in the archipelago.[37] Bulosan depicts the visual imaginary of empire in the reverse direction by means of an Amianan migrant carrying Baguio to the United States. Furthermore, by mentioning the overlap of the Cordilleras and Tewa land, this passage attests to the still ambiguous status of the American West as a contiguous "metropolitan" space. As "primitive" (rather than civilized urban) beauty in the New Mexico region, this passage attests to the ongoing settler colonialism in the continent even while the United States expanded overseas into the Philippines.[38]

An increasingly internationalist disposition marks the Allos in parts three and four of *America Is in the Heart*. After wandering in part one and then becoming involved in communist and labor union politics through the 1930s, Allos takes on a Westernized name: Carlos. Under this name, he joins the manong generation as a field hand, the diasporic dandies engaging in petty crime in Chinatowns, and worker unions in the fever of the Popular Front. Allos/Carlos cites friends who travel to the Soviet Union to learn about communism, and watches closely as the Spanish Civil War implodes and General Francisco Franco's fascist regime seizes the state.

The internationalism of Allos/Carlos inevitably brings him back to the Philippines in homely ways. At a particular point of despair, he opts to read fairy tales in order to immerse himself in happier activities. He peruses "*Arabian Nights,* Grimm's *Fairy Tales,* Andersen's *Tales,* Aesop's *Fables,* Lewis Carroll's *Alice in Wonderland.*" Crossing the core tales of different cultures across history, Allos/Carlos remarks on the resonances that return him not just to the archipelago but also to the Amianan: "These books stimulated me to go back to the folklore of my own country. I discovered with amazement that Philippine folklore was uncollected, that native writers had not assimilated it into their writings. This discovery gave me an impetus to study the common roots of our folklore, and upon finding it in the tales and legends of the pagan Igorots in the mountains of Luzon, near my native province, I blazed with delight at this new treasure. Now I must live and integrate Philippine folklore in our struggle for liberty!"[39] In reality, Philippine folklore had been—or at least had begun to be—systematically collected decades prior by Bulosan's Ilokano intellectual forebear. Whether or not Bulosan himself was aware of the work of Isabelo de los Reyes, he nonetheless imbues within Allos/Carlos the ethic of de los Reyes's folklore project. Indeed, Allos/Carlos' move to nationalize Philippine folklore in the diasporic imagination is to produce a racial archive.

Insidiously, folklore leads Allos/Carlos to not merely preserve the local cultures but also accumulate "pagan" stories into imagining a diasporic vision of being Filipino in America. Allos/Carlos cultivated a sense of what the Filipino was, particularly through the hypermobile lifestyle he leads in part two. Through those inland migrations in the circulatory infrastructures of the American West, he connects with workers from other Philippine regions (such as a fictional Frank Mancao), participating in collective activities in cities. The "our" register lets slip who Allos/Carlos's (and perhaps Bulosan's) intended audience could be. On one hand, Allos/Carlos could be speaking to a wider international audience to connect Philippine folklore with global stories. On the other hand, he might be addressing a Filipino diasporic community, constituting itself through the compilation and formation of racial archives. The collection of folklore, then, serves as a means to construct the Filipino, with the central story—"the mainsprings of our history"—being the nationalist martyr José Rizal.[40] This Philippine folklore is not a cross-ethnic democratizing one; Allos/Carlos opts instead to subsume Indigenous stories into a nationalized set of "Filipino heroes."

Allos/Carlos never does shed Northern Luzon completely. But until the end, there remains a battle between his regional roots and his commitment to American liberalism. By the end of part three, when he (like the novel's author) is diagnosed with tuberculosis, his brother Macario calls him by his native name for the first time in years. In using the native Ilokano name, Allos interprets Macario's invocation as a call to be the native colonized writer in America and commits to a transpacific writerly practice: "I knew that [Macario] would help me live for a while so that I could write about our anguish and our hopes for a better America."[41] The appropriation of a diasporic Filipinoness into the mission of improving America may be the limits of the insurgent ethnologies of *America Is in the Heart*. Once the Filipino community is formed in the American diaspora, as immigrant workers for the United States rather as transpacific colonial subjects, Philippine folklore becomes a means for primitive accumulation toward a singular "our history" rather than diverse and equal. This liberal turn by the end of the novel can be evidenced by the narrator's tenacious faith in America "and to become a part of her great tradition, and to contribute something toward her final fulfillment."[42] The call to be subsumed into the developmental teleology of "making America" coconstitutes a uniform and hegemonic Filipino. Perhaps a liberal commitment to America, or Filipino America, is the counterinsurgency to Bulosan's insurgent ethnologies.

Conclusion

A Tale of Two Mountains

Hegel remarks somewhere that all great world-historical facts and
personages appear, so to speak, twice. He forgot to add: the first time
as tragedy, the second time as farce.

—Karl Marx, *The Eighteenth Brumaire of Louis Bonaparte*, 1852

Few countries give the observer a deeper feeling of historical vertigo
than the Philippines.

—Benedict Anderson, "The First Filipino," 1997

During Holy Week in March 1972, an Ilokano political leader ascended the
Gran Cordillera *bundok* to a Jesuit retreat in the city of Baguio. In his diaries,
he wrote of his attempted communications with God to mull over the possibility of declaring martial law. He had already served two terms as president,
and the Philippine Constitution had forbidden reelection for a third term
and beyond. He feared that his stronghold over Philippine politics and the
plunder that his family had illegally amassed over decades were in danger
from the specter of communist masses threatening to overthrow him. Enrap-
tured by his reflections in his retreat, he jotted down what he believed to be a
message from God: "'This is your principal mission in life—save the country
again from the Maoists, the anarchists and the radicals.' This is the message
that I deduce from the visions that I see asleep and awake. 'Subordinate
everything to this,' God seems to be saying to me. 'And you are the only person who can do it,' He says. 'Nobody else can. So do not miss the opportunity
given you.'"[1] This Ilokano was the Philippine dictator Ferdinand Marcos. A
few months after this Cordillera sojourn, Marcos declared martial law across
the country. Overnight, his regime exercised complete control over Philippine politics and society, eliminating the most vocal forces of resistance that
had plagued his first two terms: college students, rival politicians, and rural
insurgents. Under martial law, the Philippine government suspended habeas
corpus, seized control over all media, and arrested all individuals and groups
deemed oppositional to direct rule. At the time, Marcos's declaration of martial law garnered popular support for its supposed introduction of social order for the sake of economic progress and swift development.

FIGURE C.1   The bust of Ferdinand Marcos in Pugo, La Union, before its bombing in 1989.

FIGURE C.2   Mount Rushmore in South Dakota, United States.

While Marcos's regime amounted to unprecedented state control over the archipelago, the techniques of conquest and consent actually drew upon tactics as old as colonialism in the Philippines itself. His supposed vision from God echoes the twin forces of Christianity and colonial rule that has along marked state politics in the Philippines. In particular, by claiming that he had direct contact with God, Ferdinand Marcos claimed complete sovereignty over the archipelago. Simultaneously, his claim to divine intervention outlined the boogeymen of his new regime: the "Maoists, the anarchists and the radicals."

By declaring the non-Christianized and rural insurgent Amianan as uniquely recalcitrant, the regime brought particularly aggressive modes of domination to Northern Luzon and the Cordilleras as well as Mindanao to the south. In the mountain ranges of Luzon, martial law brought about swift conquest, the likes of which could only have been dreamed of by the colonial governments before independence. Within a few months after declaring martial law, the government instated a full ban on headhunting and laid siege to large swaths of Cordillera land for the purposes of transportation, mining, and vanity projects.[2]

One such vanity project was the proposed 888-acre Marcos Park, stolen from 81 families of the Ibaloi tribe. The Marcos government claimed that it had fairly purchased the land, but Ibaloi leaders argued that soldiers had instead forced them to sell their land for far below market rate. In the clearing left by this martial law version of *reducción*, Marcos commissioned a new park, which he named after himself. On the nearby slope of Mt. Shontoug within the park, in the likeness of the famed Mount Rushmore in the United States, he had a bust of his face constructed out of concrete. The bust was to be made visible to mountain travelers journeying up the highways into Baguio, which were finally constructed and fortified under the Marcos regime.[3]

Upon the bust's construction and in the years that followed, media commentators remarked on the similarities of this Philippine Ozymandian monument to the famed Mount Rushmore in South Dakota across the Pacific.[4] But the similarities between Marcos Park and Mount Rushmore, I suggest, goes beyond a clear inspiration of the latter for the construction and celebration of the former. Rather, both figures are aesthetic claims to sovereignty over sites of Indigenous insurgency, thus naturalizing settler colonialism over stolen land. Both the United States and the Philippines built these busts on stolen land, the former near the sites of its own Indian Wars. The Mount Rushmore monument was built it just one hundred miles northwest of Wounded Knee Creek (Lakota, Čhaŋkpé Ópi Wakpála), the site of the 1890 massacre of hundreds of Lakotas at the hands of the US military. Likewise, the Marcos bust was built atop the Cordilleras where the colonial and postcolonial states faced formidable resistance. Long outside the absolute purview of the Philippine state, the Cordilleras finally came into control of the state under martial law and its magnification of counterinsurgency.

That the two monuments bring together the Indian Wars in the United States and the Philippine-American War (as well as the invasions in the Cordilleras) is no coincidence. As historians of US imperialism have shown, the Indian Wars did not end before imperial conquest left the continent's shores. The 7th Cavalry of the US Army, which massacred the Lakotas at Wounded Knee, finds its roots in the Battle of the Little Bighorn, otherwise known as Custer's Last Stand. Decades later the 7th Cavalry fought in the Philippine-American War, continuing its massacres of colonial peoples in Luzon and other islands. The 7th Cavalry would fight in the major imperial wars of the twentieth century, including the Pacific front in World War II, the Korean and Vietnam Wars, Operation Desert Storm in 1991, and George W. Bush's invasions of Iraq.[5] Through public commemorations, medals of honor, and popular valorization, the memory of the 7th Cavalry allowed the United States to absolve itself of its historical and contemporary crimes against humanity. To this day, the Wounded Knee Massacre is still referred to as the Battle of Wounded Knee, and Mount Rushmore continues to attract tourists in droves.[6]

This same historical disavowal can also be said of the Philippines, and indeed, the two cultures of commemoration across the Pacific are deeply entangled. In Philippine historiography, the American colonial occupation and the Philippine-American War are contained as a "period" of national history rather than as an enmeshment of various imperialist aggressions to establish domination over supposed colonial "frontiers." Colonialism and warfare are treated within discrete historical periodizations, as building blocks toward the emergence of a Philippine postcolonial modernity.[7] Likewise, Marcos, as a supposed World War II hero against the Japanese occupation of the Philippines (though this has been proven to be false), touted around these martial credentials as cultural capital to propel his presidency forward into its martial law years. Presenting himself and his regime as a national progression of Philippine history, Ferdinand Marcos simultaneously disavowed and reified the persistent influence of the myriad imperial histories that converge upon the Philippines as a whole and upon Luzon and its landscapes in particular. This study thus supplements the scholarship of US historians who trace settler colonial warfare in American imperial spaces by showing the violent continuities between imperial powers in a colonial hinterland. By doing so, we might denationalize the processes of imperial conquest, such as race and capitalism, and certainly these two public monuments, and suture together their inherent transnational relationships.

Another thread tethers together these two sites. As this study has shown, imperial cultural productions, particularly those that have been nationalized as American racial formations or "ethnicity," find their roots in the long historical processes of capitalism and its logics of dispossession. Whereas I focused on racial economies of the colonial archives, from ephemeral and visual media to the myriad acts of archiving, we can find these phenomena in contemporary contexts and inscribed into the extractive industrial landscape. The smooth flow of capitalism in the continental United States as well as in the Philippines was founded upon the dispossession of native peoples and the disavowal of this dispossession through a nation-state's claims to sovereignty and right to extract resources from that land. In the vicinity of Mount Rushmore and the Marcos bust, the Philippines, the United States, Canada, and other countries have built infrastructures for mining, petroleum, and natural gas extraction. The Benguet Mines in the Philippines and other quarries employ both lowland and highland native workers alike, all of whom have lost access to clean water, arable land, and the slopes and valleys of their home. In 2010 through North and South Dakota all the way up to Alberta and Saskatchewan, the North American energy company TC Energy Corporation commissioned the construction of the binational Keystone Pipeline System. A related project, the Coastal GasLink Pipeline, was proposed to cross the British Columbia mountains and transport crude oil to the West Coast. In both contexts across the Pacific, states declare Indigenous lives as disposable, as they are in the way of these projects. In the Philippines, Canada, and the United States, the respective states continue to send militarized police and death squads against Indigenous peoples and allies standing in protest of these extractive regimes. As with the mountain roads and highways in Luzon, these contemporary petroleum pipeline "highways" organize native life around them as expendable *homo sacer* to the sovereignty of transnational capitalism and therefore subject to death.[8]

Thus, the two mountain monuments suggest not only magnified state rule in these regions but also the entry of exploited labor power to further the projects of industrialization in these frontiers. In both cases, this labor power is sustained by the circulation of dispossessed subjects from the Philippine lowlands as agricultural and industrial workers in settler colonial regimes. West of the Mississippi River and in Hawaiʻi, colonial labor that came to be known as "Filipino" sustained the various industries of American capitalism, from sugar and fruit to mining and railroads. The Filipino worker coalesced— and indeed continues to be reimagined—vis-à-vis the industries of empire.

The bust of Ferdinand Marcos and the four presidential busts on Mount Rushmore both aesthetically assert state sovereignty over stolen land. Philippine and American subjects come to rally around these public monuments as national symbols or, at the very least, as sites of tourism and leisure. The native peoples—the Ibalois and Lakotas, respectively—from whom this land was stolen to build these vanity projects are deemed disposable to the mutual projects of "Filipino" and "American" national identity formation. As a result, "American" and "Philippine" identity politics and the racial economies behind their formations also emerge within the maelstrom of these coeval colonialisms across the Pacific.

WHILE I HAVE DEMONSTRATED the radical possibilities of a regional and native history of Filipino diaspora, a vernacular history of the nation and diaspora is not in itself radical. As the history of Marcos demonstrates, regional specificity—within the rubrics of empire and nation-state—can and has been deployed for colonial ends. In the Philippine context, political historian Megan C. Thomas has argued that the specificity of folk and region through ethnology has been deployed by native intellectuals to articulate different forms of colonial subjectivity and alternatives to cosmopolitan Philippine nationalism.[9] However, as cultural theorist Neferti X. Tadiar has argued, racialization without a radical critique of imperialism renders what theorist Jodi Melamed calls "racial liberalism."[10] In other words, with race simply as culture and with racial inequality as a matter of cultural difference, as that which has structured discourses of official diversity and multiculturalism in the United States and the Philippines alike after World War II, the racializations "associated with slavery and colonialism" has been characterized as "(ultimately) disappearing."[11] Racialization under empire does not a radical subject make. The transhistorical creation of the Filipino subject is thus a matter of who counts as a subject and who is disposable as an impediment to economic, national, and racial progress.

Unlike the *hermanos de los selváticos* before him, Isabelo de los Reyes and Carlos Bulosan, Ferdinand Marcos seized control over the postcolonial state. As historian Vicente Rafael notes, despite Ferdinand Marcos's Ilokano background, he was the first president to deliver his inaugural address in Tagalog and gave subsequent speeches in English. Thus, his political rhetoric reified linguistic hierarchies of the Philippine nation-state even as he deployed Tagalog to communicate to the imagined (Tagalicized) "masses."[12] Nonetheless, the Marcoses leaned into their regional non-Manila origins to acquire cult following in the Amianan and its diasporas, into Hawai'i and North America. This is evident in the tenacity of pro-Marcos communities all over the world, with strongholds among Ilokano diasporic communities such as Honolulu, and even in Ilokano cultural studies curricula and scholarship. In doing so, the Marcoses succeeded in capitalizing on the racial transits of plantation capitalism and the Filipino diaspora.[13]

These racial transits persist in the twenty-first century. In 2017 as a Fulbright Scholar to the University of Hawaiʻi, I attended a lecture at the East-West Center delivered by Philippine historian Ambeth Ocampo on the Ferdinand Marcos diaries. These documents have not yet been released to the public but are held by the Presidential Commission on Good Government. In preparation for full publication, Ocampo had been annotating the text with supplementary sources and delivered a lecture to promote the forthcoming work. The room was packed: scholars and nonacademic communities alike attended the lecture. Ocampo shared some excerpts from the diaries, including the Baguio entry that opened this conclusion. In Ocampo's lecture, he laid out his provisional argument about the religious dimensions of declaring martial law, evidenced by Marcos's extended period of retreat in a Cordillera monastery.

During the question-and-answer period, an elderly woman who claimed to be Marcos's nurse stood up. Despite the textual evidence laid out, she turned to the audience and pleaded for understanding and innocence: "Even when we got airlifted out of Malacañang [Palace], we did not know where we were going! . . . Mr. Ocampo, if you say you are a historian, then you have a responsibility to show the truth." Shortly thereafter, a middle-aged man stood up to address the speaker. "Mr. Ocampo," the man began, "I am from the North. You are Kapampangan, from the South. Do you support Marcos?" Ocampo turned to him and said, "Sir, I do not." The man turned away and sat down smugly. The rest of the question-and-answer period alternated between such personal moments of confrontation and scholarly questions, with the former drowning out the latter.

The persistence of historical revisionism among global Ilokano communities, such as the one in Hawaiʻi, points to the abuses of regionalism in the Filipino diaspora. In this way, Marcos embodies the lowlands *indio* completely subsumed by the nation-state, military imperialism, and global capitalism. His genealogy is that of the indio recruited by the Spanish and American empires into the polo to enforce Catholic rule into the highland frontiers or the landowning *principalías* of the Spanish Philippines who acquired dynastic status and capital during the American and postwar periods as the country's ruling caciques. But in Ferdinand and Imelda Marcos's ability to perform national and economic development as well as capitalize on the media technologies of the mid to late twentieth century, they could obfuscate their plunder and capitalize on their clout as regional political leaders and charismatic figureheads of the nation. As the history and contemporary legacy of the Marcos regime demonstrates, neither regionalism nor vernacular culture equate to inherently radical politics. As the specter of insurgency and anarchy became that of an imagined communist threat, the Philippine state doubled down on counterinsurgency in the hinterlands and Cold War modernization. Obscuring class relations of land and labor in favor of a pan-regional nationalist culture laid the grounds for the Marcoses to seize power and for the manifestations of *caciquismo* that persist today.[14]

Throughout this book, I have emphasized the importance of Indigenous particularity and vernacular epistemologies in the study of the Philippines and its global diasporas. But the nation-state form and its colonizing technologies can also overrun the possibilities afforded with diasporic regionalism. With the help of the United States and Filipino diasporas in America, the Marcoses maintained their stronghold over not only Philippine politics and economy but also the usurpation of the Marcoses in the Filipino popular imagination. As recently as 2019, films about the Marcoses treat them as ethnographic and filmic curiosities and only belatedly expose the human rights abuses of the regime, thus serving the purpose of stoking nostalgia for martial law.[15] The nostalgia for the glory days of Marcos boiled over into the post–People Power era, into the twenty-first century. In 2016, Filipinos elected Rodrigo Duterte, another non-Manileño elite, to the presidency. Hailing from the regions of southern Leyte and Davao (in Mindanao), Duterte campaigned on his thirty-year punitive style of mayoral governance to be brought the archipelago as a whole, converting the country into a militarized police state for the sake of economic redevelopment and disciplinary order. Having seized control of Davao in 1988, Duterte became infamous for his collaboration with the vigilante Davao Death Squad. While national martial law effectively ended with the People Power Revolution, it continued (and indeed began long before Marcos) in supposedly "insurgent" places such as Mindanao.[16] Naturally, then, during the elections Duterte chose a familiar running mate from the opposite end of the archipelago, Ferdinand "Bongbong" Marcos Jr.

And six years later in 2022, with Sara Duterte (the daughter of the elder statesman) as his running mate, Bongbong Marcos was elected as the president of the Philippines.

DESPITE THEIR INHERENT PITFALLS, writing histories of the Philippines and Filipino diaspora from the bundok allows us to glean other possibilities of insurgency and radical possibility. That is, a native and regional critique that refuses the techniques of the nation-state offers possibilities beyond the Filipinization and Americanization of social justice. Examples of such a critique can be found by bringing our focus back to the two mountains under investigation. Both monuments have been subjected to iconoclasm, from graffiti and satire to bombing and militant occupation. Visual culture scholar W. J. T. Mitchell has argued that "iconoclasm is more than just the destruction of images; it is a 'creative destruction,' in which a secondary image of defacement or annihilation is created at the same moment that the 'target' image is attacked."[17] That is, the destruction of an icon does not eliminate the image but instead creates the conditions for its multiplication through the creation of secondary images of the target of iconoclasm. Thus, defacing the Marcos bust and Mount Rushmore do not only create an image of the defilement but also circulate the afterimage of the original.

However, both monuments have also been targets of Indigenous iconoclasm markedly different from other forms, namely in the ways that they center Indigenous resurgence and the reclamation of stolen land from settler states. Recognizing that Mount Rushmore and the bust of Ferdinand Marcos are themselves defacements of sacred mountains, I suggest that the following modes of iconoclastic activism do not simply lay the ground for replicating the images of their respective public monuments. Instead, they seek to propagate the image of Indigenous land and lifeways by gesturing toward the illegitimacy of the settler state itself. This image is that of a decolonial one of land before—and against—the empty landscapes of terra nullius.[18] Terra nullius, as itself an aesthetic claim of empire, depicts the frontier as an empty and conquerable space, devoid of Indigenous life and economy. As a Spanish and American colony and as a semi-independent postcolonial nation, the Philippines lays claim to the valleys and mountain slopes of highland peoples. The Philippine nation-state as well as a cosmopolitan and transnational Filipino identity alike claims possession over Ibaloi land and other highland Cordillera territories. Indigenous interventions at colonial monuments such as the one at Marcos Park thus seek to reassert sovereignty by highlighting their experience with the moment of primitive accumulation: land theft and colonial dispossession.

Figure 8.3 is a popular image of iconoclastic resistance against Marcos. The photograph shows demonstrators protesting the vice presidency bid of Bongbong Marcos in the 2016 elections. Demonstrators have sprawled signs over the scaffolding of the bust and hold up a banner that reads "NEVER AGAIN to Martial Law! NO To Bong²/BBMII!" (Bongbong/Ferdinand Marcos II). This image and the political intervention it depicts targets the Marcoses' theft of the national economy and the reinstitution of the oligarchy. The bust had been felled to its current state in 2002 by treasure hunters who suspected that the family had hidden treasure in the monument.[19]

FIGURE C.3 Protest against Bongbong Marcos organized by martial law–era victims of human rights abuses.

Since the overthrow of the Marcoses from Malacañang Palace, news reports began to report the extent to which the Marcoses plundered the Philippines to enrich their family wealth: Imelda Marcos's infamous shoe collection, foreign investments into real estate, rare works of art, and more.[20] Unlike an earlier explosion in 1989 by supposed leftist radicals that left the bust cracked and charred, this second and more powerful detonation points to an explicitly economic critique (and a sort of counterplunder) of the Marcoses' vanity. These photographs not only suggest action against the re-emergence of an infamous ruling family (and the violence of martial law) into national politics but also gesture to a critique against economic plunder and national ruination.

While the interventions above hinge on twin axes of social order and national economy, the countercritiques by the Marcoses are also able to use these same logics for their own ends. When the bust was bombed in 2002, Imelda Marcos mourned the desecration of her late husband's likeness: "When anything that symbolizes something positive, something beautiful, something right is destroyed, it is always very sad."[21] Her daughter, politician Imee Marcos, lamented the "breakdown of law and order in the Cordilleras and Northern Luzon and in many parts of the country."[22] Imelda and Imee as well as Bongbong's 2016 campaign hinged on a claim for the restoration of beauty and prosperity through the institution of brutal order. Like his father before him and like a presidential candidate in 2016 across the Pacific, Bongbong sought to make the Philippines great again. In particular, Imee's statement conceals within it a political unconscious of the long genealogy of insurgency in the Amianan, from early colonial rule through the nineteenth and twentieth centuries. In Imee's political imagination, the Northern Luzon hinterlands continue to be a state of exception, to be disciplined according to the martial logics of Marcosian rule. Martial law and national restoration, on both sides of the political spectrum, thus draw upon the nation-state's claim to land at its frontiers.

If nation and capital are at stake with these two instances of iconoclasm at the Marcos bust, none of them grapple with the original sin that the bust represents: the theft of Ibaloi homelands and sovereignty. On March 10, 1986, roughly two weeks after the People Power Revolution that overthrew Ferdinand Marcos from power, Ibaloi leaders gathered at the bust for a *cañao*. During the cañao, they slit the throat of a black pig and poured its drained blood on the bust. This event drew ample media attention to the issues of land theft, and the revolutionary government of Corazon Aquino pledged to return the 888 acres back to the Ibaloi tribe.[23] However, the bust remained on the mountain even after its first bombing by anarchists in 1989, and despite its second bombing thirteen years later, its scaffolding remains today.[24]

Unlike the anti-Marcos activists and the post-2002 ruins, few images exist of the 1986 cañao. According to the photographer Kim Komenich, the bottom of the frame of figure 8.3 depicts the preparations for the cañao, though they are drowned out by the flag bearers atop the bust.[25] However, at the time, the cañao took place with another incident fresh in the Cordilleran memory. Shortly after declaring martial law, Marcos commissioned the Chico River Dam Project to cut across Kalinga territory, without consultation from Indigenous leaders. By 1974, the National Power Corporation began to conduct surveys on Kalinga villages' property in order to build a World Bank–funded hydroelectric dam. This dam would have laid waste to the extensive rice terraces near the Chico River and the many *ilis* (villages) of the Kalinga and Bontoc peoples. Macli-ing Dulag, a Butbut Kalinga elder, spoke out publicly against the Marcos regime and the encroachment of the dam project. Joined by other Cordillera tribes in solidarity, Dulag spoke of the increasingly violent harassment of the martial law state against his people: "Such arrogance to say that you own the land when you are owned by it! How can you own that which outlives you? Only the people own the land because only the people live forever. To claim a place is the birthright of everyone. Even the lowly animals have their own place.... How much more when we talk of human beings?"[26] Here, Dulag makes visible a different ontology of the land by appealing to an anticapitalist vision of the commons. By positing the commons as the prevailing and primordial image defiled by conquest and landownership, Dulag evoked a refusal of capitalist and colonial state visions of landscape as that which can be beholden and owned. For the settler state to lay claim to the land, that landscape must be cleared for free use both physically and in the political imagination. That settler landscape was made mundane through the aesthetic, discursive, and political creation of Indigenous disposability, clearing the land for the smooth conquest of capital and empire.

These landscapes also facilitate the unabated transmission of ideologies, finance, commodities, and people; more accurately, they might be considered what media studies scholar Arjun Appadurai calls scapes of global cultural flow.[27] During the Marcos regime, as a resource hinterland beholden to the extractive regimes of 1970s neoliberal capitalism, these Northern Luzon scapes took (and continue to take) myriad forms. As mediascapes and ideoscapes, the land can be seized and deployed to reinforce the ideologies of Marcos-era nationalism and fascism; we see this enacted in the development of the Marcos bust. As technoscape, the Cordilleras could be seized for the development of infrastructure to extract and circulate resources. Whereas it had been tobacco in the nineteenth century and mining and tourism in the early twentieth century, the dam signified an emphasis toward the extraction of energy, or what environmental studies scholar Laurence Selina calls an energyscape.[28] As Dulag pleaded before his death, "Should the need for electric power be a reason for our death?"[29] Thus, by making Indigenous disposability—not to mention Indigenous resistance—visible in the Philippine and global imagination, Cordilleran activism against Marcos sheds light on the underlying slaughter behind the creation of late twentieth-century scapes in Northern Luzon.

For the state, Dulag was nonetheless disposable. On April 24, 1980, Marcos's soldiers assassinated him in his home. However, the activism of Macliing Dulag against the Chico Dam had given other Cordillera tribes, global Indigenous peoples, and allies around the world a figure around whom they could mobilize. The World Bank repealed funding and destabilized Marcosian narratives of progress under martial law, and the United Nations denounced the Marcos regime for its human rights abuses. While anti-Marcos activists in Manila and other Philippine nationalists seized upon Dulag as a martyr for the antimartial law cause, the work of Dulag and the Ibaloi exorcism six years after Dulag's assassination point to a critique beyond the imagined community of the Philippines. Specifically, these events provided a rubric of Indigenous activism against disposability in the late capitalist moment.[30]

Thus, the activism and memory of Dulag and the cañao of Ibaloi leaders at the Marcos bust reoriented the projects of economic development and public monuments as themselves defilements of a Cordillera commons under the stewardship of its Indigenous peoples. In this case, the target was not public artwork or nationalist iconography but rather the political aesthetics of the capitalist state itself: land theft for the purposes of building economies of extraction at the expense of Indigenous lives. This appeal to a commons provides insights into lowland Filipino solidarity with the highlands, overseas Filipino workers' solidarity with Indigenous peoples at their temporary places of work, and the Filipino diaspora with the Indigenous people upon whose stolen lands they have become settlers. As job creation continues to be used as a justification for Indigenous dispossession and extermination, a critique of capitalism behind the creation of Filipino identity and Philippine ethno-nationalism reveals the inequities rendered by those dispossessed into abstract labor (as globalized workers) and those now called Indigenous peoples. The mutual loss of land and sovereignty conditions the histories of the Filipino present.

WHO COUNTS AS A FILIPINO? I began this study from the outside of those *ilustrado* imaginaries in the nineteenth century who centered a Tagalog bourgeois world in their forging of a revolutionary ethno-nationalism. The rubrics for who would become a Filipino, I argued, could be traced from the bundok in the north. Native peoples' relationship to colonial industry determined the archiving practices to which they were subject, producing the visual and discursive rubrics from which Filipino America emerged in the early twentieth century. Writers, photographers, performers, and agricultural workers subject to these racializations responded in kind. Some, such as Felingao in the fairs and Francisco on 'Ōla'a, left traces of labor politics in the archival productions of the period. Others, such as Isabelo de los Reyes, produced their own. From these multimedia conflicts, different stakeholders imagined from a constellation of visions what a Filipino America could look like.

As this project followed, the Filipino was—and continues to be—a labored construct. Throughout Manila's history, the working-class Chinese became Filipino through their economic, cultural, and culinary contributions. In the

1970s, the *balikbayan* were made Filipino through their propensity to spend American dollars on tourist versions of the Philippines. Later still, the overseas Filipino worker became Filipino through the commodification of that very exile and through the ruling class's desire for the overseas worker's votership.[31]

But not everyone continues to identify as Filipino today. One only needs to listen to the Kalinga *mambabatok* Whang-Od, who condemns the invasions of the Japanese and Filipino armies in the same breath.[32] We hear it in the Lumad anti-imperial activisms in the twenty-first century against the resource extraction regimes of Barrick Gold, from which the supposedly liberal University of Toronto, my alma mater and settler dwelling, draws its capital.[33] Northern Luzon remains a resource hinterland, with its mountains under illegal occupation by a militarized Philippine government. The cultural resources of Northern Luzon also season cosmopolitan Philippine and Filipino diasporic culture with indigenized spice as the nation-state continues to poison the land and water of *katutubo* and *katawhang lumad* all over the archipelago.

To ask who counts as a Filipino, at any given point in time, must itself be an insurgent ethnology. This brings the nation-state and its imperial afterlives of "ethnicity" in North America under constant scrutiny. The question of who counts as a Filipino challenges us to step beyond neoliberal notions of diversity by holding Filipino histories accountable to their belabored roots: the irreducible kinships that empire cannot erase.

Notes

Prologue

1. Chandlee, *De Los Reyes*; and Anderson, *Under Three Flags*.

2. Bulosan, *America Is in the Heart*, 26.

3. San Juan, *Carlos Bulosan and the Imagination of the Class Struggle*; and Espiritu, *Five Faces of Exile*.

4. English: "The fraternity between Ilocanos and Igorots."

5. Vergara, *Displaying Filipinos*; Rafael, *White Love and Other Events in Filipino History*; and Kramer, *The Blood of Government*.

6. Kramer, *The Blood of Government*.

7. Ileto, *Pasyon and Revolution*; Takaki, *Strangers from a Different Shore*; Vergara, *Displaying Filipinos*; Anderson, *The Spectre of Comparisons*; Fujita-Rony, *American Workers, Colonial Power*; Kramer, *The Blood of Government*; Jung, *Reworking Race*; Chang, *Pacific Connections*; and Labrador, *Building Filipino Hawai'i*.

8. Vergara, *Displaying Filipinos*; Hoganson, *Fighting for American Manhood*; Kaplan, *The Anarchy of Empire in the Making of U.S. Culture*; Kramer, *The Blood of Government*; Brody, *Visualizing American Empire*; Baldoz, *The Third Asiatic Invasion*; Rice, *Dean Worcester's Fantasy Islands*; and McKenna, *American Imperial Pastoral*.

9. Espiritu, *Five Faces of Exile*; Anderson, *The Spectre of Comparisons*; Kramer, *The Blood of Government*; Bender, *American Abyss*; Rice, *Dean Worcester's Fantasy Islands*; and McKenna, *American Imperial Pastoral*.

Introduction

1. Rafael, *The Promise of the Foreign*; and Blanco, *Frontier Constitutions*.

2. Thomas, *Orientalists, Propagandists, and Ilustrados*.

3. In her study of Philippine historical experience, cultural theorist Neferti X. M. Tadiar attempts to privilege those discarded by elite nationalist histories. Whereas she studies these disposed historical experiences through the recovery of subaltern literature, I further locate them latently within the myriad productions of colonial and diasporic archives. See Tadiar, *Things Fall Away*.

4. In the canon of United States history, perhaps the most relevant predecessor to this work is Paul Kramer's magisterial study, *The Blood of Government*. Also, many thanks to Joan Flores-Villalobos, Joy Sales, Christine Noelle Peralta, Ashanti Shih, Nayan Shah, and Takashi Fujitani for this framing.

5. Kramer acknowledges this limitation in an early version of his work, a 1999 article in the *Radical History Review* in which he footnotes the necessity for a "subaltern history" of the World's Fairs, as opposed to his own focus on administrators and transnational stakeholders. See Kramer, "Making Concessions."

6. Besides Kramer, other scholars who fall under these frameworks include Anderson, *Colonial Pathologies*; McCoy, *Policing America's Empire*; and Immerwahr, *How to Hide an Empire*.

7. Like many nationalist histories, Kramer frames his study of the Philippines with the national hero José Rizal, who predominantly spoke European languages but whose Tagalog was infamously bad. See Rafael, *The Promise of the Foreign*.

8. By replicating the vertical logic of racial formations as well as the racisms of colonial elites themselves, the extent to which *The Blood of Government* conducts a treatment of Indigenous histories in the Philippines is limited to their utility as the savage foil to the civilized subject. Even as Kramer brings under scrutiny the bifurcation of "Christian" and "non-Christian" peoples (effectively, lowland natives and Indigenous highlanders), it reifies this dyad all the same and hands control over it to elites during the American period. To be sure, Kramer traces these initial anxieties around Igorot exposition to late nineteenth-century Spanish and mestizo racial images. See Kramer, *The Blood of Government*, 167, 259.

9. Kramer, *The Blood of Government*, 69.

10. In works listed above, I locate this problem in the framing of colonial histories as transnational ones, that is, "the United States," "the Philippines."

11. Kramer, *The Blood of Government*, 69, 111, 171, 196.

12. In their methodological advancement of transimperial history, US historians Kristin L. Hoganson and Jay Sexton critique imperial history's imperializing tendency of "opening up" nation-centered histories to the world. Likewise, Hoganson and Sexton emphasize the limitations of the transnational in studying deeply infranational (yet highly global) historical phenomena as well as the ways that the international reifies the nation-state as the unit of history. See Hoganson and Sexton, *Crossing Empires*.

13. To borrow from Frantz Fanon, the state "uses a language of pure violence [in colonial frontiers]. . . . [T]he proximity and frequent, direct intervention by the police and military ensure the colonized are kept under close scrutiny, and contained by rifle butts and napalm." See Fanon, *The Wretched of the Earth*, 4.

14. In Philippine studies, exemplary scholarship that deploys transimperial critique understands the archipelago and its diverse peoples as a multiply colonized place and has long offered effective models for such inquiry. Working in the archipelago's south, Philippine ethnohistorians Oona Paredes and Michael C. Hawkins, scholars of the Lumad and Moro peoples, respectively, offer critical practices that center native agency under colonial duress far from the metropole. In the archipelago's north, Renato Rosaldo and Rebecca Tinio McKenna, scholars of the Sierra Madre mountains and Baguio, respectively, account not only for Spanish and American empires but also the globalizing reach of Japanese and German imperial actions in Southeast Asia. See Rosaldo, *Ilongot Headhunting, 1883–1974*; Hawkins, *Making Moros*; Paredes, *A Mountain of Difference*; and McKenna, *American Imperial Pastoral*.

15. Indigenous peoples in the Philippines know this well; for example, the famed Kalinga tattoo artist Whang-Od Oggay recalls her days as a World War II insurgent against the continuities of plunder, from the Japanese occupation through the American and then the Philippine colonial state: "During the war and the Japanese occupation, we were not only scared of the Japanese, but also from the Philippine soldiers, who abused us by taking food in exchange for nothing." "Whang Od: The Kalinga Tattoo Maker," YouTube, January 28, 2016, https://www.youtube.com/watch?v=570zdNDqDKM.

16. Here, ethnic studies scholar Dylan Rodriguez has built the foundations for my critique to take place. He describes the Filipino condition as one of suspended apocalypse: the foreclosure of decolonial liberation for the colonial diaspora brought about by Filipino diaspora's Asian Americanization. For Rodriguez, the classification and study of Filipinos under Asian America undermines the particular colonial violence at the heart of the Filipino diaspora, the very same processes of violence in the bundok. He argues instead for a genealogy of Filipino racialization that reckons with US colonial pasts and presents. Suspended apocalypse recenters Filipino genocide in the making of Filipino America, in communion with the genocidal past and present of the United States. Two particular historiographies lie at the center of Rodriguez's critique of Asian American studies: the "wave" models of Asian migrant arrival to the United States and the creation of an Asian American panethnicity. For Rodriguez, the wave model reifies the United States as a place of arrival rather than settler colonial genocide and panethnicity homogenizes diasporic migration into one Asian subject. See Rodriguez, *Suspended Apocalypse*; Takaki, *Strangers from a Different Shore*; and Espiritu, *Asian American Panethnicity*.

17. Rodriguez, *Suspended Apocalypse*, 155–56.

18. Schurz, *The Manila Galleon*; Ventura, "American Empire, Agrarian Reform and the Problem of Tropical Nature in the Philippines, 1898–1916"; Seijas, *Asian Slaves in Colonial Mexico*; and Giraldez, *The Age of Trade*.

19. Ventura, "American Empire, Agrarian Reform and the Problem of Tropical Nature in the Philippines, 1898–1916"; and Bender, *American Abyss*.

20. España-Maram, *Creating Masculinity in Los Angeles's Little Manila*; Mabalon, *Little Manila Is in the Heart*; Espiritu, *Home Bound*; Takaki, *Strangers from a Different Shore*; and Choy, *Empire of Care*.

21. Casid, *Sowing Empire*; Arnold, *The Tropics and the Traveling Gaze*; Jung, *Coolies and Cane*; Gary Okihiro, *Pineapple Culture*; Sharma, *Empire's Garden*; Besky, *The Darjeeling Distinction*; and Moore, *Capitalism in the Web of Life*.

22. For a primer on Manila as an "imperial" site for the Philippine food and agricultural systems, see de Jesus, *The Tobacco Monopoly in the Philippines*; Fradera, *Filipinas, la colonia más peculiar*; and Doeppers, *Feeding Manila in Peace and War, 1850–1945*.

23. Scott, *The Discovery of the Igorots*; and McKenna, *American Imperial Pastoral*.

24. Scott, *Barangay*.

25. Kramer, *The Blood of Government*.

26. While Karl Marx advanced how primitive accumulation created a (waged male) proletarianized working population, political scientist Glen Sean Coulthard reminds us that global manifestations of primitive accumulation are also a continuous and uneven process of colonial dispossession through the expropriation of land and the expropriation of native labor. Marx, *Capital, Volume 1*, 873–76; and Coulthard, *Red Skin, White Masks*, 11.

27. Robinson, *Black Marxism*, 21.

28. For more on *reducción* in Luzon, see Scott, *The Discovery of the Igorots*; and Blanco, *Frontier Constitutions*.

29. Foucault, *Discipline and Punish*.

30. Particular (but not exclusive) to the United States, according to literary scholar Lisa Lowe, is how "capital [maximizes] its profits not through rendering labor 'abstract' but precisely through the social productions of 'difference.'" See Lowe, *Immigrant Acts*, 27–28.

31. See, *The Filipino Primitive*.

32. For example, the Dean Conant Worcester photographs are dispersed across the United States. The US National Archives includes them within the reports of the Bureau of Insular Affairs, the Newberry Library in Chicago acquired them through purchase into the Edward Ayer collection, and the University of Michigan stores them within both the anthropological collections and the Bentley Historical Library (since Worcester's former employer was the University itself).

33. Punzalan, "Archival Diaspora."

34. Later chapters lay out exactly how the mountainous archives were made and the difficulty of their production. Ethnological expeditions in the Philippine Cordilleras doubled as military counterinsurgency trips. Guns and photographs, in equal measure, shot the bodies of natives in the regions, who in turn responded by taking advantage of the difficult Cordilleran terrain.

35. I return to the racial economy of multimedia colonial archives in chapter 2.

36. Derrida, *Archive Fever*, 1–23.

37. Derrida, *Archive Fever*, 11.

38. Stoler, "Colonial Archives and the Arts of Governance."

39. Lowe, *The Intimacies of Four Continents*, 2.

40. From Lowe, *The Intimacies of Four Continents*: "I employ the concept of intimacy as a way to develop a 'political economy' of intimacies, by which I mean a particular calculus governing the production, distribution, and possession of intimacy. This understanding unsettles the meaning of intimacy as the privileged sign of liberal interiority or domesticity, by situating this more familiar meaning in relation to the global processes and colonial connections that are the conditions of its production. . . . This involves considering scenes of close connection in relation to a global geography that one more often conceives in terms of vast spatial distances" (18).

41. Lowe, *The Intimacies of Four Continents*, 3.

42. On colonial amnesia, see Rafael, *White Love and Other Events in Filipino History*.

43. Lowe, *The Intimacies of Four Continents*, 6.

44. To understand racial and political images as a constellation with roots in labor and archives, I draw upon the Honduras-based work of Coleman, *A Camera in the Garden of Eden*.

45. In recent years Filipino cultural studies has taken up the project of critical archive reading in histories of diaspora and imperial rule. Through museums and photographic collections from the colonial Philippines, scholars emphasize unruly—indeed insurgent—ways of reading the dispersed archives of diasporic peoples in order to complicate how dispersal has reified capitalist images of race. Balce, *Body Parts of Empire*; and See, *The Filipino Primitive*.

46. On interimperial collaborations and infrastructures, especially on migration and empire, see Neptune, *Caliban and the Yankees*; Chang, *Pacific Connections*; and Shah, *Stranger Intimacy*.

47. Once referring only to Spanish-born people in the islands, the "Filipino" in its modern iteration was articulated by the young elite *ilustrado* revolutionaries who traveled to Europe as migrant students. While certainly the "Filipino" spread among peasants around Manila through revolutionary literature, by and large identification as "Filipino" remained

piecemeal across the archipelago. See Rafael, *The Promise of the Foreign*; Mojares, *Brains of the Nation*; and Thomas, *Orientalists, Propagandists, and* Ilustrados. On nonmetropolitan and nonelite people on the archipelago, see Ileto, *Pasyon and Revolution*; and Mojares, *The War against the Americans*. In chapters 5 and 6, I trace Ilokanos mobilized as migrant workers in the US empire, often forging ideas of Filipino community through their encounters with capital or otherwise through their self-forging of diasporic nationalisms.

48. As literary scholar Victor Bascara argues, the "Filipino American" subject stands "at the intersection of the immigrant and the colonized, and at the overlap of the waning of territorial empire and the waxing of neocolonialism." See Bascara, "Up from Benevolent Assimilation."

49. Manalansan and Espiritu, *Filipino Studies*.

50. Chu, *The Chinese and Chinese Mestizos of Manila*; and Chu, *Chinese Merchants of Binondo in the Nineteenth Century*.

51. Vergara, *Displaying Filipinos*; and Kramer, "Making Concessions." Two historians who synthesize race and labor together are Bender, *American Abyss*; and McKenna, *American Imperial Pastoral*.

52. Lowe, *The Intimacies of Four Continents*, 35.

53. See, *The Filipino Primitive*, is a prime example of understanding Philippine indigeneity and American capitalism together.

54. Maile Arvin's study on settler colonial whiteness in Oceania is a particularly powerful demonstration of the entanglements between race, indigeneity, and settler colonial science. See Arvin, *Possessing Polynesians*.

55. Paredes, "Indigenous vs. Native"; Hirano, "Thanatopolitics in the Making of Japan's Hokkaido"; Barclay, *Outcasts of Empire*; Espiritu and Ruanto-Ramirez, "The Philippine Refugee Processing Center"; and Mostiller, "The Nexus of Asian Indigeneity, Refugee Status, and Asian Settler Colonialism in the Case of Indigenous Cham Muslim Refugees."

56. Rodriguez, *Suspended Apocalypse*; and Salvador-Amores, "Re-examining Igorot Representation."

57. Fujikane and Okamura, *Asian Settler Colonialism*; Day, *Alien Capital*; and Gandhi, *Archipelago of Resettlement*.

58. Two examples from Asian American studies that also conduct this work include Le, *Unsettled Solidarities*; and Hu-Pegues, *Space-Time Colonialism*.

Chapter One

1. Much of the social history in this chapter is thanks to the work of the late Ilokano historian Grace Estela C. Mateo, whose dissertation is the most comprehensive study of early modern Ilokano and Northern Luzon history to date. See Mateo, "A History of Ilocos."

2. Flannery, "Battlefield Diplomacy and Empire-Building in the Indo-Pacific World during the Seven Years' War."

3. The monopoly in Luzon was modeled after the earlier one in Mexico. For a broad synthesis of the former, see de Jesus, *The Tobacco Monopoly in the Philippines*. On the latter, see Deans-Smith, *Bureaucrats, Planters, and Workers*.

4. For a longer discussion on the *babaknang*, see Mateo, "A History of Ilocos."

5. Lowe, *Immigrant Acts*, writes that "in the history of the United States, capital has maximized its profits not through rendering labor 'abstract' but precisely through the social productions of 'difference,' of restrictive particularity and illegitimacy marked by race, nation, geographical origins, and gender" (28). This chapter, as in the rest of this study, extends Lowe's thesis into transimperial terrain, recognizing that the production of capital and social difference began in the Global South well before the United States occupied the Philippines.

6. Here as throughout this book, I think with the insights of cultural theorist Sarita See, whose work on Filipino exhibits in American colonial museums reveals how the US occupation's projects of primitive accumulation also included that of racial knowledge. However, we find these projects not particular to American occupation, and indeed, the United States drew upon earlier palimpsests of primitive accumulation at different points during the late Spanish occupation. It is my hope that the foundations of her revelations in the American museum can be inferred from this work. See See, *The Filipino Primitive*.

7. Scott, *Barangay*.

8. Scott, *Barangay*.

9. Agoncillo, *History of the Filipino People*.

10. Agoncillo, *History of the Filipino People*.

11. Giraldez, *The Age of Trade*.

12. Abinales and Amoroso, *State and Society in the Philippines*, 60–62.

13. Abinales and Amoroso, *State and Society in the Philippines*, 60–61. On churches as sites of knowledge production and local discipline, see Rafael, *Contracting Colonialism*.

14. Abinales and Amoroso, *State and Society in the Philippines*, 62.

15. Acabado, "The Archaeology of the Pericolonialism."

16. Paredes, *A Mountain of Difference*.

17. Mateo, "A History of Ilocos," 255.

18. Mateo, "A History of Ilocos," 257–81.

19. Ilocano remains the lingua franca there, albeit with regional variations in the fertile lowlands, across highland peoples, and in the coastal regions. See Keeping, *The Ethnohistory of Northern Luzon*; Flores, "Amianan Studies."

20. Mateo, "A History of Ilocos," 254–55.

21. Rafael, *Contracting Colonialism*.

22. Scott, *The Discovery of the Igorots*.

23. De Jesus, *The Tobacco Monopoly in the Philippines*.

24. After the Seven Years' War, the Spanish government in the Philippines immediately sought to discipline natives into enacting early experiments of the tobacco monopoly through increased policing. The government had some successes with coercing people to surrender land and commerce to the state but almost as soon as it enacted such efforts noted the proliferation of "vagabonds" and "contrabandists." Letter from José Basco, May 12, 1786, Filipinas 391 N. 49, General Archive of the Indies, Sevilla, Spain.

25. Scott, *The Discovery of the Igorots*; and de Jesus, *The Tobacco Monopoly in the Philippines*.

26. De Jesus, *The Tobacco Monopoly in the Philippines*.

27. *Discurso 6*, May 6, 1781, Filipinas 593, General Archive of the Indies, Sevilla, Spain.

28. *Actas del Sociedad Económica*, 1787, Filipinas 593, General Archive of the Indies, Sevilla, Spain.

29. Letter from José de Galvez, June 18, 1783, Filipinas 593, General Archive of the Indies, Sevilla, Spain.

30. *Actas del Sociedad Económica.*

31. De Jesus, *The Tobacco Monopoly in the Philippines.*

32. De Jesus, *The Tobacco Monopoly in the Philippines.*

33. De Jesus, *The Tobacco Monopoly in the Philippines; Actas del Sociedad Económica*; and Letter from José Basco, June 2, 1783, Filipinas 593, General Archive of the Indies, Sevilla, Spain. For more on the criminalization of nonproductivity, see Foucault, *Madness and Civilization.* For archival techniques in the American colonial Philippines such as photography and censuses, see Rafael, *White Love and Other Events in Filipino History.*

34. De Jesus, *The Tobacco Monopoly in the Philippines.*

35. Letter from José Basco, May 15, 1787, Filipinas 593, General Archive of the Indies, Sevilla, Spain.

36. Filipinas 591 N.49, General Archive of the Indies, Sevilla, Spain.

37. De Jesus, *The Tobacco Monopoly in the Philippines*; and Mateo, "A History of Ilocos."

38. Mateo, "A History of Ilocos"; and Pertierra, "Lured Abroad."

39. De Jesus, *The Tobacco Monopoly in the Philippines*; de Jesus, "Control and Compromise in the Cagayan Valley"; and Mateo, "A History of Ilocos."

40. Kerkvliet, *Manila Workers' Unions, 1900–1950.*

41. Scott, *The Discovery of the Igorots*; Rafael, *The Promise of the Foreign*; and Clemente, "Guanxi in Chinese Commerce."

42. Martinez de Zúñiga, *Historia de las islas Filipinas.*

43. McKenna, *American Imperial Pastoral.*

44. Letter from José Basco, December 22, 1779, Filipinas 593, General Archive of the Indies, Sevilla, Spain.

45. Scott, *The Discovery of the Igorots*; Mateo, "A History of Ilocos"; and McKenna, *American Imperial Pastoral.*

46. Spanish: "Pero es tal el descuido en Filipinas para el buen cultivo del tabaco, que al señalar las plantas para semilla dejan indistintamente en la sementera cualesquiera matas sin elegir las más robustas y de una misma clase; la cogen después sin hacer ninguna separación, la solean y guardan sin ningún esmero dejándola llena de suciedad, de tierra, de polvo, de palillos y partículas délas gárgolas ó celdillas en que se contiene y así la dejan hasta la cosecha siguiente. Con bastante más cuidado la he visto conservar á los indios salvajes que siembran tabaco en los bosques, y observado que los frutos que crian son mejores en calidad, tamaño y bondad, no pocas veces. / Diré ahora el modo racional y útil de coger buena semilla y la manera de conservarla en buen estado de una para otra sementera." Garcia Lopez, *Manual para el cultivo y beneficio del tabaco en Filipinas, por el alcalde mayor Colector de la provincia de Cagayan,* 66–67, George Arents Tobacco Collection, New York Public Library. Translation by the author.

47. Liébana y Trincado, *Apuntes sobre el camino militar emprendido desde la provincia de Abra á la de Cagayaen en la Isla de Luzon.*

48. De Jesus, *The Tobacco Monopoly in the Philippines*, 33.

49. Thomas, *Orientalists, Propagandists, and* Ilustrados.

50. Chapter 4 explores the visual aftermath of racial archiving in the tobacco monopoly through the Philippine Commission (1898–1914).

51. Chu, *The Chinese and Chinese Mestizos of Manila.*

52. Chu, *Chinese Merchants in Binondo in the Nineteenth Century.*

53. Escoto, "Expulsion of the Chinese and Readmission to the Philippines."

54. Rafael, *The Promise of the Foreign*; and Blanco, *Frontier Constitutions.*

55. Escoto, "Expulsion of the Chinese and Readmission to the Philippines."

56. Letter from José Basco, December 22, 1779, Filipinas 593, General Archive of the Indies, Sevilla, Spain.

57. Chu, *The Chinese and Chinese Mestizos of Manila.*

58. *Actas del Sociedad Económica*; Letter, May 3, 1783, Filipinas 593, General Archive of the Indies, Sevilla, Spain; and Fradera, *Filipinas, la colonia más peculiar.*

59. Clemente, "Guanxi in Chinese Commerce."

60. Blanco, *Frontier Constitutions*; Chu, *Chinese Merchants of Binondo in the Nineteenth Century.*

61. Spanish: plantation owners.

62. De Jesus, *The Tobacco Monopoly in the Philippines.*

63. De Jesus, *The Tobacco Monopoly in the Philippines*; and de Jesus, "Control and Compromise in the Cagayan Valley."

64. Letter from José Basco, June 10, 1782, Filipinas 593, General Archive of the Indies, Sevilla, Spain.

65. Letter from Patricio Daruin, December 31, 1795, Filipinas 593, General Archive of the Indies, Sevilla, Spain.

66. Letter, December 30, 1789, Filipinas 593, General Archive of the Indies, Sevilla, Spain.

67. De Jesus, *The Tobacco Monopoly in the Philippines.* The feminization of the final cigar product, as commodity of empire and as women's work, appears in some nineteenth-century literature and popular culture. For instance, in an 1886 poem titled "The Betrothed," Rudyard Kipling's speaker jocularly professes his love for the cigar ("the great god Nick o' Teen") and his distaste for his fifty-year-old wife. The wife, Maggie, declares an ultimatum: choose between his marriage and his nicotine addiction. The speaker evidently chooses a harem of cigar "brides" that would be the envy of "the Moor and the Mormon." Among his many brown brides are the commodities of empire: tea, vanilla, and tobacco from Spanish colonies. The Manila cigar offers the speaker an exotic, feminine alternative to his white wife: "mild" and with a "wifely smile." The Philippines became known by international smoking connoisseurs for its Manila-rolled cigars, but the plantations that fortified this industry are obscured. However, Kipling's feminization of tobacco unwittingly reveals a gendered and racialized system that lies at the political unconscious of this commodity. Through the gendered division of labor in the Spanish Empire's tobacco-producing colonies, poetic imaginaries and tastes emerged, such as those represented as far away as Kipling's bourgeois England.

68. Robles, *The Philippines in the Nineteenth Century*; and Flannery, "Battlefield Diplomacy and Empire-Building in the Indo-Pacific World during the Seven Years' War."

69. Mateo, "A History of Ilocos."

70. Martinez de Zúñiga, *Historia de las islas Filipinas*; de Jesus, *The Tobacco Monopoly in the Philippines*; and Mateo, "A History of Ilocos."

71. De Jesus, "Control and Compromise in the Cagayan Valley."

72. Blumentritt, *The Philippines*, 26–27.

73. De Jesus, *The Tobacco Monopoly in the Philippines.*

74. In 1912, Dean C. Worcester commissioned the development of a film in the Philippines depicting ongoing activities from Tabacalera. Correspondence, 1912, Dean Conant Worcester papers, Bentley Historical Library, Ann Arbor, MI.

75. The Italian word for "farm." (Factory is *fabricca.*) The false cognate suggests the industrial and agri-business nature of colonial farm systems and the industrial labor behind the making of pastoral landscapes.

76. Doeppers, *Feeding Manila in Peace and War, 1850–1945*; and Ventura, "From Small Farms to Progressive Plantations."

77. Paredes, *A Mountain of Difference.*

Chapter Two

1. Blanco, *Frontier Constitutions.*

2. Vergara, *Displaying Filipinos*; Rafael, *The Promise of the Foreign*; Blanco, *Frontier Constitutions*; Brody, *Visualizing American Empire*; and Rice, *Dean Worcester's Fantasy Islands.*

3. On infrastructures and cultures of looking in other colonial contexts, see Arnold, *The Tropics and the Traveling Gaze.*

4. On globalization and accelerated circulation, see Appadurai, *Modernity at Large*; and Anderson, *Imagined Communities.*

5. Blanco, *Frontier Constitutions.*

6. Mojares, *Brains of the Nation.*

7. Kramer, *The Blood of Government*; Mojares, *Brains of the Nation*; and Thomas, *Orientalists, Propagandists, and* Ilustrados.

8. Kramer, *The Blood of Government*; and Mojares, *Brains of the Nation.*

9. Mojares, *Brains of the Nation*; and Thomas, *Orientalists, Propagandists, and* Ilustrados.

10. Dean Conant Worcester, a University of Michigan zoologist and later secretary of the interior of the Philippines, was among those who drew upon Scheerer's work in his own writings. H. Otley Beyer, the founder of the Department of Anthropology at the University of the Philippines, likewise established his school through Scheerer's influence.

11. I consider the diasporic dandy in chapter 6, starting with the ilustrados and moving toward the *manongs.*

12. Chang, *Pacific Connections.* I also gesture toward three recent dissertations on transpacific steamships and Pacific imperialism: Patrick Chung (Department of American Studies, Brown University, 2017), Minyong Lee (Department of History, University of Chicago, 2018), and Will Riddell (Department of History, University of Toronto, 2018).

13. Brody, *Visualizing American Empire.*

14. Letter from Alex R. Webb to Joseph Beale Steere in Manila, December 26, 1888, Correspondence 1881–1890, Joseph Beale Steere Papers, Bentley Historical Library, Ann Arbor, MI.

15. Kramer, *The Blood of Government*; and Rice, *Dean Worcester's Fantasy Islands* (2014).

16. Letter from Alex R. Webb to Joseph Beale Steere in Manila, December 26, 1888, Correspondence 1881–1890, Joseph Beale Steere Papers, Bentley Historical Library, Ann Arbor, MI.

17. Kaplan, *The Anarchy of Empire in the Making of U.S. Culture*; Kramer, *The Blood of Government*; and Gonzalez, *Securing Paradise.*

18. Some examples of these memoirs include Fiske, *The Story of the Philippines*; and Davis, *Our Conquests in the Pacific.*

19. Thank you to the Bentley Historical Library staff for some research into these acquisitions.

20. Robert R. Rudd Papers, folder 3, box 1, Schomburg Center for Research in Black Culture, New York, NY. An in-depth analysis of *The Igorrotes of Benguet* and its relationship with civilian ethnologists appears in chapter 4.

21. Office of the Chief Engineer to Robert R. Rudd, June 5, 1900, Robert Rudd Papers, folder 3, box 1, Schomburg Center for Research in Black Culture, New York, NY.

22. Expeditions are covered further in chapter 4.

23. Solheim, "Formosan Relationships with Southeast Asia," notes the long-extant scholarship between the two locations and that Formasa has served as a popular site for anthropological study since the late nineteenth century.

24. Scheerer, *Zur ethnologie der inselkette zqischen Luzon und Formosa.*

25. Scheerer, *Zur ethnologie der inselkette zwischen Luzon und Formosa*; and Scheerer, *Batan Texts with Notes.*

26. Letter from Shinji Ishii to David Barrows, Dean Conant Worcester Papers, Box 1, "Correspondence 1907–1911," Bentley Historical Library, University of Michigan.

27. Ching, *Becoming "Japanese."*

28. Reid, "Who Are the Negritos?"

29. Thomas, *Orientalists, Propagandists, and* Ilustrados.

30. Here, as in the larger concept of the racial economy, I critically examine the cultural geographies of archival circulation, not just production. On colonial archives and its uses and abuses, see Stoler, *Along the Archival Grain.*

31. Kramer, *The Blood of Government.*

32. Discussed in chapter 1.

33. On arithmetic counting and state power, see Rancière, *Disagreement.*

34. *Annual Report of the Philippine Commission, 1900–1906.*

35. Rafael, *White Love and Other Events in Filipino History*, chap. 1.

36. Kramer, *The Blood of Government*; and McCoy, *Policing America's Empire.*

37. Chapter 4 discusses colonial blueprints in depth.

38. Coleman, James, and Sharma, "Photography and Work."

39. Box 1, folder 3, Robert R. Rudd papers, Schomburg Center for Research in Black Culture, New York.

40. Rafael, *White Love and Other Events in Filipino History*, chap. 1.

41. On geometric counting, see Rancière, *Disagreement.*

42. Scott, *The Art of Not Being Governed.*

43. Vergara, *Displaying Filipinos*; Kramer, *The Blood of Government*; Brody, *Visualizing American Empire*; and Rice, *Dean Worcester's Fantasy Islands.*

44. Benjamin, *Illuminations.*

45. Benjamin, *Illuminations.*

46. Walter Benjamin would call this the "optical unconscious." See Benjamin, *Illuminations.*

47. Barthes, *Camera Lucida*; and Coleman et al., "Photography and Work."

48. Rice, *Dean Worcester's Fantasy Islands.*

49. Salvador-Amores, "Afterlives of Dean C. Worcester's Colonial Photographs."

50. For other examples in Global South contexts in South Asia and South America, see Poole, *Vision, Race, Modernity*; and Chaudhary, *Afterimage of Empire*.

51. Papers, 1911–1913, concerning the production of a film on the Philippines, Dean Conant Worcester Papers, Bentley Historical Library, Ann Arbor, MI.

52. Letter from Douglas Flattery (Loew's Theatrical Enterprises) to Dean Worcester, December 31, 1912, Correspondence, 1911–1912, Dean Conant Worcester Papers, Bentley Historical Library, Ann Arbor, MI.

53. A specific conflict over distribution rights versus physical film rights appears in correspondences between G. Magie and William Dinwiddie (the film representative of Worcester), June 23, 1922, Correspondence, 1907–1911, Dean Conant Worcester Papers, Bentley Historical Library, Ann Arbor, MI.

54. Correspondence, 1912, Dean Conant Worcester Papers, Bentley Historical Library, Ann Arbor, MI.

55. Chapter 3 explores the labor regimes behind the visual economy of the Kodak Zone.

56. Letter from Dean C. Worcester to Edward Ayer (May 26, 1905), Edward Ayer Papers, box 1, folder 10 (1905). Newberry Library, Chicago.

57. *Annual Report of the Philippine Commission, 1900–1906.*

58. Kramer, "Making Concessions"; Davis, *Late Victorian Holocausts*; and Ventura, "Medicalizing *Gutom*."

59. See chapter 3 for the expansion of this visual and labor economy of the World's Fairs. See also Rodgers, *Atlantic Crossings*; and Rydell, *All the World's a Fair*.

60. "The Tobacco growing industry in the Phil.," Dean Conant Worcester Papers, box 1, folder "Concerning the Production of a Film on the Philippines," Bentley Historical Library, University of Michigan.

61. These migrant men—the *sakadas* and the manongs—are covered in chapters 5 and 6. See also Baldoz, *The Third Asiatic Invasion*.

Chapter Three

1. Kramer, *The Blood of Government*; Bender, *American Abyss*; and McKenna, *American Imperial Pastoral*.

2. Quote in Vergara, *Displaying Filipinos*, 1.

3. Handheld camera producers such as Kodak encouraged the average American to purchase cameras and become amateur traveling photographers in their own right. See *The Cyclist* (1891).

4. Kaplan, *The Anarchy of Empire in the Making of U.S. Culture*.

5. Rafael, *White Love and Other Events in Filipino History*; and Balce, *Body Parts of Empire*.

6. Poole, *Vision, Race, Modernity*.

7. Vergara, *Displaying Filipinos*.

8. Rafael, *White Love and Other Events in Filipino History*.

9. Brody, *Visualizing American Empire*; and Rice, *Dean Worcester's Fantasy Islands*.

10. Afable, "Journeys from Bontoc to the Western Fairs, 1904–1915"; and Salvador-Amores, "Afterlives of Dean C. Worcester's Colonial Photographs."

11. Poole, *Vision, Race, Modernity*.

12. Vergara, *Displaying Filipinos*; Rafael, *White Love and Other Events in Filipino History*; Rice, *Dean Worcester's Fantasy Islands*; and Balce, *Body Parts of Empire*.

13. Coleman, "The Photos We Don't Get to See"; and Coleman, "The Right Not to Be Looked At."

14. Coleman, *A Camera in the Garden of Eden*; Coleman, "The Photos We Don't Get to See"; and Coleman, "The Right Not to Be Looked At."

15. Azoulay, *The Civil Contract of Photography*, 85–86.

16. Beckert, "American Danger."

17. Kaplan, *The Anarchy of Empire in the Making of U.S. Culture*; and Friedman, *Covert Capital*.

18. Mirzoeff, *The Right to Look*. Mirzoeff elaborates on these challenges to imperial capitalist visuality, calling the challenges within heterotopic spaces "countervisuality," under which we find evidence of the visual economies of subaltern working lives.

19. Poole, *Vision, Race, Modernity*; and Scott, "The Contested Spaces of the Subterranean."

20. Scott, *The Discovery of the Igorots*, 9–39.

21. Acabado, "The Archaeology of Pericolonialism."

22. Spanish: "útiles á la sociedad y aptos para recibir la Religion." *Plan de misiones para reducir a los Igorrotes de Nueva-Vizcaya, Isabela y Cagayan*.

23. The debate between missionary-led reducción and military reducción for road building is outlined in reports written in the 1880s. For secondary literature on the late Spanish and early American occupations of the region, see Scott, *The Discovery of the Igorots*; Kramer, *The Blood of Government*; and McKenna, *American Imperial Pastoral*, 23.

24. Dean C. Worcester, "The Lepanto Igorrotes," Series 9, box 47–48, Dean C. Worcester Photographs, Newberry Library.

25. Dean C. Worcester, "Igorrotes of Benguet," Series 10, box 48–54, Dean C. Worcester Photographs, Newberry Library.

26. Letter from Dean C. Worcester to Edward Ayer, December 19, 1904, box 1, folder 9, Ayer Collection Correspondence, Newberry Library.

27. An analogous case can be found in Scott, "The Contested Spaces of the Subterranean."

28. Vergara, *Displaying Filipinos*; and Kramer, *The Blood of Government*.

29. Lowe, *Immigrant Acts*; and Day, *Alien Capital*.

30. Olin, *Touching Photographs*.

31. Azoulay, *The Civil Contract of Photography*, 93–94.

32. Brown, *The Corporate Eye*; and Lawrie, *Forging a Laboring Race*.

33. McCoy, *Policing America's Empire*.

34. Prentice, *The Lost Tribe of Coney Island*.

35. Dean C. Worcester, "Notes and Documents, 1901 Jan. 1—June 30," 106, Dean C. Worcester Philippine Collection, Special Collections Library, University of Michigan.

36. Dean C. Worcester, "Notes and Documents, 1901 Jan. 1—June 30," 108–09.

37. Rice, "His Name Was Don Francisco Muro."

38. Rice, "His Name Was Don Francisco Muro," 56.

39. Rice, "His Name Was Don Francisco Muro," 57.

40. Filipinos across the islands were being mobilized for public works projects. See McKenna, *American Imperial Pastoral*, 49–73; and Ventura, "From Small Farms to Progressive Plantations."

41. Rice, *Dean Worcester's Fantasy Islands*.

42. Blanco, "Memory-Work and Empire," 53.

43. Scott, *The Discovery of the Igorots*, 267–303.

44. Warren, *Buffalo Bill's America*; and Blanchard et al., *Human Zoos*.

45. At the turn of the twentieth century, many publications were released that celebrated America's new overseas empire and sought to provide profiles of the acquisitions to popular audiences. See, for example, Olivares, *Our Islands and Their People as Seen with Camera and Pencil*.

46. Kramer, "Making Concessions"; and Afable, "Journeys from Bontoc to the Western Fairs, 1904–1915." I thank Christopher Capozzola for reminding me of this point.

47. Kramer, *The Blood of Government*, 68–71.

48. Edwards, "Photography and the Making of the Other."

49. Edwards, "Photography and the Making of the Other." For more on the vulgarization of racial sciences and social Darwinism, see Bender, *American Abyss*.

50. Edwards, "Photography and the Making of the Other"; and Blanchard et al., *Human Zoos*.

51. Afable, "Journeys from Bontoc to the Western Fairs, 1904–1915."

52. Gonzalez, "Head-Hunter Itineraries."

53. Kramer, "Making Concessions"; Kramer, *The Blood of Government*; and *The Complete Portfolio of Photographs of the World's Fair, St. Louis, 1904*.

54. Afable, "Journeys from Bontoc to the Western Fairs, 1904–1915."

55. Kramer, *The Blood of Government*, 260–84.

56. Translated by the author.

57. Liébana y Trincado, *Apuntes sobre el camino militar emprendido desde la provincia de Abra á la Cayagan en la Isla de Luzon*.

58. McKenna, *American Imperial Pastoral*, 127–34.

59. McKenna, *American Imperial Pastoral* 128; and Worcester, "The Non-Christian Peoples of the Philippine Islands," 1200.

60. Davis, *Late Victorian Holocausts*; Ventura, "Medicalizing *Gutom*."

61. "Strike On at Igorrote Village; "'No Dog, No Work,' Says Swarthy Chieftian [*sic*]," n.d., 23, Richard Schneidewind Papers, Oversize Volume 2, Bentley Historical Library, University of Michigan.

62. For more on urban dogs in the Anglo-American world, see Ritvo, *The Animal Estate*; and Grier, *Pets in America*.

63. "Contracts and Licenses, 1905–1907," Richard Schneidewind Papers, box 1, Bentley Historical Library, University of Michigan. On Felingao (or Falikao), see Afable, "Journeys from Bontoc to the Western Fairs, 1904–1915."

64. "Igorrotes Strike for Dog Feast before Working, September 13, 1907," 55, Richard Schneidewind Papers, Oversize Volume 2, Bentley Historical Library, University of Michigan.

65. *The Complete Portfolio of Photographs of the World's Fair, St. Louis, 1904*.

66. "An Act Providing for the Regulation and Licensing of Emigration Agents," 1908, box 3, Volume 11, folder 13, Dean Worcester Papers, University of Michigan Hatcher Graduate Library.

67. "Enclosure to the 2nd Endorsement, Ex. B. 98762-Al," April 9, 1907, box 2, Volume 3, folder 29, Dean Worcester Papers, University of Michigan Hatcher Graduate Library. For

more on the language of personal liberty and contractual labor, see Stanley, *From Bondage to Contract*. For more on Filipinos as "nationals," see Poblete, *Islanders in the Empire*.

68. "Exhibition of Igorots (clippings & documents), box 3, folder 29, Dean Worcester Papers, University of Michigan Graduate Library.

69. Third Philippine Legislature, Act No. 2486, 1915.

70. Lowe, *Immigrant Acts*; Kramer, *The Blood of Government*, 347–431; and Baldoz, *The Third Asiatic Invasion*.

71. Gonzalez, "Head-Hunter Itineraries."

72. Manila-based photographer Jake Verzosa's photos of Kalinga women and their tattoos made their way to Toronto in the summer of 2016 under the title "The Last Tattooed Women of Kalinga" for the Royal Ontario Museum's special exhibition *Tattoos: Ritual. Identity. Obsession. Art.*

73. Afable, "Journeys from Bontoc to the Western Fairs, 1904–1915"; and Kramer, *The Blood of Government*.

74. "REPUBLIC ACT NO. 8485: An Act to Promote Animal Welfare in the Philippines, Otherwise Known as 'The Animal Welfare Act of 1998'," Section 6, No. 1.

75. I continue the trail to find its location, and in the meantime, for lack of acquiring permissions to use this photograph, I cannot include it here.

76. Buck-Morss, *The Dialectics of Seeing*.

Chapter Four

1. Kramer, "Making Concessions"; and Prentice, *The Lost Tribe of Coney Island*.

2. David Barrows to Fred Atkinson (May 4, 1903), David Barrows Papers, box 1, BANC MSS C-B 1005, Bancroft Library, Berkeley, CA.

3. Rosaldo, *Ilongot Headhunting, 1883–1974*.

4. On the circulation of racializations in photographic cultures, see Chaudhary, *Afterimage of Empire*. On popular consumption from empire and its effects on American mass culture, see Hoganson, *Consumers' Imperium*.

5. For instance, in Manila, colonial public health and its "sanitary regimes" developed out of wartime destruction and environmental conditions of scarcity. See Anderson, *Colonial Pathologies*; and Ventura, "Medicalizing *Gutom*."

6. On calibrated colonialism in the American Colonial Philippines, see Kramer, *The Blood of Government*.

7. For a longer discussion on Ilokano peasantry and imperial racialization, see chapter 5.

8. Bender, *American Abyss*, chap. 2.

9. Bender, *American Abyss*, chap. 2.

10. Liébana y Trincado, *Apuntes sobre el camino militar emprendido desde la provincia de Abra á la de Cagayaen en la Isla de Luzon*; and de Jesus, *The Tobacco Monopoly in the Philippines*.

11. Scott, *The Discovery of the Igorots*; and de Jesus, *The Tobacco Monopoly in the Philippines*.

12. Hoganson, *Fighting for American Manhood*; Rafael, *White Love and Other Events in Filipino History*; and Kramer, *The Blood of Government*.

13. Bender, *American Abyss*, chap. 2; McCoy, *Policing America's Empire*; and Capozzola, "The Secret Soldiers' Union."

14. Scott, *The Discovery of the Igorots*; Rosaldo, *Ilongot Headhunting, 1883–1974*; and McKenna, *American Imperial Pastoral*.

15. *Report of the Philippine Commission to the President, January 31, 1900*; and Kramer, *The Blood of Government*.

16. Otto Scheerer, "Igorrotes of Benguet," June 20, 1900, box 1, Volume 1, Dean C. Worcester Papers, Hatcher Graduate Library, University of Michigan.

17. Scheerer, "Igorrotes of Benguet," 20.

18. Scheerer, "Igorrotes of Benguet," 2.

19. Scheerer, "Igorrotes of Benguet," 20.

20. On swidden agriculture and highlands anarchism in Southeast Asia, see Scott, *The Art of Not Being Governed*.

21. On conservation and anti-Indigenous spatial politics, see Sunseri, "Reinterpreting a Colonial Rebellion."

22. Scheerer, "Igorrotes of Benguet," 8.

23. Scheerer, "Igorrotes of Benguet," 20.

24. Scheerer, "Igorrotes of Benguet," 5.

25. Scheerer, "Igorrotes of Benguet," 7.

26. Scott, *The Art of Not Being Governed*; and Ventura, "From Small Farms to Progressive Plantations." For more on arithmetic versus geometric ways of counting people, see Rancière, *Disagreement*.

27. Scott, *Seeing Like a State*, 12.

28. Scott, *The Art of Not Being Governed*.

29. "Ilongots and Ibilaos," box 1, folder 17, Dean C. Worcester Papers, Hatcher Graduate Library, University of Michigan, 2–3.

30. Scheerer, "Igorrotes of Benguet," 9.

31. Rafael, *White Love and Other Events in Filipino History*, chap. 1.

32. Dean Worcester to Governor General (October 6, 1911), Dean C. Worcester Papers, box 1, folder "Concerning disciplinary cases of government officials (1)," Bentley Historical Library, University of Michigan.

33. Scheerer, "Igorrotes of Benguet," 20.

34. Rancière, *Disagreement*.

35. On industrial capitalism and punishing nonproductive lifeways, see Foucault, *The Punitive Society*.

36. Vergara, *Displaying Filipinos*.

37. "Ilongotes and Ibilaos," Dean C. Worcester Papers, box 1, Volume 1, folder 17, Hatcher Graduate Library, University of Michigan.

38. McKenna, *American Imperial Pastoral*.

39. Jeff Gallman to Dean Worcester (November 1, 1911), Tomlinson Papers, box 1, folder "Tomlinson Papers, 1911–1912," Bentley Historical Library, University of Michigan.

40. Gallman to Worcester (November 1, 1911), Tomlinson Papers, Bentley Historical Library; and Gonzalez, *Securing Paradise*, chap. 2; and McKenna, *American Imperial Pastoral*.

41. De Leon, "Working the Kodak Zone."

42. Kramer, "Making Concessions"; and Olivera, "Colonial Ethnology and the Igorrote Village at the AYP."

43. Olivera, "Colonial Ethnology and the Igorrote Village at the AYP."

44. Kramer, "Making Concessions"; Rice, *Dean Worcester's Fantasy Islands*; and De Leon, "Working the Kodak Zone."

45. Caption for 2-c 37 1/2, *Index to Worcester Photographs, Vol. 1* (1905), Newberry Library.

46. On photography, ethnological knowledge, and accumulation of artifacts, see Rafael, *White Love and Other Events in Filipino History*; Rice, *Dean Worcester's Fantasy Islands*; Balce, *Body Parts of Empire*; and See, *The Filipino Primitive*.

47. See, *The Filipino Primitive*.

48. Rosaldo, *Ilongot Headhunting, 1883–1974*.

49. Kramer, *The Blood of Government*; McCoy, *Policing America's Empire*; and Capozzola, "The Secret Soldiers' Union."

50. Balce, "The Filipina's Breast"; and Winkelmann, "Rethinking the Sexual Geography of American Empire in the Philippines."

51. Dean C. Worcester to Governor General (October 6, 1911), Dean C. Worcester Papers, box 1, folder "Concerning disciplinary cases of government officials (1)," Bentley Historical Library, University of Michigan.

52. For instance, the Newberry photographic index contains fewer than three boxes of Ilongot photographs, while there are four boxes of Ifugao photographs. In the Hatcher Graduate Library's Cordillera blueprints, the most completely (and intricately) mapped, with the most detail on budgeting for road building, are in the Cordillera Central (e.g., Ibaloi, Ifugao, Bontoc land).

53. Explored in this chapter's discussions on Cornelis de Witt Willcox's travelogues.

54. Liébana y Trincado, *Apuntes sobre el camino militar emprendido desde la provincia de Abra á la de Cagayan en la Isla de Luzon*; de Jesus, *The Tobacco Monopoly in the Philippines*; and Rosaldo, *Ilongot Headhunting, 1883–1974*.

55. "The Ilongote," *Index to Worcester Photographs, Volume 1*, Newberry Library; and "Ilongote and Ibilao."

56. Rosaldo, *Ilongot Headhunting, 1883–1974*.

57. "Ilongote and Ibilao," 1.

58. Scott, *Seeing Like a State*; and Scott, *The Art of Not Being Governed*.

59. "Ilongote and Ibilao," 39–40.

60. "Ilongote and Ibilao," 50.

61. "Ilongote and Ibilao," 15.

62. Caption to 2-a 21, *Index to Worcester Photographs, Volume 1*, Newberry Library.

63. Caption to 2-b 46, *Index to Worcester Photographs, Volume 1*, Newberry Library.

64. "Ilongote and Ibilao," 9.

65. Thanks to Roneva Keel at the University of Washington for sharing her chapter notes. Sonza, *Sugar Is Sweet*; Larkin, *Sugar and the Origins of Modern Philippine Society*; and Merleaux, *Sugar and Civilization*.

66. On Western conquest and ethnology in the popular imagination, see Warren, *Buffalo Bill's America*; and Blackhawk, *Violence over the Land*.

67. "Ilongote and Ibilao," 13.

68. "Ilongote and Ibilao," 2.

69. "Ilongote and Ibilao," 3.

70. "Ilongote and Ibilao," 2–3.

71. *Index to Worcester Photographs, Volume 1,* Edward Ayer Philippine Collection, Newberry Library, 39.

72. Caption to 2-a 20, *Index to Worcester Photographs, Volume 1,* Newberry Library.

73. On hegemonic ways of ascribing meanings to photographs (e.g., captions), see Barthes, *Camera Lucida.*

74. "Ilongote and Ibilao."

75. Rosaldo, *Culture and Truth.*

76. Gonzalez, *Securing Paradise,* chap. 2.

77. Acabado, "The Archaeology of Pericolonialism."

78. Scheerer, "Igorrotes of Benguet"; and McCoy, *Policing America's Empire.*

79. McCoy, *Policing America's Empire.* On cognate cases of Ibaloi cooperation, see McKenna, *American Imperial Pastoral.*

80. From various captions taken in and of Banaue and Kiangan, in Owen A. Tomlinson Albums, Box 2, Bentley Historical Library, University of Michigan.

81. On landscape and visual imperial possession, see Mitchell, *Landscape and Power*; and Casid, *Sowing Empire.*

82. Nanon Fay Leas Worcester diary, Bentley Historical Library, University of Michigan, 7–8.

83. On landscape and colonial labor, see Casid, *Sowing Empire*; Arnold, *The Tropics and the Traveling Gaze*; Sharma, *Empire's Garden*; and Besky, *The Darjeeling Distinction.*

84. Worcester diary, Bentley Historical Library, 57.

85. Mitchell, *Landscape and Power*; and Casid, *Sowing Empire.*

86. David Barrows to Fred Atkinson (May 4, 1903), David Barrows Papers, box 1, BANC MSS C-B 1005, Bancroft Library, Berkeley, CA.

87. "Series 7—The Ifugaos," *Index to Worcester Photographs, Vol. 1* (1905), Newberry Library, 144.

88. Worcester diary, Bentley Historical Library, 7.

89. Gonzalez, *Securing Paradise,* chap. 2.

90. Acabado, "The Archaeology of Pericolonialism."

91. "Series 7—The Ifugaos," *Index to Worcester Photographs, Vol. 1* (1905), Newberry Library, 144.

92. "Series 7—The Ifugaos," 144.

93. Rosaldo, *Ilongot Headhunting, 1883–1974*; Kramer, *The Blood of Government*; and McCoy, *Policing America's Empire.*

94. Scheerer, "Igorrotes of Benguet."

95. McCoy, *Policing America's Empire.*

96. Jeff Gallman to Dean Worcester (October 20, 1910), Dean C. Worcester Papers, box 3, Volume 15, folder 2/4, Hatcher Graduate Library, University of Michigan.

97. Gallman to Worcester (October 20, 1910), Hatcher Graduate Library.

98. On the progenitor concepts of the reserve army of labor, see Engels, *The Condition of the Working Class in England in 1844*; and Marx, *Capital, Volume 1,* chap. 25. On penalizing vagrancy and unproductivity in the age of industry, see Foucault, *Madness and Civilization*; and Foucault, *The Punitive Society.*

99. "Constabulary Record of Major Owen A. Tomlinson," Owen Tomlinson Papers, box 1, folder "1917–1920," Bentley Historical Library, University of Michigan.

100. Jeff Gallman to Dean Worcester (November 1, 1911), Tomlinson Papers, box 1, folder "Tomlinson Papers, 1911–1912," Bentley Historical Library, University of Michigan.

101. Gallman to Worcester (November 1, 1911), Bentley Historical Library.

102. On colonial governance of abstract and concrete marketplaces in the Cordilleras, see McKenna, *American Imperial Pastoral.*

103. "Biographical Sketches of the Subprovince of Ifugao," Owen Tomlinson Papers, Box 1, approx. date 1915.

104. "Biographical Sketches of the Subprovince of Ifugao"; and McKenna, *American Imperial Pastoral.*

105. For instance, in "Biographical Sketches of the Subprovince of Ifugao," Tomlinson profiles a Banaue leader as follows: "Balu-gat. Presidente of Banaue, Ifugao, residence of Bocos, Banaue, Mt. about 59 yrs of age appointed as Presidente Aug. 16, 1910, by Lieut. Gov. Jeff D. Gallman, is a rich man; owns 3 houses, large sementeries [sic], hogs, chickens and Buji, total all properties valued P2480.00, a loyal man, wealthy and brave. Has within 12 yrs killed and taken heads of 5 men, in actual combat at Banaue, 1-of Dalican 1-of Lugu, 1-of Anao, 1-of Nungaua and 1-of Umalbong, when they wanted to enter Banaue, was cabecilla during the Spanish time."

106. Thanks to Diana Bachman and Malgosia Myc, archivists at the Bentley Historical Library, for this information on the acquisition history.

107. On feminine nudity in the Philippine visual archive, see Balce, "The Filipina's Breast."

108. Bell to Tomlinson (October 4, 1911), Owen Tomlinson Papers, box 1, folder "Tomlinson Papers, 1911–1912), Bentley Historical Library, University of Michigan.

109. Winkelmann, "Rethinking the Sexual Geography of American Empire in the Philippines."

110. Barton, "Ifugao Economics."

111. On the optical unconscious of the image and the image's surplus value, see Mitchell, "The Surplus Value of Images."

112. Letter from David Barrows to Fred Atkinson (May 4, 1903), David Barrows Papers, box 1, Bancroft Library, University of California Berkeley.

113. Owen Tomlinson Papers, box 2, Bentley Historical Library, University of Michigan.

114. Caption to 7-b 72, *Index to Worcester Photographs, Vol. 1* (1905), Newberry Library.

115. Caption to 7-b 73, *Index to Worcester Photographs, Vol. 1* (1905), Newberry Library (emphasis added).

116. Caption to 7-b 73, *Index to Worcester Photographs, Vol. 1* (1905), Newberry Library (emphasis added).

117. Caption to 7-b 78 and 7-b 79, *Index to Worcester Photographs, Vol. 1* (1905), Newberry Library (emphasis added).

118. Caption to 7-b 77, *Index to Worcester Photographs, Vol. 1* (1905), Newberry Library.

119. For more on free indirect discourse and its cognitive properties, see Reboul, Delfitto, and Fiorin, "The Semantic Properties of Free Indirect Discourse."

120. Rosaldo, *Culture and Truth,* 2.

121. The caption reads "In 7-b 75 the headless trunk may be seen in a sitting position. The arms and legs have been bound against the front of the body with a burial blanket, knotted behind, in the middle of the back. The blanket was first chopped full of holes with head

knives by the friends of the deceased, who informed the corpse that they would serve his enemies at they were serving the blanket." *Index to Worcester Photographs, Vol. 1* (1905), Newberry Library.

122. Willcox, *The Head Hunters of Northern Luzon*, 62.

123. Willcox, *The Head Hunters of Northern Luzon*, 70.

124. Discussed in chapter 3. For the 1915 act, see Third Philippine Legislature, Act No. 2486.

125. "The Life of the Ifugaos," Dean C. Worcester Papers, box 1, folder "Papers, 1911–1913, concerning the production of a film on the Philippines," Bentley Historical Library, University of Michigan.

126. Douglass Flattery (Loew's Theatrical Enterprises) to Dean Worcester (December 31, 1912), Dean C. Worcester Papers, box 1, folder "Correspondence, 1912," Bentley Historical Library, University of Michigan.

127. Rice, *Dean Worcester's Fantasy Islands*.

128. Rosaldo, *Ilongot Headhunting, 1883–1974*; and Gonzalez, *Securing Paradise*, chap. 2.

129. Salvador-Amores, *Tapping Ink, Tattooing Identities*.

130. Hoganson, *Consumers' Imperium*.

131. Kramer, *The Blood of Government*.

132. Baldoz, *The Third Asiatic Invasion*.

Chapter Five

1. I alternate between 'Ōla'a and Olaa in this chapter, with the former signifying the Hawaiian spelling for the eastern rainy regions of the island of Hawai'i and the latter signifying the plantation company name that stretched as far as Puna (later taking on "Puna" as the name) and Mountain View.

2. Puna Sugar Company Correspondences, Letter #292 (January 24, 1907), PSC 3A/1, Bishop & Co. Letters, 1907–1908.

3. Puna Sugar Company Correspondences, Letter #399 (August 10, 1907), PSC 3A/1, Bishop & Co. Letters, 1907–1908.

4. Alcantara, *Filipino History in Hawai'i before 1946*, chap. 1.

5. Anderson, *Under Three Flags*.

6. In the World's Fairs, a Filipino label extracted from decontextualized savage iconography, derived from ethnological and geological surveys in the Cordilleras, served to delegitimize Igorots' claims to Cordilleran gold and natural resources and "Filipinos'" ability to self-govern. For more on the World's Fairs, multiethnicity, and techniques of delegitimizing Filipino self-rule, see Vergara, *Displaying Filipinos*; Rafael, *White Love and Other Events in Filipino History*; and Kramer, *The Blood of Government*.

7. On savage images of the Igorot, see Vergara, *Displaying Filipinos*.

8. The best systematic history of the Ilocos and of the migratory Ilokanos is the dissertation of the late Grace Estela C. Mateo. This study is indebted to her meticulous research and dazzling syntheses. See Mateo, "A History of Ilocos."

9. Miguel G. Abaya, "The History of Candon," National Library of the Philippines, April 24, 1953; and Kerkvliet, *The Huk Rebellion*.

10. For more on despotic versus infrastructural power, see Gerstle, "A State Both Strong and Weak."

11. Anderson, "Cacique Democracy and the Philippines"; and Anderson, *The Spectre of Comparisons*.

12. Mateo, "A History of Ilocos."

13. For more on war capitalism in the eighteenth century, see Beckert, *Empire of Cotton*.

14. Anderson, "Cacique Democracy and the Philippines"; and Chiba, "Cigar-Makers in American Colonial Manila."

15. Anderson, "Cacique Democracy and the Philippines"; and Chiba, "Cigar-Makers in American Colonial Manila."

16. Sharma, "Towards a Political Economy of Emigration from the Philippines"; Pertierra, "Lured Abroad"; and Davis, *Late Victorian Holocausts*.

17. Pertierra, "Lured Abroad."

18. Kramer, *The Blood of Government*; Mojares, *Brains of the Nation*; Bender, *American Abyss*; and Okihiro, *Pineapple Culture*.

19. Blumentritt, *The Philippines*, 26–27.

20. Worcester, *The Philippine Islands and Their People*, 81–82.

21. Ventura, "Medicalizing *Gutom*."

22. Ventura, "From Small Farms to Progressive Plantations."

23. Some examples of popular literature during the Philippine-American War include White, *Our New Possessions*; Davis, *Our Conquests in the Pacific*; and de Olivares, *Our Islands and Their People as Seen with Camera and Pencil*. See also Brody, *Visualizing American Empire*.

24. Kramer, *The Blood of Government*; and McCoy, *Policing America's Empire*.

25. McCoy, *Policing America's Empire*.

26. Ventura, "From Small Farms to Progressive Plantations."

27. Kramer, *The Blood of Government*; and Rice, *Dean Worcester's Fantasy Islands*.

28. Besky, *The Darjeeling Distinction*.

29. Jung, *Coolies and Cane*.

30. Flores, "Toward the Intellectualization of the Ilokano."

31. Jung, *Coolies and Cane*; Sharma, *Empire's Garden*; and Besky, *The Darjeeling Distinction*.

32. Takaki, *Pau Hana*, 3–21; Lowe, "The Intimacies of Four Continents," 198; Jung, *Coolies and Cane*; Kauanui, *Hawaiian Blood*; and Moore, *Capitalism in the Web of Life*.

33. Susan M. Campbell and Patricia M. Ogburn, "Puna Sugar Company History," Hawaiian Sugar Planters' Association Plantation Archives, 1992, http://www2.hawaii.edu/~speccoll/p_puna.html.

34. Okihiro, *Cane Fires*.

35. Okihiro, *Cane Fires*.

36. Alcantara, *Filipino History in Hawai'i before 1946*.

37. #224 (August 9, 1906), PSC 14A/4 Bishop & Co. Letters, 1906; Okihiro, *Cane Fires*.

38. Puna Sugar Company Correspondences, Letter #621 (August 20, 1906), PSC 14A/4 Bishop & Co. Letters, 1906.

39. Puna Sugar Company Correspondences, #590 (August 28, 1908), PSC 4/1 Bishop & Co. Letters, 1908.

40. Bender, *American Abyss*.

41. Puna Sugar Company Correspondences, #600 (August 2, 1906), PSC 14A/1 Bishop & Co. Letters, 1906. In order to promote white settlement during the republic period (1894–1898), President Sanford B. Dole's government passed the Land Act in 1895 in order to repur-

pose public lands—appropriated in the mid-nineteenth century from the kingdom—into homesteads with 99-year leases. Kanaka Maolis also qualified for these leases but only had access to the least cultivable tracts of land. With the provision that homesteaders needed to make money from the land in order to keep it, many Kanaka Maolis lost their titles or otherwise sold their plots to haoles for cash. See Kauanui, *Hawaiian Blood*.

42. Puna Sugar Company Correspondences, No number (February 1, 1907), PSC 3A/1 Bishop & Co. Letters, 1907–1908 (emphasis added).

43. Rafael, *White Love and Other Events in Filipino History*; Kramer, *The Blood of Government*; Poblete, *Islanders in the Empire*; and Kirsch, "Insular Territories."

44. Mateo, "A History of Ilocos"; and Galam, "Through the Prism of Seamen's Left-Behind Wives."

45. Puna Sugar Company Correspondences, #292 (January 24,), PSC 3A/1 Bishop & Co. Letters, 1907–1908.

46. Poblete, *Islanders in the Empire*.

47. Galam, "Through the Prism of Sea-men's Left-Behind Wives."

48. Poblete, *Islanders in the Empire*.

49. Annual Report of the Olaa Sugar Company, April 30, 1900. Hawaiian Sugar Planters Association Archives, Hawaiian and Pacific Collections, Hamilton Library.

50. Puna Sugar Company Correspondences, #506 (March 27, 1908), PSC 3/3 Bishop & Co. Letters, 1908.

51. Puna Sugar Company Correspondences, No number (August 29, 1899), PSC 1/10 Alexander & Baldwin Letters, 1899.

52. Puna Sugar Company Correspondences, #653 (January 25, 1909), PSC 4/2 Bishop & Co. Letters, 1909; #1486 (March 12, 1909), PSC 4/2 Bishop & Co. Letters, 1909; "Hawaii Mill Co to Bishop & Co" (May 6, 1909), PSC 4/2 Bishop & Co. Letters, 1909; and #703 (May 13, 1909), PSC 4/2 Bishop & Co. Letters, 1909.

53. Puna Sugar Company Correspondences, #284 (January 7, 1907), PSC 3A/1 Bishop & Co. Letters, 1907–1908.

54. Puna Sugar Company Correspondences, No number (September 24, 1910), PSC 60/3 Bishop & Co. Letters, 1910.

55. Puna Sugar Company Correspondences, Letter #1468 (February 16, 1909), PSC 4/2 Bishop & Co. Letters, 1909; and Letter #2250 (February 25, 1914), PSC 4/2 Bishop & Co. Letters, 1909.

56. Puna Sugar Company Correspondences, Letter #978 (January 8, 1914), PSC 4/4 Bishop & Co. Letters, 1914 (emphasis added).

57. Puna Sugar Company Correspondences, Letter #2240 (February 25, 1914), PSC 4/4 Bishop & Co. Letters, 1914.

58. #284 (January 7, 1907), PSC 3A/1 Bishop & Co. Letters, 1907–1908.

59. #690 (April 12, 1909), PSC 4/2 Bishop & Co. Letters, 1909; and #2240 (February 25, 1914), PSC 5/3 Bishop & Co. Letters, 1914.

60. Alcantara, *Filipino History in Hawai'i before 1946*.

61. On the American political home front, the Republicans had had a stronghold over the Philippine Commission's activities and governance of the islands. Upon his election, Democratic president Woodrow Wilson appointed Francis Burton Harrison as the archipelago's governor-general. The Democratic government instated a "Filipinization" policy, which

gradually encouraged Filipino (elite) participation in the American colonial government and continued the colonization project. See Kramer, *The Blood of Government*.

62. Poblete, *Islanders in the Empire*.

63. Puna Sugar Company Correspondences, Letter #879 (January 8, 1914, 1914), PSC 5/3 Bishop & Co. Letters, 1914; #2240 (February 25, 1914); #897 (February 26, 1914); and Poblete, *Islanders in the Empire*).

64. On the corporate sovereignty of the HSPA in Hawai'i and other American sugar companies around the Pacific and Caribbean, see Merleaux, *Sugar and Civilization*.

65. Puna Sugar Company Correspondences, Letter #510 (June 11, 1911), PSC 4/4 Bishop & Co. Letters, 1911–1912.

66. Puna Sugar Company Correspondences, Letter #510 (June 11, 1911), PSC 4/4 Bishop & Co. Letters, 1911–1912.

67. Puna Sugar Company Correspondences, Letter #813 (March 1, 1907), PSC 3A/1 Bishop & Co. Letters, 1907–1908.

68. Kelley, *Race Rebels*; Gilmore, *Gender and Jim Crow*; and Camp, *Closer to Freedom*.

69. Okihiro, *Cane Fires*.

70. Jung, *Reworking Race*; and Jung, *Coolies and Cane*.

71. Stanley, *From Bondage to Contract*.

72. Puna Sugar Company Correspondences, #1291 (March 24, 1908), PSC 3/3, Bishop & Co. Letters, 1908. On contract work in road-building schemes in Benguet, see McKenna, *American Imperial Pastoral*.

73. Puna Sugar Company Correspondences, #1291 (March 24, 1908), PSC 3/3, Bishop & Co. Letters, 1908; and #464 (January 10, 1908), PSC 3/3, Bishop & Co. Letters, 1908.

74. Poblete, *Islanders in the Empire*; Simon Ygloria Papers, Hawaiian Evangelical Association Archives, Hawaiian Historical Society; and Puna Sugar Company Correspondences, #1096 (September 10, 1907), PSC 3A/1, Bishop & Co. Letters, 1907–1908.

75. PSC 3A/1, 1907–1908, translated by the author and Joan De Leon.

76. Puna Sugar Company Correspondences, #1096 (September 10, 1907), PSC 3A/1, Bishop & Co. Letters, 1907–1908.

77. #1096 (September 10, 1907); #1191 (December 27, 1907); #460 (December 30, 1907), PSC 3A/1, Bishop & Co. Letters, 1907–1908.

78. Olaa Sugar Company Treasurer's Report, April 30, 1900. Hawaiian Sugar Planters Association Archives, Hawaiian and Pacific Collections, Hamilton Library.

79. #1291, PSC 3A/1, Bishop & Co. Letters, 1907–1908.

80. #723 (June 28, 1909); #1291, PSC 4/2, Bishop & Co. Letters, 1909. For more on the American belief of a contaminant and vagrant working-class city at the turn of the twentieth century, see Bender, *American Abyss*.

81. #506 (March 27, 1908), PSC 3/3, Bishop & Co. Letters, 1908.

82. #474 (January 23, 1908), PSC 3/3, Bishop & Co. Letters, 1908.

Chapter Six

1. For more on Bulosan's life, see San Juan, *Carlos Bulosan and the Imagination of the Class Struggle*; and Espiritu, *Five Faces of Exile*. On ethnic writers and the Cultural Front, see Denning, *The Cultural Front*; and Briones, *Jim and Jap Crow*.

2. Bulosan, *America Is in the Heart.*

3. On human media, see Tadiar, "Decolonization, 'Race,' and Remaindered Life under Empire."

4. On mobility and working-class masculinities, I am especially indebted to the work of España-Maram, *Creating Masculinity in Los Angeles' Little Manila*; Fajardo, *Filipino Crosscurrents*; and Asaka, "The Unsettled City." Fajardo especially focuses on an ethnography of masculinity in a steamship infrastructure, and I am indebted to his insights to take on a project in an oral historical context.

5. Larkin, "The Politics and Poetics of Infrastructure."

6. Ingold, "The Temporality of the Landscape"; and Oetelaar and Meyer, "Movement and Native American Landscapes."

7. On analyzing a history of the affect of time, speed, and modernity, I draw from Harootunian, *Overcome by Modernity.*

8. See Fujikane and Okamura, *Asian Settler Colonialism in Hawai'i*; Day, *Alien Capital*; and Karuka, *Empire's Tracks.*

9. Historians of enslaved Black folk in the United States provide cognate examples of racialized rhythms and time. See Hahn, *A Nation under Our Feet*; and Camp, *Closer to Freedom.*

10. For more on capitalism and ecology, see Reichman, *The Broken Village*; Besky, *The Darjeeling Distinction*; and Moore, *Capitalism in the Web of Life.*

11. Hämäläinen, *The Comanche Empire*; Hämäläinen, "The Politics of Grass"; and Hämäläinen, "What's in a Concept?"

12. Raibmon, *Authentic Indians.*

13. For a primer on violence, trauma, and uneven capitalist development, see Blackhawk, *Violence over the Land.*

14. Byrd, *The Transit of Empire: Indigenous Critiques of Colonialism.* In the case of Kānaka Maolis in Hawai'i and the technics of blood quantum to reduce natives into a disappearing racial minority, see Kauanui, *Hawaiian Blood.*

15. White, *Railroaded.*

16. Worster, *Dust Bowl*; Worster, *Rivers of Empire*; Hundley, *The Great Thirst*; Fitzgerald, *Every Farm a Factory*; Guthman, *Agrarian Dreams*; and Tucker, *Insatiable Appetites.*

17. For instance, in Mexico City, industrial meat was only able to be implemented in earnest by the 1990s due to local political resistance by butchers based on people's tastes. See Pilcher, *The Sausage Rebellion.*

18. Cronon, *Nature's Metropolis.*

19. Interviews with Jesus Yambao and Chris Mensalvas, Rosalia and Juan Mendoza, and Prudencio Mori, FANHS.

20. Hahn, *A Nation under Our Feet*; Camp, *Closer to Freedom*; Smallwood, *Saltwater Slavery*; and Johnson, *River of Dark Dreams.*

21. Some examples include Stanley, *From Bondage to Contract*; Jung, *Coolies and Cane*; Hahamovitch, *No Man's Land*; Lowe, *The Intimacies of Four Continents*; and Bender and Lipman, *Making the Empire Work.*

22. Mintz, *Sweetness and Power*; Davis, *Late Victorian Holocausts*; Mudry, *Measured Meals*; Besky, *The Darjeeling Distinction*; Veit, *Modern Food, Moral Food*; and Ventura, "Medicalizing *Gutom.*"

23. Baldoz, *The Third Asiatic Invasion*; and Poblete, *Islanders in the Empire*.

24. Fujita-Rony, *American Workers, Colonial Power*; Interview with Prudencio Mori, September 17, 1981, Cassette P181-FIL-001DC, Filipino American National Historical Society (FANHS).

25. *Oxford English Dictionary*, s.v. "Adventure."

26. Tagalog: financially parsimonious, cheap, closely guarded with money.

27. Sharma, "Towards a Political Economy of Emigration from the Philippines"; and Pertierra, "Lured Abroad."

28. Cassette FIL-KNG 76-42dc, National Pinoy Archives, FANHS; Fujita-Rony, *American Workers, Colonial Power*; and Asaka, "The Unsettled City."

29. On baseball and American imperialism, see Burgos, *Placing America's Game*; and Antolihao, "From Baseball Colony to Basketball Republic."

30. Cronon, *Nature's Metropolis*.

31. Interview with Mariano Angeles, November 6, 1975, Cassette FIL-KNG75-32cm, FANHS.

32. For more on the American-language teachers and colonial education, see Roma-Sianturi, "'Pedagogic Invasion'"; and Rafael, "The War of Translation."

33. Interview with Teodoro Aguinaldo Ranjo, Cassette FIL-KNG76-41cm, FANHS.

34. Interview with Rudolfo M. Andres, June 27, 1981, Cassette BA/C81-FIL-004-4HMH-1, FANHS.

35. Ilokano: north. Another term for the Ilocos homeland.

36. Interview with Trinidad Rojo, February 18 and 19, 1975, Cassette FIL-KNG75-17ck, National Pinoy Archives, FANHS.

37. Interview with Sinforoso L. Ordoña, June 25, 1981, Cassette PNW81-FIL-015NK, FANHS.

38. Bulosan, *America Is in the Heart*, 63.

39. Bulosan, *America Is in the Heart*, 70.

40. Interview with John Mendoza, FANHS.

41. On colonial nursing and health education, see Choy, *Empire of Care*.

42. Choy, *Empire of Care*. On steamships and masculinity, see Fajardo, *Filipino Crosscurrents*.

43. Tagalog: fellow countryperson.

44. Cassette PNW82-FIL-032DC, National Pinoy Archives, FANHS.

45. Poblete, *Islanders in the Empire*.

46. Fujita-Rony, *American Workers, Colonial Power*; and Chang, *Pacific Connections*.

47. Fujita-Rony, *American Workers, Colonial Power*.

48. Interviews with Rudolfo Andres, Prudencio Mori, and Rosalia and Juan Mendoza, FANHS.

49. For more on the American and global sugar industry in the region, see Mintz, *Sweetness and Power*; Fiset, "Thinning, Topping, and Loading"; and Merleaux, *Sugar and Civilization*.

50. Interview with Rosalia and Juan Mendoza, FANHS.

51. Interview with Prudencio Mori in Las Piñas, Metro Manila, Cassette P181-FIL-001DC, September 17, 1981, FANHS.

52. Interview with Rudolfo Andres, FANHS.

53. Interview with Rosalia and Juan Mendoza, FANHS.

54. Interview with Prudencio Mori, FANHS.

55. On tramping, hobos, and immigrant labor, see Peck, *Reinventing Free Labor*; Cresswell, *The Tramp in America*; Higbie, *Indispensable Outcasts*; and Bender, *American Abyss*.

56. Interview with Teodoro Ranjo, FANHS.

57. Interview with Rosalia and Juan Mendoza, FANHS.

58. Fujita-Rony, *American Workers, Colonial Power*; and Conversations with Dorothy Cordova, February 2018.

59. Interview with Prudencio Mori, FANHS.

60. For more on landscape, imperialism, and capitalism, see Casid, *Sowing Empire*; Mirzoeff, *The Right to Look*; and McKenna, *American Imperial Pastoral*.

61. Bulosan, "As Long as the Grass Shall Grow," 38.

62. The most prominent example of these claims is the work of Ronald Takaki, whose discussions of the Filipino American community elude the settlement models of the Chinese and Japanese American groups. See Takaki, *Strangers from a Different Shore*. For critiques of those claims, see España-Maram, *Creating Masculinity in Los Angeles's Little Manila*; and Mabalon, *Little Manila Is in the Heart*.

63. Bulosan, "As Long as the Grass Shall Grow," 38.

64. Fujita-Rony, *American Workers, Colonial Power*, 126.

65. The expulsion of Japanese Americans paved the way for African American and Filipino tenancy in those abandoned spaces. See España-Maram, *Creating Masculinity in Los Angeles's Little Manila*; and Kurashige, *The Shifting Grounds of Race*.

66. Interview with Jesus Yambao and Chris Mensalvas, February 10 and 11, 1975, Cassette FIL-KNG-1CK, FANHS.

67. Interview with Jesus Yambao and Chris Mensalvas.

68. España-Maram, *Creating Masculinity in Los Angeles's Little Manila*.

69. Cassette PNW82-FIL-032DC, FANHS.

70. Interview with Rudolfo Andres, FANHS. On zoot suits and ethnic minorities in the United States, see Alvarez, "From Zoot Suits to Hip Hop." My thanks to my second reader, in whose report and feedback I came to understand the cultural distinctions behind rakish sportswear.

71. Benjamin, *The Arcades Project*; Buck-Morss, *The Dialectics of Seeing*; and Coates, "Key Figure of Mobility."

72. Mirzoeff, *The Right to Look*; and Coleman, *A Camera in the Garden of Eden*.

73. To get a sense of the social lives of the ilustrados, see Mojares, *Brains of the Nation*; and Thomas, *Orientalists, Propagandists, and Ilustrados*.

74. In a visual and prewar diasporic context, I extend the insights made in the groundbreaking cultural history Hau, *Elites and Ilustrados in Philippine Culture*.

75. Fujita-Rony, *American Workers, Colonial Power*, chap. 5.

76. Fujita-Rony, *American Workers, Colonial Power*; and España-Maram, *Creating Masculinity in Los Angeles's Little Manila*.

77. Frank Mancao, the subject of chapter 7, was one such kuripot Pinoy.

78. Wenning, "On Gambling."

79. See España-Maram, *Creating Masculinity in Los Angeles's Little Manila*; and Bernardo, "From 'Little Brown Brothers' to 'Forgotten Asian Americans.'"

80. España-Maram, *Creating Masculinity in Los Angeles's Little Manila*; Baldoz, *The Third Asiatic Invasion*; Burns, *Puro Arte*, chap. 2.

81. Interview with Julian Ebat, February 5, 1982, Cassette SC82-FIL-007-GE, FANHS.

82. Interview with Teodoro Aguinaldo Ranjo, FANHS.

83. Interview with Frank Mancao, FANHS.

84. España-Maram, *Creating Masculinity in Los Angeles's Little Manila*.

85. *Nakem* is Ilokano for "consciousness"; *kamalayan* is Tagalog for "consciousness." Both exhibit different qualities.

86. Ilokano: for townmates and fellow Ilokanos.

87. Ilokano: his first cousin from Bauang, at La Union.

88. Valer Laigo is the father of Dorothy Cordova, the archivist and executive director of FANHS.

89. For more on Filipinos' "tongues not their own," see Rafael, *Motherless Tongues*.

90. Ilokano, roughly: Manong Teodolo Ranjo came from Pasuquin in Ilocos Norte. Left as an orphan, Manong Teodolo was raised by his aunt. He left for Seattle by ship. His first job was in a box factory in Cosmopolis, having been told about the Western Washington opportunity by a friend. The two friends met in the town of Batac, also in Ilocos Norte. But when he received a letter from his first cousin, he recalled how hard and lonely it was living in America.

91. Ilokano: he said to Cynthia Mejia, a woman from the Demonstration Project for Asian Americans.

92. Ilokano: Manong Teodolo sobbed, this young man, without any family or province-mate with him.

93. Ilokano: Manong Teodolo was able to speak English and Ilokano when he was a new arrivant to the United States, but he did not how to speak Tagalog. He learned Tagalog with different Pilipino groups, often without any other Ilokanos.

94. Tagalog, roughly: When Manong Teodolo learned Tagalog, he was able to speak with his fellow countrypeople. Furthermore, he was able to discover a new category of kinship, outside of the homeland: Pilipino or, perhaps, Pinoy. At Dimas-Alang, one of the fraternity groups that proliferated in Pilipino communites in cities, he became Pilipino. His nakem (consciousness) became kamalayan (consciousness).

95. Interview with Teodoro Aguinaldo Ranjo, FANHS.

96. Rafael, *Motherless Tongues*.

97. Shuto, *Migration, Regional Integration and Human Security: The Formation and Maintenance of Transnational Spaces*, chaps. 9–12; and Kerkvliet, "Mutual Aid and Manila Unions."

98. Fujita-Rony writes extensively about the social history of nationalism and mutual aid societies. See Fujita-Rony, *American Workers, Colonial Power*, chap. 5. See also Lim, "Asian American Youth Culture"; and Hau, *Elites and Ilustrados in Philippine Culture*.

99. On the nationalization of *utang na loob*, see Mariano, "Doing Good in Filipino Diaspora."

Chapter Seven

1. A racial capitalist perspective expands on the sliding scales of civilization in the American colonial Philippines, posited by Kramer, *The Blood of Government*.

2. See Thomas, *Orientals, Propagandists, and* Ilustrados.

3. Thomas, *Orientals, Propagandists, and* Ilustrados, 97–140.

4. Mojares, *Brains of the Nation*; and Thomas, *Orientals, Propagandists, and* Ilustrados.

5. Spanish: "Hermano de los selváticos, aetas, igorrotes y tinguianes y nacido en esta apartada colonia española, donde la civilización brilla aún con luz muy tenue, confieso sinceramente que muy poco ó mas bien dicho, nada sé yo de la nueva ocupación del pensamiento humano llamado Folk-Lore." De los Reyes y Florentino, *El Folk-lore Filipino*, 20.

6. Thomas, *Orientals, Propagandists, and* Ilustrados.

7. Thomas, *Orientals, Propagandists, and* Ilustrados, 22.

8. Thomas, *Orientals, Propagandists, and* Ilustrados, 24.

9. Mojares, *Brains of the Nation*.

10. de los Reyes y Florentino, *Historia de Ilocos*, 39.

11. The Spanish term used is *paisanos*.

12. De los Reyes y Florentino, *El Folk-lore Filipino*, 58–60.

13. De los Reyes y Florentino, *El Folk-lore Filipino*, 472–538.

14. De los Reyes y Florentino, *El Folk-lore Filipino*, 52.

15. Thomas, *Orientals, Propagandists, and* Ilustrados.

16. Thomas, *Orientals, Propagandists, and* Ilustrados, 114.

17. Anderson, *Under Three Flags*.

18. San Juan, *Carlos Bulosan and the Imagination of the Class Struggle*, 1.

19. San Juan, *Carlos Bulosan and the Imagination of the Class Struggle*, 2.

20. San Juan, *Carlos Bulosan and the Imagination of the Class Struggle*.

21. Here, I am drawing upon Augusto Espiritu's "two shores" approach in Filipino American transnational history, but I expand on it by focusing not just on the "shores" of the Philippine archipelago, but the specificities of the provincial and native roots of Bulosan's life. See Espiritu, "Transnationalism and Filipino American Historiography."

22. See, "Gambling with Debt."

23. Bulosan, *America Is in the Heart*, 23.

24. Bulosan, *America Is in the Heart*, 26.

25. Bulosan, *America Is in the Heart*, 27.

26. Bulosan, *America Is in the Heart*, 39.

27. Bulosan, *America Is in the Heart*, 40.

28. For a discussion of penal ethnologies against Ifugaos' agricultural off-seasons, see chapter 4.

29. Bulosan, *America Is in the Heart*, 67.

30. Balce, "The Filipina's Breast."

31. Bulosan, *America Is in the Heart*, 69.

32. Rafael, *Motherless Tongues*.

33. Bhabha, "Of Mimicry and Man."

34. Bulosan, *America Is in the Heart*, 69.

35. Bulosan, *America Is in the Heart*, 71.

36. Bulosan, *America Is in the Heart*, 168.

37. McKenna, *American Imperial Pastoral*.

38. On the mutuality of overseas empire and contiguous settler colonialism, see Goldstein, *Formations of United States Colonialism*. Another resonance, beyond the confines of

this project, can be found through the Tewa anthropologist Edward Dozier, who was famous for studying the Philippine Cordilleras after World War II.

39. Bulosan, *America Is in the Heart*, 260.

40. Bulosan, *America Is in the Heart*, 260.

41. Bulosan, *America Is in the Heart*, 261.

42. Bulosan, *America Is in the Heart*, 327.

Conclusion

1. William C. Rempel and Richard E. Meyer, "The Marcos Diary: A Lust for Power, an Eye on Glory," *Los Angeles Times*, February 6, 1989.

2. In their ethnographies, Michelle and Renato Rosaldo lay out some of the consequences of martial law in the Cordilleras. See Rosaldo, *Knowledge and Passion*; and Rosaldo, *Ilongot Headhunting, 1883–1974*.

3. Criselda Yabes, "Tribesmen 'Exorcise' Marcos Bust with PM-Philippines, Bjt," Associated Press, March 10, 1986.

4. Steve Lohr, "Twilight of the Marcos Era," *New York Times*, January 6, 1985.

5. Kramer, "Race-Making and Colonial Violence in the U.S. Empire."

6. The story of Lakota sovereignty struggles and the broken US treaties, from Custer's Last Stand through Wounded Knee, is beyond the scope of this book. For a primer, see Treuer, *The Heartbeat of Wounded Knee*.

7. Michael C. Hawkins lays out this historiography and how it reifies colonial violence in the Philippine hinterlands. See Hawkins, *Making Moros*.

8. On Indigenous critiques of pipeline colonialism, see Simpson, *As We Have Always Done*; and Estes, *Our History Is the Future*.

9. Thomas, *Orientalists, Propagandists, and Ilustrados*.

10. Melamed, "The Spirit of Neoliberalism."

11. Tadiar, "Decolonization, 'Race,' and Remaindered Life under Empire," 139–40.

12. Rafael, *White Love and Other Events in Filipino History*, 197.

13. Some scholars in the fledgling field of Amianan studies continue to refer to Ferdinand Marcos as "Apo," an Ilokano honorific. See, for example, Flores, "Amianan Studies."

14. Benedict Anderson identifies transimperial Philippine governance by the elites as "*cacique* democracy." See Anderson, "Cacique Democracy and the Philippines."

15. Laura Greenfield, director, *The Kingmaker* (2019).

16. Diaz, "Following *La Pieta*."

17. Mitchell, *What Do Pictures Want?*, 18.

18. On terra nullius as an aesthetic of empire allowing for the free passage of colonial conquest, see Byrd, *The Transit of Empire*.

19. For some of the latest work on transnational anti-Marcos activism, see Zarsadiaz, "Raising Hell in the Heartland"; and Sales, "#NeverAgainToMartialLaw."

20. For example, within a few days to a month after the People Power Revolution and the overthrow of Marcos, major US newspapers published analyses of the Marcoses' looting of the Philippines. See Clyde Haberman, "Manila after Marcos: Problems Already Popping Up; Once Forbidden Malacanang Palace Lures People of Manila to Its Grounds," *New York*

Times, February 27, 1986); and Dale Russakoff, "The Philippines: Anatomy of a Looting," *Washington Post*, March 30, 1986.

21. Artemio Dumlao, "Marcos Bust Blasted," *PhilStar*, December 30, 2002.

22. Dumlao, "Marcos Bust Blasted."

23. Yabes, "Tribesmen 'Exorcise' Marcos Bust with PM-Philippines, Bjt."

24. Dumlao, "Marcos Bust Blasted."

25. Anika Burgess, "Stark Photos of the 1986 Philippine Revolution That Took Down a Dictator," *Atlas Obscura*, February 27, 2016.

26. "Dulag, Macli-ing," Bantayog Foundation, October 15, 2015, https://bantayog .foundation/dulag-macli-ing.

27. Appadurai, "Disjuncture and Difference in the Global Cultural Economy."

28. Delina, "Indigenous Environmental Defenders and the Legacy of Macli-ing Duyag."

29. "Dulag, Macli-ing," Bantayog Foundation.

30. Delina, "Indigenous Environmental Defenders and the Legacy of Macli-ing Duyag."

31. Rafael, *White Love and Other Events in Filipino History*.

32. "Whang Od: The Kalinga Tattoo Maker," YouTube, January 28, 2016, https://www .youtube.com/watch?v=57ozdNDqDKM.

33. Katherine Achacoso investigates the intersection the geontologies of trans-Indigenous activism, mineral resource transits, and Canadian imperial capitalism in Surigao and Tkaronto.

Bibliography

Archival Collections

American Historical Collection, Rizal Library, Ateneo de Manila University. Quezon City, Philippines.

Archivos del Sociedad Económica de los Amigos del País (Filipinas), Archivo General de Indias. Seville, Spain.

Ateneo Library of Women Writers, Rizal Library, Ateneo de Manila University. Quezon City, Philippines.

Carlos Bulosan Papers, Special Collections, University of Washington Library. Seattle, WA.

David P. Barrows Papers, Bancroft Library, University of California Berkeley. Berkeley, CA.

Dean Conant Worcester Papers, Hatcher Graduate Library, University of Michigan. Ann Arbor, MI.

Edward E. Ayer Collection, Newberry Library. Chicago, IL.

George Arents Tobacco Collection, Special Collections, New York Public Library. New York, NY.

Hawaiian Evangelical Association Archives, Mission Houses Museum, Honolulu, HI.

Hawaiian Sugar Planters Association Archives, Hawaiian and Pacific Collections, Hamilton Library. Honolulu, HI.

National Pinoy Archives, Filipino American National Historical Society. Seattle, WA.

Owen Tomlinson Papers, Bentley Historical Library, University of Michigan. Ann Arbor, MI.

Philippine Archives Collection, National Archives and Records Administration. College Park, MD.

Record Group 350, Records of the Bureau of Insular Affairs, National Archives and Records Administration. College Park, MD.

Theophilius Gould Steward Papers, Schomburg Center for Research in Black Culture, New York Public Library. New York, NY.

Trinidad Rojo Papers, Special Collections, University of Washington Library. Seattle, WA.

Worcester Philippine History Collection, Bentley Historical Library, University of Michigan. Ann Arbor, MI.

Published Primary Sources

Annual Reports of the Philippine Commission, 1900–1906. Washington, DC: US Government Printing Office, 1906.

Blumentritt, Ferdinand. The Philippines: A Summary Account of Their Ethnographical, Historical and Political Conditions. Trans. David J. Doherty. Chicago: Donohue, 1900.

Bulosan, Carlos. *America Is in the Heart: A Personal History*. Seattle: University of Washington Press, 1973.

———. "As Long as the Grass Shall Grow." *Common Ground* (Summer 1949): 38–43.

The Complete Portfolio of Photographs of the World's Fair, St. Louis, 1904. Chicago: Educational Company, 1904.

Davis, Oscar K. *Our Conquests in the Pacific*. New York: Stokes, 1899.

De los Reyes y Florentino, Isabelo. *El Folk-lore Filipino*. Manila: Tipo-Litografía de Chofré, 1889.

———. *Historia de Ilocos*, Vol. 1. 2nd ed. Manila: Establecimiento tipográfico La Opinión, 1890.

De Olivares, José. *Our Islands and Their People as Seen with Camera and Pencil*. New York: N. D. Thompson, 1899.

Fiske, Amos K. *The Story of the Philippines*. New York: Mershon, 1898.

Garcia Lopez, Don Rafael. *Manual para el cultivo y beneficio del Tabaco en Filipinas, por el alcalde mayor Colector de la provincia de Cagayan*. George Arents Tobacco Collection, New York Public Library, New York, 1860.

Liébana y Trincado, D. Evaristo. *Apuntes sobre el camino military emprendido desde la provincial de Abra a la de Cagayan en la Isla de Luzon*. Madrid: Imprenta del Memorial de Ingenieros, 1882.

Martinez de Zúñiga, Joaquín. *Historia de las islas Filipinas*. Sampaloc: Impreso de Sampaloc, 1803.

Plan de misiones para reducir a los Igorrotes de Nueva-Vizcaya, Isabela y Cagayan. Newberry Library, 1880.

Report of the Philippine Commission to the President, January 31, 1900. Washington, DC: US Government Printing Office, 1900.

Scheerer, Otto. *Batan Texts with Notes*. Manila: Bureau of Printing, 1914.

———. *Zur ethnologie der inselkette zwischen Luzon und Formosa*. Tokyo: Hobunsha, 1906.

White, Trumbull. *Our New Possessions: A Graphic Account, Descriptive and Historical, of the Tropic Islands of the Sea*. Philadelphia: Fidelity, 1898.

Worcester, Dean Conant. *The Philippine Islands and Their People*. New York: Macmillan, 1898.

Secondary Sources

Abaya, Miguel G. "The History of Candon." Manila: National Library of the Philippines, 1953.

Abinales, Patricio N., and Donna J. Amoroso. *State and Society in the Philippines*. Lanham, MD: Rowman & Littlefield, 2005.

Acabado, Stephen. "The Archaeology of Pericolonialism: Responses of the 'Unconquered' to Spanish Conquest and Colonialism in Ifugao, Philippines." *International Journey of Historical Archaeology* 21, no. 1 (March 2017): 1–26.

Afable, Patricia O. "Journeys from Bontoc to the Western Fairs, 1904–1915: The 'Nikimalika' and Their Interpreters." *Philippine Studies: Historical and Ethnographic Viewpoints* 52, no. 4 (2004): 445–73.

Agoncillo, Teodoro. *History of the Filipino People*. Quezon City: R. P. Garcia, 1960.

Alcantara, Ruben. *Filipino History in Hawai'i before 1946: The Sakada Years of Filipinos in Hawai'i*. Honolulu, HI: University of Hawai'i Press, 1988.

Alvarez, Luis. "From Zoot Suits to Hip Hop: Towards a Relational Chicana/o Studies." *Latino Studies* 5, no. 1 (2007): 53–75.

Anderson, Benedict. "Cacique Democracy and the Philippines: Origins and Dreams." *New Left Review* 169 (May 1988): 3–31.

———. *Imagined Communities: Reflections on the Origin and Spread of Nationalism*. London: Verso, 2006.

———. *The Spectre of Comparisons: Nationalism, Southeast Asia, and the World*. London: Verso, 1998.

———. *Under Three Flags: Anarchism and the Anti-Colonial Imagination*. London: Verso, 2005.

Anderson, Warwick. *Colonial Pathologies: American Tropical Medicine, Race, and Hygiene in the Philippines*. Durham, NC: Duke University Press, 2006.

Antolihao, Lou. "From Baseball Colony to Basketball Republic: Post-Colonial Transition and the Making of a National Sport in the Philippines." *Sport in Society* 15, no. 10 (December 2012): 1396–412.

Appadurai, Arjun. "Disjuncture and Difference in the Global Cultural Economy." *Theory, Culture & Society* 7 (1990): 295–310.

———. *Modernity at Large: Cultural Dimensions of Globalization*. Minneapolis: University of Minnesota Press, 2006.

Arnold, David. *The Tropics and the Traveling Gaze: India, Landscape, and Science, 1800–1856*. Seattle: University of Washington Press, 2006.

Arvin, Maile. *Possessing Polynesians: The Science of Settler Colonial Whiteness in Hawai'i and Oceania*. Durham, NC: Duke University Press, 2019.

Asaka, Megan. "The Unsettled City: Migration, Race, and the Making of Seattle's Urban Landscape." PhD dissertation, Department of American Studies, Yale University, 2014.

Azoulay, Ariella. *The Civil Contract of Photography*. New York: Zone Books, 2008.

Balce, Nerissa. *Body Parts of Empire: Visual Abjection, Filipino Images, and the American Archive*. Ann Arbor: University of Michigan Press, 2016.

———. "The Filipina's Breast: Savagery, Docility, and the Erotics of the American Empire." *Social Text* 24 (2006): 89–110.

Baldoz, Rick. *The Third Asiatic Invasion: Migration and Empire in Filipino America, 1898–1946*. New York: New York University Press, 2011.

Barclay, Paul. *Outcasts of Empire: Japan's Rule on Taiwan's "Savage Border," 1874–1945*. Berkeley: University of California Press, 2017.

Barthes, Roland. *Camera Lucida: Reflections on Photography*. Trans. Richard Howard. New York: Hill and Wang, 1981.

Barton, R. F. "Ifugao Economics." *American Archaeology and Ethnology* 15, no. 5 (April 12, 1922): 385–446.

Bascara, Victor. "Up from Benevolent Assimilation: At Home with the Manongs of Bienvenido Santos." *MELUS* 29, no. 1 (Spring 2004): 61–78.

Beckert, Sven. "American Danger: United States Empire, Eurafrica, and the Territorialization of Industrial Capitalism, 1870–1950." *American Historical Review* 122, no. 4 (October 2017): 1137–70.

———. *Empire of Cotton: A Global History*. New York: Knopf, 2014.

Bender, Daniel E. *American Abyss: Savagery and Civilization in the Age of Industry*. Ithaca, NY: Cornell University Press, 2009.

Bender, Daniel E., and Jana K. Lipman, eds. *Making the Empire Work: Labor and United States Imperialism*. New York: New York University Press, 2015.

Benjamin, Walter. *The Arcades Project*. Cambridge, MA: Belknap, 2002.

———. *Illuminations*. New York: Bodley Head, 2015.

Bernardo, Joseph. "From 'Little Brown Brothers' to 'Forgotten Asian Americans': Race, Space, and Empire in Filipino Los Angeles." PhD dissertation, Department of History, University of Washington, 2014.

Besky, Sarah. *The Darjeeling Distinction: Labor and Justice on Fair-Trade Tea Plantations in India*. Berkeley: University of California Press, 2013.Bhabha, Homi.

Bhabha, Homi K. "Of Mimicry and Man: The Ambivalence of Colonial Discourse." *October* 28 (1984): 125–33.

Blackhawk, Ned. *Violence over the Land: Indians and Empires in the Early American West*. Cambridge, MA: Harvard University Press, 2008.

Blanchard, Pascal, et al., eds. *Human Zoos: Science and Spectacle in the Age of Colonial Empires*. Liverpool: Liverpool University Press, 2008.

Blanco, Alda. "Memory-Work and Empire: Madrid's Philippines Exhibition (1887)." *Journal of Romance Studies* 5 (2005): 53–63.

Blanco, John D. *Frontier Constitutions: Christianity and Colonial Empire in the Nineteenth-Century Philippines*. Berkeley: University of California Press, 2009.

Briones, Matthew M. *Jim and Jap Crow: A Cultural History of 1940s Interracial America*. Princeton, NJ: Princeton University Press, 2012.

Brody, David. *Visualizing American Empire: Orientalism and Imperialism in the Philippines*. Chicago: University of Chicago Press, 2010.

Brown, Elspeth. *The Corporate Eye: Photography and the Rationalization of American Commercial Culture, 1884–1929*. Baltimore: Johns Hopkins University Press, 2005.

Buck-Morss, Susan. *The Dialectics of Seeing: Walter Benjamin and the Arcades Project*. Cambridge, MA: MIT Press, 1989.

Burgos, Adrian. *Playing America's Game: Baseball, Latinos, and the Color Line*. Berkeley: University of California Press, 2007.

Burns, Lucy Mae San Pablo. *Puro Arte: Filipinos on the Stages of Empire*. New York: New York University Press, 2012.

Byrd, Jodi. *The Transit of Empire: Indigenous Critiques of Colonialism*. Minneapolis: University of Minnesota Press, 2011.

Camp, Stephanie. *Closer to Freedom: Enslaved Women and Everyday Resistance in the Plantation South*. Chapel Hill: University of North Carolina Press, 2004.

Capozzola, Christopher. "The Secret Soldiers' Union: Labor and Soldier Politics in the Philippine Scouts Mutiny of 1924." In *Making the Empire Work: Labor and United States Imperialism*, ed. Daniel E. Bender and Jana K. Lipman, 85–103. New York: New York University Press, 2015.

Casid, Jill. *Sowing Empire: Landscape and Colonization*. Minneapolis: University of Minnesota Press, 1999.

Chandlee, H. Ellsworth. *De Los Reyes: Supreme Bishop in the Philippines*. New York: National Council, 1962.

Chang, Kornel. *Pacific Connections: The Making of the U.S.-Canadian Borderlands.*
Berkeley: University of California Press, 2012.

Chaudhary, Zahid R. *Afterimage of Empire: Photography in Nineteenth-Century India.*
Minneapolis: University of Minnesota Press, 2012.

Chiba, Yoshihiro. "Cigar-Makers in American Colonial Manila: Survival during Structural
Depression in the 1920s." *Journal of Southeast Asian Studies* 36, no. 3 (October 2005):
373–97.

Ching, Leon. *Becoming "Japanese": Colonial Taiwan and the Politics of Identity Formation.*
Berkeley: University of California Press, 2001.

Choy, Catherine Ceniza. *Empire of Care: Nursing and Migration in Filipino American
History.* Durham, NC: Duke University Press, 2003.

Chu, Richard T. *The Chinese and Chinese Mestizos of Manila: Family, Identity, and Culture,
1860s–1930s.* London: Brill, 2010.

Chu, Richard T. *Chinese Merchants of Binondo in the Nineteenth Century.* Manila:
University of Santo Tomas Press, 2010.

Clemente, Tina S. "Guanxi in Chinese Commerce: Informal Enforcement in the Spanish
Philippines." *Seoul Journal of Economics* 26, no. 2 (2013): 203–37.

Coates, Jamie. "Key Figure of Mobility: The *Flâneur*." *Social Anthropology* 25, no. 1 (2017):
28–41.

Cohen, Lizabeth. *Making a New Deal: Industrial Workers in Chicago, 1919–1939.* Cambridge:
Cambridge University Press, 1990.

Coleman, Kevin. *A Camera in the Garden of Eden: The Self-Forging of a Banana Republic.*
Austin: University of Texas Press, 2016.

———. "The Photos We Don't Get to See: Sovereignties, Archives, and the 1928 Massacre
of Banana Workers in Colombia." In *Making the Empire Work: Labor and United States
Imperialism,* ed. Daniel E. Bender and Jana K. Lipman, 104–135. New York: New York
University Press, 2015.

———. "The Right Not to Be Looked At." *Estudios Interdisciplinarios de América Latin y el
Caribe* 25, no. 2 (2015): 43–63.

Coleman, Kevin, Daniel James, and Jayeeta Sharma. "Photography and Work." *Radical
History Review* 2018, no. 132 (2018): 1–22.

Coulthard, Glen Sean. *Red Skin, White Masks: Rejecting the Colonial Politics of Recognition.*
Minneapolis: University of Minnesota Press, 2014.

Cresswell, Tim. *The Tramp in America.* London: Reaktion Books, 2001.

Cronon, William. *Nature's Metropolis: Chicago and the Great West.* New York: Norton,
1991.

Davis, Mike. *Late Victorian Holocausts: El Niño Famines and the Making of the Third World.*
London: Verso, 2000.

Day, Iyko. *Alien Capital: Asian Racialization and the Logic of Settler Colonial Capitalism.*
Durham, NC: Duke University Press, 2016.

Deans-Smith, Susan. *Bureaucrats, Planters, and Workers: The Making of the Tobacco
Monopoly in Bourbon Mexico.* Austin: University of Texas Press, 1992.

De Jesus, Ed. C. "Control and Compromise in the Cagayan Valley." In *Philippine Social
History: Global Trade and Local Transformations,* ed. Alfred W. McCoy and Ed. C de
Jesus, 21–38. Quezon City: Ateneo de Manila University Press, 1982.

———. *The Tobacco Monopoly in the Philippines: Bureaucratic Enterprise and Social Change, 1766–1880*. Quezon City: Ateneo de Manila University Press, 1998.

Delina, Laurence. "Indigenous Environmental Defenders and the Legacy of Macli-ing Duyag: Anti-Dam Dissent, Assassinations, and Protests in the Making of the Philippine Energyscape." *Energy Research & Social Science* 65 (2020): 1–13.

Denning, Michael. *The Cultural Front: The Laboring of American Culture in the Twentieth Century*. London: Verso, 1996.

Derrida, Jacques. *Archive Fever: A Freudian Impression*. Trans. Eric Prenowitz. Chicago: University of Chicago Press, 1996.

Diaz, Josen Masangkay. "Following *La Pieta*: Toward a Transpacific Feminist Historiography of Philippine Authoritarianism." *Signs: Journal of Women in Culture and Society* 44, no. 3 (2019): 693–716.

Doeppers, Daniel F. *Feeding Manila in Peace and War, 1850–1945*. Madison: University of Wisconsin Press, 2016.

Edwards, Elizabeth. "Photography and the Making of the Other." In *Human Zoos: Science and Spectacle in the Age of Colonial Empires*, ed. Pascal Blanchard et al., 239–46. Liverpool: Liverpool University Press, 2008.

Engels, Friedrich. *The Condition of the Working Class in England in 1844*. New York: John W. Lovell, 1847.

Escoto, Salvador P. "Expulsion of the Chinese and Readmission to the Philippines: 1764–1799." *Philippine Studies* 47, no. 1 (1999): 48–76.

España-Maram, Linda. *Creating Masculinity in Los Angeles's Little Manila: Working-Class Filipinos and Popular Culture, 1920s–1950s*. New York: Columbia University Press, 2006.

Espiritu, Augusto. "Transnationalism and Filipino American Historiography." *Journal of Asian American Studies* 11, no. 2 (2008): 171–84.

Espiritu, Augusto Fauni. *Five Faces of Exile: The Nation and Filipino American Intellectuals*. Stanford, CA: Stanford University Press, 2005.

Espiritu, Yen Le. *Asian American Panethnicity: Bridging Institutions and Identities*. Philadelphia: Temple University Press, 1992.

———. *Home Bound: Filipino American Lives across Cultures, Communities, and Countries*. Berkeley: University of California Press, 2003.

Espiritu, Yen Le, and J. A. Ruanto-Ramirez. "The Philippine Refugee Processing Center: The Relational Displacements of Vietnamese Refugees and Indigenous Aetas." *Verge: Studies in Global Asias* 6, no. 1 (2020): 118–42.

Estes, Nick. *Our History is the Future: Standing Rock versus the Dakota Access Pipeline, and the Long Tradition of Indigenous Resistance*. London: Verso, 2019.

Fajardo, Kale Bantigue. *Filipino Crosscurrents: Oceanographies of Seafaring, Masculinities, and Globalization*. Minneapolis: University of Minnesota Press, 2011.

Fanon, Frantz. *The Wretched of the Earth*. Trans. Richard Philcox. New York: Grove, 2004.

Final Proceedings of the 2006 Nakem Centennial Conference. Honolulu: Ilokano and Philippine Drama and Film Program, University of Hawai'i at Mānoa, 2006.

Fiset, Louis. "Thinning, Topping, and Loading: Japanese Americans and Beet Sugar in World War II." *Pacific Northwest Quarterly* 90, no. 3 (1999): 123–39.

Fitzgerald, Deborah Kay. *Every Farm a Factory: The Industrial Ideal in American Agriculture.* New Haven, CT: Yale University Press, 2003.

Flannery, Kristie P. "Battlefield Diplomacy and Empire-Building in the Indo-Pacific World during the Seven Years' War." *Itinerario* 40, no. 3 (December 2016): 467–88.

Flores, Abraham R., Jr. "Toward the Intellectualization of the Ilokano: Practices and Philosophies." *EXPLORATIONS* 11, no. 1 (Spring 2011): 51–62.

Flores, Ma. Crisanta. "Amianan Studies: Theory and Perspectives." In *Final Proceedings of the 2006 Nakem Centennial Conference,* 40–54. Honolulu: Ilokano and Philippine Drama and Film Program, University of Hawai'i at Mānoa, 2006.

Foucault, Michel. *Discipline and Punish: The Birth of the Prison.* New York: Pantheon Books, 1977.

———. *Madness and Civilization: A History of Insanity in the Age of Reason.* New York: Random House, 1965.

———. *The Punitive Society: Lectures at the Collège de France, 1972–1972.* Trans. Arnold I. Davidson. New York: Palgrave Macmillan, 2016.

Fradera, Josep. *Filipinas, la colonia más peculiar: La hacienda pública en la definición de la política colonial, 1762–1868.* Madrid: Consejo Superior de Investigaciones Científicas, 1999.

Friedman, Andrew. *Covert Capital: Landscapes of Denial and the Making of U.S. Empire in the Suburbs of Northern Virginia.* Berkeley: University of California Press, 2013.

Fujita-Rony, Dorothy. *American Workers, Colonial Power: Philippine Seattle and the Transpacific West, 1919–1941.* Berkeley: University of California Press, 2003.

Galam, Roderick. "Through the Prism of Seamen's Left-Behind Wives: Imagination and the Culture of Migration in Ilocos, Philippines." *Asian and Pacific Migration Journal* 24, no. 2 (2015): 137–59.

Gandhi, Evyn Lê Espiritu. *Archipelago of Resettlement: Vietnamese Refugee Settlers and Decolonization across Guam and Israel-Palestine.* Durham, NC: Duke University Press, 2022.

Gerstle, Gary. "A State Both Strong and Weak." *American Historical Review* 115, no. 3 (June 2010): 779–85.

Gilmore, Glenda. *Gender and Jim Crow: Women and the Politics of White Supremacy in North Carolina, 1896–1920.* Chapel Hill: University of North Carolina Press, 1992.

Giraldez, Arturo. *The Age of Trade: The Manila Galleons and the Dawn of the Global Economy.* Lanham, MD: Rowman & Littlefield, 2015.

Goldstein, Alyosha, ed. *Formations of United States Colonialism.* Durham, NC: Duke University Press, 2014.

Gonzalez, Vernadette Vicuña. "Head-Hunter Itineraries: The Philippines as America's Dream Jungle." *Global South* 3, no. 2 (2009): 144–72.

———. *Securing Paradise: Tourism and Militarism in Hawai'i and the Philippines.* Durham, NC: Duke University Press, 2013.

Grier, Katherine C. *Pets in America: A History.* Chapel Hill: University of North Carolina Press, 2010.

Guthman, Julie. *Agrarian Dreams: The Paradox of Organic Farming in California.* Berkeley: University of California Press, 2004.

Hahamovitch, Cindy. *No Man's Land: Jamaican Guestworkers in America and the Global History of Deportable Labor*. New York: Oxford University Press, 2011.

Hahn, Steven. *A Nation under Our Feet: Black Political Struggles in the Rural South from Slavery to the Great Migration*. Cambridge, MA: Harvard University Press, 2003.

Hämäläinen, Pekka. *The Comanche Empire*. New Haven, CT: Yale University Press, 2008.

———. "The Politics of Grass: European Expansion, Ecological Change, and Indigenous Power in the Southwest Borderlands." *William and Mary Quarterly* 67, no. 2 (April 2010): 173–208.

———. "What's in a Concept? The Kinetic Empire of the Comanches." *History and Theory* 52, no. 1 (February 2013): 81–90.

Harootunian, H. D. *Overcome by Modernity: History, Culture, and Community in Interwar Japan*. Princeton, NJ: Princeton University Press, 2000.

Hau, Caroline S. *Elites and Ilustrados in Philippine Culture*. Quezon City: Ateneo de Manila University Press, 2017.

Hawkins, Michael C. *Making Moros: Imperial Historicism and American Military Rule in the Philippines' Muslim South*. DeKalb: Northern Illinois University Press, 2013.

Higbie, Frank Tobias. *Indispensable Outcasts: Hobo Workers and Community in the American Midwest*. Urbana: University of Illinois Press, 2003.

Hirano, Katsuya. "Thanatopolitics in the Making of Japan's Hokkaido: Settler Colonialism and Primitive Accumulation." *Critical Historical Studies* 2, no. 2 (2015): 191–218.

Hoganson, Kristin L. *Consumers' Imperium: The Global Production of American Domesticity, 1865–1920*. Chapel Hill: University of North Carolina Press, 2007.

———. *Fighting for American Manhood: How Gender Politics Provoked the Spanish-American and Philippine-American Wars*. New Haven, CT: Yale University Press, 1998.

Hoganson, Kristin L., and Jay Sexton, eds. *Crossing Empires: Taking U.S. History into Transimperial Terrain*. Durham, NC: Duke University Press, 2020.

Hundley, Norris. *The Great Thirst: Californians and Water, 1770s–1990s*. Berkeley: University of California Press, 1992.

Hu-Pegues, Juliana. *Space-Time Colonialism: Alaska's Indigenous and Asian Entanglements*. Chapel Hill: University of North Carolina Press, 2021.

Ileto, Reynaldo C. *Pasyon and Revolution: Popular Movements in the Philippines, 1840–1910*. Quezon City: Ateneo de Manila University Press, 1979.

Immerwahr, Daniel. *How to Hide an Empire: A History of the Greater United States*. New York: Farrar, Strauss and Giroux, 2019.

Ingold, Tim. "The Temporality of the Landscape." *World Archaeology* 25, no. 2 (October 1993): 152–74.

Johnson, Walter. *River of Dark Dreams: Slavery and Empire in the Cotton Kingdom*. Cambridge, MA: Harvard University Press, 2013.

Jung, Moon-Ho. *Coolies and Cane: Race, Labor and Sugar in the Age of Emancipation*. Baltimore: Johns Hopkins University Press, 2006.

———. *Reworking Race: The Making of Hawai'i's Interracial Labor Movement*. New York: Cambridge University Press, 2006.

Kaplan, Amy. *The Anarchy of Empire in the Making of U.S. Culture*. Cambridge, MA: Harvard University Press, 2002.

Karuka, Manu. *Empire's Tracks: Indigenous Nations, Chinese Workers, and the Transcontinental Railroad*. Berkeley: University of California Press, 2019.

Kauanui, J. Kēhaulani. *Hawaiian Blood: Colonialism and the Politics of Sovereignty and Indigeneity*. Durham, NC: Duke University Press, 2008.

Keeping, Felix M. *The Ethnohistory of Northern Luzon*. Stanford, CA: Stanford University Press, 1962.

Kelley, Robin D. G. *Race Rebels: Culture, Politics, and the Black Working Class*. New York: Free Press, 1994.

Kerkvliet, Benedict. *The Huk Rebellion: A Study of Peasant Revolt in the Philippines*. Berkeley: University of California Press, 1977.

Kerkvliet, Melinda Tria. *Manila Workers' Unions, 1900–1950*. Quezon City: New Day Publishers, 1982.

———. "Mutual Aid and Manila Unions." *Wisconsin Papers on Southeast Asia* (1982).

Kirsch, Scott. "Insular Territories: U.S. Colonial Science, Geopolitics, and the (Re) Mapping of the Philippines." *Geographic Journal* 182, no. 1 (March 2016): 2–14.

Kramer, Paul. *The Blood of Government: Race, Empire, the United States, and the Philippines*. Chapel Hill: University of North Carolina Press, 2006.

———. "Making Concessions: Race and Empire Revisited at the Philippine Exposition, St. Louis, 1901–1905." *Radical History Review* 73 (Winter 1999): 75–114.

———. "Race-Making and Colonial Violence in the U.S. Empire: The Philippine-American War as Race War." *Diplomatic History* 30, no. 2 (2006): 169–210.

Kurashige, Scott. *The Shifting Grounds of Race: Black and Japanese Americans in the Making of Multiethnic Los Angeles*. Princeton, NJ: Princeton University Press, 2008.

Labrador, Roderick. *Building Filipino Hawai'i*. Urbana: University of Illinois Press, 2015.

Larkin, Brian. "The Politics and Poetics of Infrastructure." *Annual Review of Anthropology* 42 (October 2013): 327–43.

Larkin, John. *Sugar and the Origins of Modern Philippine Society*. Berkeley: University of California Press, 1993.

Lawrie, Paul. *Forging a Laboring Race: The African American Worker in the Progressive Imagination*. New York: New York University Press, 2016.

Le, Quynh Nhu. *Unsettled Solidarities: Asian and Indigenous Cross-Representations in the Américas*. Philadelphia: Temple University Press, 2019.

Lim, Shirley Jennifer. "Asian American Youth Culture." *Journal of Asian American Studies* 11, no. 2 (2008): 211–28.

Lowe, Lisa. *Immigrant Acts: On Asian American Cultural Politics*. Durham, NC: Duke University Press, 1995.

———. "The Intimacies of Four Continents." In *Haunted by Empire: Geographies of Intimacy in North American History*, ed. Ann Laura Stoler, 191–212. Durham, NC: Duke University Press, 2006.

———. *The Intimacies of Four Continents*. Durham, NC: Duke University Press, 2015.

Mabalon, Dawn Bohulano. *Little Manila Is in the Heart: The Making of the Filipina/o American Community in Stockton, California*. Durham, NC: Duke University Press, 2013.

Manalansan, Martin F., and Augusto Espiritu, eds. *Filipino Studies: Palimpsests of Nation and Diaspora*. New York: New York University Press, 2016.

Mariano, Joyce. "Doing Good in Filipino Diaspora: Philanthropy, Remittances, and Homeland Returns." *Journal of Asian American Studies* 20, no. 2 (2017): 219–44.

Marx, Karl. *Capital, Volume 1: A Critique of Political Economy*. New York: Penguin Books, 1992.

Mateo, Grace Estela C. "A History of Ilocos: A Study of the Regionalization of Spanish Colonialism." PhD dissertation, Department of History, University of Hawaiʻi at Mānoa, 2004.

McCoy, Alfred. *Policing America's Empire: The United States, the Philippines, and the Rise of the Surveillance State*. Madison: University of Wisconsin Press, 2009.

McKenna, Rebecca Tinio. *American Imperial Pastoral: The Architecture of US Colonialism in the Philippines*. Chicago: University of Chicago Press, 2017.

Melamed, Jodi. "The Spirit of Neoliberalism: From Racial Liberalism to Neoliberal Multiculturalism." *Social Text* 24, no. 4 (Winter 2006): 1–24.

Merleaux, April. *Sugar and Civilization: American Empire and the Cultural Politics of Sweetness*. Chapel Hill: University of North Carolina Press, 2015.

Mintz, Sidney. *Sweetness and Power: The Place of Sugar in Modern History*. New York: Penguin Books, 1985.

Mirzoeff, Nicholas. *The Right to Look: A Counterhistory of Visuality*. Durham, NC: Duke University Press, 2013.

Mitchell, W. J. T., ed. *Landscape and Power*. 2nd ed. Chicago: University of Chicago Press, 2002.

———. "The Surplus Value of Images." *Mosaic* 35, no. 3 (2002): 1–23.

———. *What Do Pictures Want? The Lives and Loves of Images*. Chicago: University of Chicago Press, 2005.

Mojares, Resil B. *Brains of the Nation: Pedro Paterno, T. H. Pardo de Tavera, Isabelo de los Reyes, and the Production of Modern Knowledge*. Honolulu: University of Hawaiʻi Press, 2006.

———. *The War against the Americans: Resistance and Collaboration in Cebu, 1899–1906*. Quezon City: Ateneo de Manila University, 1999.

Moore, Jason W. *Capitalism in the Web of Life: Ecology and the Accumulation of Capital*. London: Verso, 2015.

Mostiller, Marimas Hosan. "The Nexus of Asian Indigeneity, Refugee Status, and Asian Settler Colonialism in the Case of Indigenous Cham Muslim Refugees." *Amerasia Journal* 47, no. 1 (2021): 112–18.

Mudry, Jessica. *Measured Meals: Nutrition in America*. Albany: State University of New York Press, 2009.

Neptune, Harvey. *Caliban and the Yankees: Trinidad and the American Occupation*. Chapel Hill: University of North Carolina Press, 2007.

Oetelaar, Gerald A., and David Meyer. "Movement and Native American Landscapes: A Comparative Approach." *Plains Anthropologist* 51, no. 199 (2006): 355–74.

Okihiro, Gary. *Cane Fires: The Anti-Japanese Movement in Hawaiʻi, 1865–1945*. Philadelphia: Temple University Press, 1991.

———. *Pineapple Culture: A History of the Tropical and Temperate Zones*. Berkeley: University of California Press, 2009.

Olin, Margaret. *Touching Photographs*. Chicago: University of Chicago Press, 2011.

Olivera, John. "Colonial Ethnology and the Igorrote Village at the AYP." *Pacific Northwest Quarterly* 101, nos. 3–4 (2010): 141–49.

Olivares, José de. *Our Islands and Their People as Seen with Camera and Pencil*. New York: N. D. Thompson, 1899.

Paredes, Oona. "Indigenous vs. Native: Negotiating the Place of Lumads in the Bangsamoro Homeland." *Asian Ethnicity* 16, no. 2 (2015): 166–85.

———. *A Mountain of Difference: The Lumad in Early Colonial Mindanao*. Ithaca, NY: Cornell University Press, 2013.

Peck, Gunther. *Reinventing Free Labor: Padrones and Immigrant Workers in the North American West, 1880–1930*. New York: Cambridge University Press, 2000.

Pertierra, Raul. "Lured Abroad: The Case of Ilocano Overseas Workers." *Sojourn: Journal of Social Issues in Southeast Asia* 9, no. 1 (1994): 54–80.

Pilcher, Jeffrey. *The Sausage Rebellion: Public Health, Private Enterprise, and Meat in Mexico City, 1890–1917*. Albuquerque: University of New Mexico Press, 2006.

Poblete, JoAnna. *Islanders in the Empire: Filipino and Puerto Rican Laborers in Hawai'i*. Urbana: University of Illinois Press, 2014.

Poole, Deborah. *Vision, Race, Modernity: A Visual Economy of the Andean Image World*. Princeton, NJ: Princeton University Press, 1997.

Prentice, Claire. *The Lost Tribe of Coney Island: Headhunters, Luna Park, and the Man Who Pulled Off the Spectacle of the Century*. New York: New Harvest, 2014.

Punzalan, Ricardo. "Archival Diaspora: A Framework for Understanding the Complexities and Challenges of Dispersed Photographic Collections." *American Archivist* 77, no. 2 (2014): 326–49.

Rafael, Vicente. *Contracting Colonialism: Translation and Christian Conversion in Tagalog Society under Early Spanish Rule*. Ithaca, NY: Cornell University Press, 1988.

———. *Motherless Tongues: The Insurgency of Language amid Wars of Translation*. Durham, NC: Duke University Press, 2016.

———. *The Promise of the Foreign: Nationalism and the Technics of Translation in the Spanish Philippines*. Durham, NC: Duke University Press, 2005.

———. "The War of Translation: Colonial English, American English, and Tagalog Slang in the Philippines." *Journal of Asian Studies* 74, no. 2 (2015): 283–302.

———. *White Love and Other Events in Filipino History*. Durham, NC: Duke University Press, 2000.

Raibmon, Paige. *Authentic Indians: Episodes of Encounter in the Late-Nineteenth-Century Northwest Coast*. Durham, NC: Duke University Press, 2005.

Rancière, Jacques. *Disagreement: Politics and Philosophy*. Trans. Julie Rose. Minneapolis: University of Minnesota Press, 1999.

Reboul, Ann, Denis Delfitto, and Gaetano Fiorin. "The Semantic Properties of Free Indirect Discourse." *Annual Review of Linguistics* 2, no. 1 (January 2016): 255–71.

Reichman, Daniel R. *The Broken Village: Coffee, Migration, and Globalization in Honduras*. Ithaca, NY: Cornell University Press, 2011.

Reid, Lawrence A. "Who Are The Negritos? Evidence from Human Language." *Human Biology* 85, nos. 1–3 (2013): 329–58.

Rice, Mark. *Dean Worcester's Fantasy Islands: Photography, Film, and the Colonial Philippines*. Ann Arbor: University of Michigan Press, 2014.

———. "His Name Was Don Francisco Muro: Reconstructing an Image of American Imperialism." *American Quarterly* 62, no. 1 (March 2010): 49–76.

Ritvo, Harriet. *The Animal Estate: The English and Other Creatures in Victorian England*. Cambridge, MA: Harvard University Press, 1989.

Robinson, Cedric. *Black Marxism: The Making of the Black Radical Tradition*. Chapel Hill: University of North Carolina Press, 1983.

Robles, Eilodoro G. *The Philippines in the Nineteenth Century*. Quezon City: Malaya Books, 1969.

Rodgers, Daniel T. *Atlantic Crossings: Social Politics in a Progressive Age*. Cambridge, MA: Harvard University Press, 2000.

Rodriguez, Dylan. *Suspended Apocalypse: White Supremacy, Genocide, and the Filipino Condition*. Minneapolis: University of Minnesota Press, 2010.

Roma-Sianturi, Dinah. "'Pedagogic Invasion': The Thomasites in Occupied Philippines." *Kritikal Kultura* 12 (2009): 5–23.

Rosaldo, Michelle Z. *Knowledge and Passion: Ilongot Notions of Self and Social Life*. Cambridge: Cambridge University Press, 1980.

Rosaldo, Renato. *Culture and Truth: The Remaking of Social Analysis*. Boston: Beacon, 1993.

———. *Ilongot Headhunting, 1883–1974: A Study in Society and History*. Stanford, CA: Stanford University Press, 1980.

Rydell, Robert W. *All the World's a Fair: Visions of Empire at American International Expositions, 1876–1916*. Chicago: University of Chicago Press, 1985.

Sales, Joy. "#NeverAgainToMartialLaw: Transnational Filipino American Activism in the Shadow of Marcos and the Age of Duterte." *Amerasia Journal* 45, no. 3 (2019): 299–315.

Salvador-Amores, Analyn. "Afterlives of Dean C. Worcester's Colonial Photographs: Visualizing Igorot Material Culture, from Archives to Anthropological Fieldwork in Northern Luzon." *Visual Anthropology* 29, no. 1 (2016): 54–80.

———. *Tapping Ink, Tattooing Identities: Tradition and Modernity in Contemporary Kalinga Society, North Luzon, Philippines*. Honolulu: University of Hawai'i Press, 2014.

San Juan, E., Jr. *Carlos Bulosan and the Imagination of the Class Struggle*. New York: Oriole Editions, 1972.

Schurz, Wylliam Lytle. *The Manila Galleon*. New York: Dutton, 1939.

Scott, Heidi V. "The Contested Spaces of the Subterranean: Colonial Governmentality, Mining, and the Mita in Early Spanish Peru." *Journal of Latin American Geography* (2012): 7–33.

Scott, James C. *The Art of Not Being Governed: An Anarchist History of Upland Southeast Asia*. New Haven, CT: Yale University Press, 2009.

———. *Seeing Like a State: How Certain Schemes to Improve the Human Condition Have Failed*. New Haven, CT: Yale University Press, 2005.

Scott, William Henry. *Barangay: Sixteenth-Century Philippine Culture and Society*. Quezon City: Ateneo de Manila University Press, 1997.

———. *The Discovery of the Igorots: Spanish Contacts with the Pagans of Northern Luzon*. Manila: New Day Publishers, 1974.

See, Sarita. *The Filipino Primitive: Accumulation and Resistance in the American Museum.* New York: New York University Press, 2017.

See, Sarita Echavez. "Gambling with Debt: Lessons from the Illiterate." *American Quarterly* 64, no. 3 (September 2012): 495–513.

Seijas, Tatiana. *Asian Slaves in Colonial Mexico: From Chinos to Indians.* New York: Cambridge University Press, 2014.

Shah, Nayan. *Stranger Intimacy: Contesting Race, Sexuality and the Law in the North American West.* Berkeley: University of California Press, 2011.

Sharma, Jayeeta. *Empire's Garden: Assam and the Making of India.* Durham, NC: Duke University Press, 2011.

Sharma, Miriam. "Towards a Political Economy of Emigration from the Philippines: The 1904 to 1906 Ilocano Movement to Hawai'i in Historical Perspective." *Philippine Sociological Review* 35, nos. 3–4 (1987): 15–33.

Shuto, Mokoto. *Migration, Regional Integration and Human Security: The Formation and Maintenance of Transnational Spaces.* Burlington, VT: Ashgate, 2006.

Simpson, Leanne Betasamosake. *As We Have Always Done: Indigenous Freedom through Radical Resistance.* Minneapolis: University of Minnesota Press, 2017.

Smallwood, Stephanie. *Saltwater Slavery: A Middle Passage from Africa to American Diaspora.* Cambridge, MA: Harvard University Press, 2008.

Solhem, Wilhelm G., II. "Formosan Relationships with Southeast Asia." *Asian Perspectives* 7, no. 1 (1950): 251–60.

Sonza, Demy P. *Sugar Is Sweet: The Story of Nicholas Loney.* Manila: National Historical Institute, 1977.

Stanley, Amy Dru. *From Bondage to Contract: Wage Labor, Marriage, and the Market in the Age of Slave Emancipation.* Cambridge: Cambridge University Press, 1998.

Stoler, Ann Laura. *Along the Archival Grain: Epistemic Anxieties and Colonial Common Sense.* Princeton, NJ: Princeton University Press, 2008.

———. "Colonial Archives and the Arts of Governance." *Archival Science* 2, nos. 1–2 (2002): 87–109.

Sunseri, Thaddeus. "Reinterpreting a Colonial Rebellion: Forestry and Social Control in German East Africa, 1874–1915." *Environmental History* 8, no. 3 (2003): 430–51.

Tadiar, Neferti X. "Decolonization, 'Race,' and Remaindered Life under Empire." *Qui Parle: Critical Humanities and Social Sciences* 23, no. 2 (2015): 135–60.

———. *Things Fall Away: Philippine Historical Experience and the Makings of Globalization.* Durham, NC: Duke University Press, 2009.

Takaki, Ronald. *Pau Hana: Plantation Life and Labor in Hawai'i.* Honolulu: University of Hawai'i Press, 1983.

———. *Strangers from a Different Shore: A History of Asian Americans.* Boston: Little, Brown, 1989.

Thomas, Megan C. *Orientalists, Propagandists, and Ilustrados: Filipino Scholarship at the End of Spanish Colonialism.* Minneapolis: University of Minnesota Press, 2012.

Treuer, David. *The Heartbeat of Wounded Knee: Native America from 1890 to the Present.* New York: Riverhead Books, 2009.

Tucker, Richard P. *Insatiable Appetites: The United States and the Ecological Degradation of the Tropical World.* Lanham, MD: Rowman & Littlefield, 2007.

Veit, Helen Zoe. *Modern Food, Moral Food: Self-Control, Science, and the Rise of Modern American Eating in the Early Twentieth Century*. Chapel Hill: University of North Carolina Press, 2013.

Ventura, Theresa M. "American Empire, Agrarian Reform, and the Problem of Tropical Nature in the Philippines, 1898–1916." PhD dissertation, Columbia University, 2010.

———. "Medicalizing *Gutom*: Hunger, Diet, and Beriberi during the American Period." *Philippine Studies: Historical and Ethnographic Viewpoints* 63, no. 1 (March 2015): 39–69.

———. "From Small Farms to Progressive Plantations: The Trajectory of Land Reform in the American Colonial Philippines, 1900–1916." *Agricultural History* (2016): 459–83.

Vergara, Benito. *Displaying Filipinos: Photography and Colonialism in Early 20th Century Philippines*. Manila: University of the Philippines Press, 1995.

Warren, Louis. *Buffalo Bill's America: William Cody and the Wild West Show*. New York: Penguin Books, 2006.

Wenning, Mario. "On Gambling: The Provocation of Lady Fortune." *Thesis Eleven* 143, no. 1 (2017): 82–96.

White, Richard. *Railroaded: The Transcontinentals and the Making of Modern America*. New York: Norton, 2011.

Willcox, Cornelis De Witt. *The Head Hunters of Northern Luzon: From Ifugao to Kalinda; A Ride through the Mountains of Northern Luzon*. Kansas City, MO: Franklin Hudson Publishing, 1912.

Winkelmann, Tessa O. "Rethinking the Sexual Geography of American Empire in the Philippines: Interracial Intimacies in Mindanao and the Cordilleras, 1898–1921." In *Gendering the Trans-Pacific World*, ed. Catherine Ceniza Choy and Judy Tzu-Chun Wu, 39–76 (London: Brill, 2017).

Worcester, Dean Conant. "The Non-Christian Peoples of the Philippine Islands." *National Geographic* 24, no. 11 (November 1913): 1157–256.

Worster, Donald. *Dust Bowl: The Southern Plains in the 1930s*. New York: Oxford University Press, 1979.

———. *Rivers of Empire: Water, Aridity, and the Growth of the American West*. New York: Pantheon Books, 1985.

Zarsadiaz, James. "Raising Hell in the Heartland: Filipino Chicago and the Anti-Martial Law Movement, 1972–1986." *American Studies* 56, no. 1 (2017): 141–62.

Index